THE INTEGRATION OF
WOMEN IN MANAGEMENT

THE INTEGRATION OF WOMEN IN MANAGEMENT

A Guide for Human Resources and
Management Development
Specialists

Ann-Marie Rizzo and
Carmen Mendez

Foreword by
Donald Klingner

Q

Quorum Books
New York • Westport, Connecticut • London

Library of Congress Cataloging-in-Publication Data

Rizzo, Ann-Marie, 1947–
    The integration of women in management : a guide for human
resources and management development specialists / Ann-Marie Rizzo
and Carmen Mendez ; foreword by Donald Klingner.
        p. cm.
    Includes bibliographical references.
    ISBN 0–89930–475–3 (lib. bdg. : alk. paper)
    1. Women—Employment.   2. Personnel management.   3. Organizational
change.   4. Women executives.   I. Mendez, Carmen.   II. Title.
    HD6053.R48   1990
    658.3'042—dc20   90–8422

British Library Cataloguing in Publication Data is available.

Library of Congress Catalog Card Number: 90–8422
ISBN: 0–89930–475–3

First published in 1990

Quorum Books, 88 Post Road West, Westport, CT 06881
An imprint of Greenwood Publishing Group, Inc.

Printed in the United States of America

The paper used in this book complies with the
Permanent Paper Standard issued by the National
Information Standards Organization (Z39.48–1984).

10 9 8 7 6 5 4 3 2 1

This book is dedicated to our mothers for showing us that women can succeed in the workplace, and to our fathers for providing the encouragement to do it.

Contents

Illustrations

Foreword

Organizations are often remiss in providing new supervisors with training in how to make the transition to a managerial role. This is unfortunate. A preponderance of research studies and managerial cases shows that leaders are made through training and experience, not born with innate managerial qualities. And one of the first things managers learn is that there is no "one right way" to do things—good policy and practice are tested by their appropriateness to the manager's personality, employee expectations, the demands of the situation, and the organization's climate.

In the United States, the 1980s were significant because it was the first time in recorded history that more women were in the workforce than in the home. This trend will continue. *The Integration of Women in Management* by Ann-Marie Rizzo and Carmen Mendez makes a critical contribution to the field of administrative behavior and management by discussing, with both breadth and clarity, how changes in the role of women during this century in the United States have changed the way organizations and managers must behave in order to remain effective.

Several types of changes are necessary. First, organizations will need to draw increasingly upon the skills of women to remain competitive globally. Second, to do this successfully, managers—both male and female—need to change some of their stereotypes about the characteristics of women as workers and managers. Third, this increased investment in human assets will force managers to recognize that the character of the relationships between managers and employees, and among employees, is the most important nontechnological factor affecting organizational productivity.

These authors have contributed by showing how changes in managerial attitudes and behavior toward women can create an organizational climate where all employees work more productively because their needs and feelings are respected. Moreover, they show how managers can design and implement the human resource management systems that help make this possible.

Donald Klingner

Preface

Writing this book has required a great deal of help and caring from our colleagues, student researchers, and support staff at Florida International University. Without their concentrated efforts a completed manuscript would have not been possible.

We owe a profound debt to Roy Van Wyck and Neal Burgess who conducted the library research and personal interviews. Roy in particular, with his dedication to finding everything he could about a subject, was instrumental in providing information that crossed such a wide spectrum.

Thanks to Sandi Boudreaux, Delores Bell, Sylvia Tuman, and Dawn Minisall who were always willing to answer our questions on computer software and convert our disks. Special thanks to Sandi and Benigno S. Mendez for their contributions in the way of data input and computer design of technical material. Without Peggy Bradley, her magic printer, and her ability to know where commas belong, our task would have been impossible.

Our colleagues in the School of Public Affairs and Services, Howard Frank, Manny Lorenzo, Milan Dluhy, and Donald Klingner are an unusually perceptive and caring support group. Their ideas and suggestions were provided generously and with great enthusiasm. And to Allan Rosenbaum, who has provided access to computer equipment and release time, our heartfelt thanks and appreciation. Without their concern and desire to see us succeed, our efforts would have taken longer and come at a greater personal cost. No book is written solely by its authors, and this one is no exception.

THE INTEGRATION OF
WOMEN IN MANAGEMENT

Introduction

For the past ten years or so, we have attentively followed popular as well as academic literature that has documented trends and changes in the American workforce. Often, we have regarded these findings with a mixture of interest, skepticism, and wonder. Particularly with respect to how women have been received and treated in the workplace, this literature has reflected a diversity of cultural responses ranging from accounts of sexual harassment to the "mommy track." In the past several years, however, we have found evidence of a changing regard for the American worker generally. Review this sampling of recent thought (Solomon, 1989, p. B1; italics added for emphasis):

The American work force, rapidly becoming more diverse, will present managers with one of their biggest challenges in the 1990s and beyond. From now till the end of the century, 88 percent of work-force growth will come from women, blacks, and people of Hispanic or Asian origin, including immigrants. White men, meanwhile, account for most retirees and are leaving the work force in record numbers. *So, companies that once grudgingly shoehorned women and minorities into their ranks are now finding them indispensable.*

And this:

As slowing work-force growth puts women in a seller's market, the challenge for many companies isn't just finding and hiring talented women—it's holding on to them. Mobil and some other employers that once required women to adapt to the corporation are beginning to take pains to be more accommodating and create more opportunities. (Trost, 1989, pp. B–1, B–4)

So, is the revolution over? Have women and minorities already scored the final victory, of which the press is only now taking notice? Some evidence indicates that, due to economic necessities, workers formerly tolerated by management may be prized in the future. Witness these predicted trends from *Workforce 2000*:

- According to some projections, by the Year 2000, population growth could increase as little as 12 percent, the slowest rate in American history. Immigrants may help to fill the gap created by this decline in growth, with changes in federal immigration policy responding to this need. Similarly, qualified minorities and women with credentials in the right fields will enjoy greater access to employment opportunities.

- The greatest increase in the number of jobs will be in professional, technical, and sales areas. As long as workers possess the credentials and qualifications in those and related fields, there will be a demand for their talents. (Johnston and Packer, 1987)

Trends such as these indicate that, in order to thrive in the economic marketplace of the 1990s, those directing the work organization of the future will be required to work diligently to recruit and retain qualified workers. And this effort will not simply involve competing with other employers in attractive pay, benefits, and working conditions, but in cultural enhancements as well. Given that this emerging workforce will tend to be composed primarily not of white males but larger numbers of minorities, women, and immigrants as well, we conclude that in the future workplace, people will need more than ever before to be able to work cooperatively and in ways that acknowledge and capitalize on their special talents, experience, and background.

In large measure, addressing that need is what compelled us to write this book. To us, persuading people in work institutions to accept and appreciate the notion of differences in people—rather than the all-too-common sentiments of expecting employees to conform to white male standards—was a welcome challenge. Still, in exploring how to arrive at an integrated workforce, we needed to find the answers to some serious questions. What people skills are involved? What political strategies are required? What knowledge and information will be needed about a given work culture to make the right decisions and choose the appropriate strategies? And even, what does an "integrated" organization look like? In addressing these issues, employers will need to work on how they attempt to involve or "integrate" employees to make the organization more effective as well as responsive.

We are particularly interested in the situation of women as a test case, a bellwether for examining how employers accomplish this goal. While we do not confine our overall argument to women, women and minorities are currently the individuals most vulnerable to changes in employment policies, so that examining how "outsiders"—provided that women generally can be described as such—may be included in a more cohesive work unit may have hidden benefits for those who already fit the prevailing white male model or standard. A related theme for this book centers on how human resource development can serve to bridge the gap between women's current status in employment, however that is construed, and their potential to become better involved and utilized in that workforce. To that end, several chapters are devoted to explaining women's role in the workplace.

In chapter 1, we look at common stereotypes of working women, as well as how these stereotypes contribute to the underutilization and devaluation of women in the workplace. Here and in chapter 2, we explore several questions about women in employment: What do we know about women at work? Do women's behavior, styles, and performance differ from men's in important and influential ways? Chapter 2 also covers historical developments that have brought about women's current conditions of employment, as well as how organizational structure, behavior, and power create or hinder opportunities for women. Similarly, chapter 5 examines women's strategies to influence others at work. Do the ways in which women negotiate their work environments differ from men's? If there are differences, do they matter? And what should interested parties do with this knowledge?

To gain some powerful insights into these issues, chapter 3 presents feminist perspectives concerning women's status, as well as epistemological explorations of how we know what we know about gender differences. This chapter also describes an important theme found later in this book, to wit, how organization members conceptualize their place in work cultures. Therefore, to crystalize how we view organizational life, we introduce the metaphor of the web in this section. Although not original with us, the notion of a web suggests people at various levels of interconnectedness with others and with authorities at the center, encountering a variety of choices in their everyday work life, each of which may lead to a different path with different outcomes. Webs possess both centers and peripheries, and, although much of the life-and-death action appears to take place at the center, many critical shaping events occur at the periphery, supporting the multicausal and reflexive version of organizations. Curiously, like work cultures, no two webs are alike. They are also like work cultures in another sense: they are constantly in flux, as lines of communication are continually being torn, repaired, or redrawn. While hierarchy accurately depicts the authority and responsibility dimensions, webs show not only the dynamics of work relationships—how power shifts, how people need to rely on changing networks of communication—but how these relationships are two-way and can be altered. Thus, in chapters 3 and especially 4, we explore what this metaphor means to people who, although they are immersed in organizational life, are trying to transform organizations.

Another theme explored in these pages reflects the attention employers devote to workers generally. To some extent, American management literature has been exploring this and related issues since the 1960s, when McGregor wrote about the predominant views of human nature in our culture, Theories X and Y (1960). Nevertheless, Americans had to encounter a more competitive international marketplace, and the Japanese economic "miracle" in particular, to resurrect human-centered considerations and assign them higher priorities in business and government circles. For those interested in putting these priorities into practice, we are faced with this question: How can Human Resource Development (HRD) specialists, managers, peers, or colleagues promote/foster the involvement and participation of employees? This issue is addressed primarily in chapter 4: What is organizational integration and what is involved in accomplishing it? Here a model is proposed that spells out the essential components needed by integrated work cultures. In chapter 5, a case study is presented and analyzed to show how women attempt to influence others at work. Commonly used and recommended strategies, emphasizing political approaches, are found in this chapter. Chapter 6 includes other ways to examine the dilemma described in the previous chapter's case study, as well as our experience experimenting with a two-day workshop to empower women managers. The workshop outlined in this chapter is followed up by the description of each method and technique in chapter 7. Questionnaires, case studies, and so on are presented here, accompanied by our recommendations and advice for the reader's use.

A third and broader theme emerges throughout these pages as we disclose our values and assumptions concerning the direction in which we want work cultures to move. As will become apparent, we are interested in changing people and collectivities in work organizations so that the workplace better approaches democratic ideals. Workplace democratization has been around for some time, and we borrow from a growing foundation of literature and an emerging record of research to guide us in describing how we want the workplace of the next century to look. While this lofty and admittedly idealistic theme underlies much of the book, it is featured most prominently in chapter 6, which covers action theory, critical theory, and dialectical analysis. While these approaches are considered first for their challenge to the customary ways to analyze the case study in the previous chapter, they also form the theoretical foundation for our experiment in empowerment training for women managers. To a lesser extent, the democratization theme re-emerges in chapter 8. Here we consider how individuals in authoritative capacities, as well as interested parties, can help to transform work cultures through working with individual employees.

While we would like to believe that *Workforce 2000* and similar projections and predictions for the future workplace will hold true and that women and minority workers will fare better then than now, we cannot entertain that as the only possible scenario. The marketplace arguably plays the major role in determining regard for and treatment of the American worker, and economic and labor conditions can change radically, defying all prognostications. No matter what the future holds, this book was written to persuade specialists in HRD, trainers, supervisors, even employees, general managers, and executives of the many ways in which they can contribute to changing and improving their respective institutions. In the pages that follow, we hope to make clear that we place our faith in the capacity and dedication of human resource professionals to be able not only to retain talented individuals, but to shape an involved and committed workforce. We hope that this book will enable and encourage them to take the appropriate steps.

REFERENCES

Johnston, W., and A. Packer. 1987. *Workforce 2000: Work and Workers for the Twenty-first Century*. Indianapolis: Hudson Institute.

McGregor, D. 1960. *The Human Side of Enterprise*. New York: McGraw-Hill.

Solomon, J. 1989. "Firms Grapple With Language Barriers." *Wall Street Journal*, November 7, B–1, B–4.

Trost, C. 1989. "New Approach Forced by Shifts in Population." *Wall Street Journal*, November 22, B–1, B–4.

PART I

Current Status of Women

To understand the current status of women, both in the working community and as members of society, one must investigate the historical base that has guided the development of women's move from traditional roles in society to nontraditional employment and relationships. In the past, women had few opportunities to stray from traditional expectations; however, with changes in the workplace and the financial necessity of two-income households, greater latitude and choices have become available.

Entrance into the job market has not come without major struggles or difficulties. In chapter 1, we describe the stereotypes that have been called upon to reinforce the limited role of women in the workplace. Though women differ physically from their male counterparts and may demonstrate different organizational behaviors, the roles they play in making and implementing decisions, in organizations both public and private, are being acknowledged. The differences that have limited professional potential for women have undergone careful scrutiny, and the subsequent results indicate that the significant differences are minor in comparison with the degree of similarities between genders.

Access does not necessarily guarantee success. Women, as described in chapter 2, must develop interpersonal skills, master technological advances, and be perceived as viable competitors in the workplace as we approach the twenty-first century. Perhaps of greatest importance are the developments of individual empowerment and strategic efforts to identify and maximize individual professional potential. These requisites will be the basis for employment options and promotional possibilities.

Chapter 1 ────────────────────────

Views of Women

The following chapter will attempt to identify and define gender-based stereotypes and provide insight into the effect of conventional and oversimplified conceptions, opinions, or beliefs on individuals and the organizations in which they work. By looking at traditional stereotypes from a perspective that incorporates a review of relevant research and an appraisal of variables used to evaluate performance, we will better understand how women have been perceived in the workplace and what must be done to overcome the barriers that have limited their access to nontraditional roles and responsibilities.

Women have traditionally held positions in the job market that were filled for the most part only by women and were at a lower rank and pay than positions held by men. In most cases, these positions were supportive by function and were an extension, outside of the home, of the woman's nurturing role. These hiring and employment practices were justified by a basic principle that men and women demonstrated their natural abilities in very different ways and that, consequently, nature had provided a division of labor based upon gender. In many cases, these classifications had standardized decision-making and minimized the need for extensive individual evaluations or review. Until recently, there had been no great outcry to question the validity of these assumptions or the impact that these assumptions had on individuals and organizations. In many ways, this simplistic use of stereotypes not only formalized personal bias into accepted organizational behavior, but limited the organizational perspective when making personnel choices.

Although stereotypes may in fact be based on a grain of truth, in reality they often conceal more than they reveal (Cohen and Bradford, 1989).

Stereotypes then, by definition, can be seen as deceptive shortcuts that are perceived to be helpful for immediate usage. However, the long-term implications for depending on oversimplified generalizations has resulted in categorized decision-making that assumes certain consistencies that do not exist. Unfortunately, assumptions based upon stereotypes have served as the cornerstone of personnel decision-making because of a dependence on these grains of truth. Their usage has survived because few people in managerial capacities exhibited nontraditional characteristics and because there was little reason or desire to doubt what they felt to be true. Those who were aware of the possibility that the stereotypes were in error felt that it was in their best interest to ignore what was concealed. Goleman, in an article on racism, describes the strength of stereotypes—both innocent and hostile—being "attributed to the mind's natural bent to seek to confirm its beliefs. While several experiences to the contrary can challenge those beliefs, an isolated experience is unlikely to do so" (Goleman, 1989, p. 2e).

At the core of many of these stereotypes was, and to some extent still is, the basic belief that men were and are better-suited for assuming decision-making responsibilities. When considering and evaluating characteristics that best described a successful manager, those in positions of authority assumed that the variables attributed to men and male behavior were those exhibited by successful managers. Schein (1973, 1975) contributes to this notion by defining the successful manager as being someone who possesses characteristics, attitudes, behaviors, and temperament more commonly ascribed to men than to women. Men were seen as being rational, decisive, and in control, while women were perceived as being too emotional and unable to act under pressure. McGregor, in his description of a successful manager, provides an even more explicit definition of the required characteristics for success and the implications of the implementation of this definition.

The model of the successful manager in our culture is a masculine one. The good manager is aggressive, competitive, firm, just. He is not feminine; he is not soft or yielding or dependent or intuitive in the womanly sense. The very expression of emotion is widely viewed as a feminine weakness that would interfere with effective business processes. Yet the fact is that all these emotions are part of the human nature of men and women alike. Cultural forces have shaped not their existence but their acceptability; they are repressed, *but this does not render them inactive.* They continue to influence attitudes, opinions, and decisions. [Emphasis added](McGregor, 1967, p. 23)

The dependence on this model may in part be attributed to a perceived investment on the part of male managers and a feeling that there will be little return for encouraging women, who will leave the workforce without contributing what is normally expected from men.

There is a strong pull to conform in this definition; model behavior in its ideal form must emulate male or masculine characteristics. With this comes an unwillingness to identify or come to terms with the reality that feminine characteristics or behavior are exhibited by both men and women, and contribute to management effectiveness. Consequently, upper-level managers who are seen as successful will be identified as having personal attributes that are more likely found in men than women (Basil, 1973). This may be attributed to the traditional definitions of managerial effectiveness that have relied on military and sport models to provide a baseline for identifying desired managerial behaviors (Shepard, 1977; Harragan, 1977; Hennig and Jardim, 1977). Because of the historical exclusion of women from both the military and competitive sports, there has been unequal access to male-dominated activities that have proven helpful in developing the skills and abilities that result in promotions, salary increases, and, more importantly, the responsibility for making decisions.

Due to this exclusion, women have been seen as having neither the preparation, the opportunity, nor the experience for consideration as candidates for managerial positions. Of course, not all men who can be characterized as successful managers have had experience in the fields of battle or competitive sports, or, conversely, that all men with such previous experience are, or desire to be, successful managers. However, men, simply because of their gender and the assumption that they would exhibit stereotypical male behavior, have been perceived as capable and responsible managers. Consequently, the stereotypical masculine standard of behavior described by McGregor in 1967 remains a powerful contributor in shaping unconscious attitudes toward men, management, and women in management.

One must wonder why the stereotypical image of a successful manager existed unquestioned by so few for years and continues even today to a lesser degree. Changing an image or an idea that is popular, though not completely accurate, requires at a minimum a level of access or opportunity to prove that the previously believed stereotypes do not hold, at least in this particular case, and that there are other examples that would support divergence from the stereotypical belief (Goleman, 1989). Further, a personal support network must be in place and responsive for the individual who acts on nontraditional expectations. Without that network, one can lose sight of the desired direction or not develop the level of political perspective that increases one's chances for success.

Along with this unquestioned masculine standard of behavior has developed a fascination with a demonstration of aggressive, and consequently male, behavior. On reviewing the research conducted by Hennig and Jardim (1977), which concludes that men have been more aggressive in vying for promotions than women, one can only ask why a woman should demonstrate aggressive behavior and request a promotion when, first, there has been little or no history of access for women to male-dominated positions and, second, no apparent support for nontraditional behavior has been exhibited in the past. Consequently, because of this lack of reinforcement and limited acceptability for aggressive behavior, women had little chance for successfully breaking the traditional, male-dominated job barriers. Women thus continued to work in job classifications that were available to them and developed the reputation for being effective in supportive positions. Since men as a group have not faced the same level or degree of exclusion from the job market, one cannot determine whether, faced with the same constraints, they would have behaved any differently.

In addition to the lack of access to the administrative or managerial track, women did not have access to or participate in the informal networks that facilitate moves up the hierarchical ladder. The ability to develop influential networks requires acceptance by and a camaraderie with fellow workers at equal or higher levels, both formally and informally. This type of personal relationship provides individual support, inside information, and access to those who make decisions that are imperative when contemplating position advancements. In retrospect, women have not been part of the informal network because there was no perceived reason or need to include them. Women were not seen as possible candidates for promotions and positions of equal status within the organization. Therefore, attempts to measure women's use of aggressive behavior in vying for promotions in areas where, by virtue of their gender, women were unable to compete, appears to be counterproductive and reaffirms stereotypical definitions.

Other studies go on to show that women were excluded from managerial positions, assuming that they had been given equal access, because they could not compete due to their lack of knowledge of the rules of the game and, more importantly, because they did not even know they were competing (Haskell, 1985). Skills and information can be learned as part of on-the-job training, management training, or academic coursework. One can adopt a work style to include a strict obedience to the rules of hierarchy and the development of strategies to ensure success (Harragan, 1977). But the more difficult task is to develop a sense of competition, as well as the skills and willingness to compete for position or power. "Women in hierarchal corporations have discovered that being competent and doing a good job is not enough. They sometimes get passed over for promotions because they don't understand the politics" (Haskell, 1985, p. 13). Understanding politics is not accomplished easily in the classroom or in support positions where the model for compliant females is generally reinforced. Where, then, can women develop the political savvy that will allow them to compete?

This lack of political understanding may not be as much a lack of astuteness in the political arena but rather an emphasis on personal relationships that has received little acknowledgment in organizational dimensions. Canter's observations clearly highlight women's striving for achievement not only as a response to organizational environments but also for the purpose of establishing or strengthening personal relationships. In contrast, men strive to succeed for a sense of individual mastery (Canter, 1982). But will striving to succeed solely for individual mastery be the optimum behavior for the twenty-first century? The emphasis on personal relationships, if truly representative of female behavior, may be an untapped resource for organizations. If the trend toward a service-based economy continues, individuals, regardless of gender, will be reinforced for developing interpersonal skills. This may be easier for women, who if successful have learned to deal with the conflict between traditional female stereotypes and prescriptions for feminine behavior and what the organization describes as desired managerial behavior (Bhatnagar, 1988). Organizations can benefit from revising preferred managerial behavior styles and encouraging individuals to do what they do best. "In an increasingly service-driven labor force and changes in the nature of work itself, there has been a reevaluation of the stereotypical 'female' managerial characteristics and of their viability in management" (Catalyst, 1987, p. 41).

Over the past twenty years, women have moved into middle- and upper-management positions with differing levels of success and acceptance. The nature of these positions is very different from those traditionally occupied by women. Responsibilities will often include management or supervision of other employees. Women as a group have approached leadership roles less confidently than their male counterparts and consequently have held lower expectations for success (Lenney, 1977). These lower levels of self-confidence have limited the progress of women in nontraditional positions by relying on institutional sanctions for influencing others rather than on persuasive strategies (Kipnis and Cosentino, 1969). By resorting to organizational sanctions, the opportunity for developing a variety of influence techniques is overlooked, and the subsequent empowerment of the individual is greatly limited. If one always depends on organizational sanctions to get what one wants, one's overall effectiveness on the job and reputation for being able to deal with a variety of difficult situations will suffer. Lower levels of self-confidence and a reliance on organizational sanctions have resulted in the unwillingness of others to entrust decision-making to individuals who have not demonstrated sufficient versatility and expertise in being able to assess situations clearly and to determine and implement optimum strategies.

Overcoming these lower levels of self-confidence has required not only an expanded repertoire of organizational behavior but also the opportunity to be evaluated based upon standards that transcend traditional expectations and that have not been weighted in favor of one gender. Though the use of preferential selection has provided women with an entree into middle and upper management, its use in lieu of merit when deciding issues of employment, promotion, or salary increases further reinforces feelings of low self-confidence and low expectations of success (Heilman et al., 1987). Merit considerations, assuming they evaluate performance accurately, can provide a mechanism for measuring self-worth. When an individual knows that the appointment, raise, or promotion was based on productivity, the individual's level of self-confidence can rise in proportion to her reinforcement. The difficulty arises in both the public and private sector when workers do not see a correlation between pay and performance. Then the ability to develop better self-confidence will depend on intangible yet valuable forms of reinforcement.

To maintain personal esteem and self-confidence, one must accurately evaluate the competency and skills of employees through the consistent use of uniform standards. Lott (1985) asserts that there is a tendency to underrate and under-reward women when they are compared to men with identical credentials. Lower evaluations for comparable work does little to improve one's self-perception and self-esteem. Long-term implications of the devaluation of women's efforts have been substantiated by Goldberg, who found that the same article, when perceived to have been written by a man, was judged as being more competent and valuable than when written by a woman (Goldberg, 1968). These results reveal the degree to which sex-role stereotypes are deeply rooted in our culture, our institutions, and are perpetuated in everyday life. Such views would have us believe that women have fewer of the qualities that contribute to effective leadership and management skills (Boverman, et al., 1972). But in reality, assumptions that have been made based on limited information can and will become inoperative when sufficient data are gathered that refute these beliefs (Kiesler, 1975).

To overcome stereotypical generalizations, one must ensure that in the process of gathering sufficient data a careful analysis is made on the implementation and interpretation of the research project. On occasion, individual researchers will arrive at conclusions that are justifiable based upon their laboratory results, yet would not be supported in the field studies. The ability to compare the behavior of multiple organizational members will provide the researcher with a clearer understanding of actual behavior rather than depending on implicit sex theories (Osborn and Vicars, 1976). Dobbins and Platz (1986), in their meta-analytical review of seventeen studies examining sex differences in leadership, find that there is little support for the proposition that a leader's gender will have an impact on his or her behavior or subordinate satisfaction. They urge a "moratorium on research that simply compares male and female leaders on measures of initiating structure, consideration, and effectiveness."

Future research should instead investigate the processes through which sex stereotypes and implicit sex theories bias a rater's evaluations of men and women leaders. This is supported by the results of a survey of a pharmaceutical manufacturing company in Montreal where "women managers were rated as no more concerned for employees than male managers, and this independently of the level of influence they were perceived to hold" (Trempe, et al., 1985, p. 46). In comparing methods of supervision used by men and women, both genders were found to use similar approaches when the access to power resources were held constant. Some examples of behavior that affirmed sex-role stereotypes in the area of social influence were found, but they were weak and of only marginal significance (Instone, et al., 1983, p. 326). Their results demonstrated that males tended to make more influence attempts ($M = 7.75$) than females ($M = 6.2$) and used a wider range of strategies ($M = 4.04$, $W = 3.32$). Self-confidence accounted for the greatest level of variance in their study with regard to the frequency of influencing attempts and the use of coercion. In reviewing this research, one is struck by the similarity of behavior that is exhibited by men and women when one measures actual behavior and holds constant other variables that would negatively affect the results.

We have highlighted ways in which stereotypes have been used to justify the positions that women generally hold in most organizational structures. These positions are lower in status and pay, and require skills that will not be rewarded by promotions or facilitate upward mobility. Though the basis for these stereotypes can be proved to be only marginally significant, no one can dispute the effects of these beliefs on hiring or promoting practices. Women have been and continue to be disadvantaged in the workplace, and this disadvantage is less a function of the differential probability of returns based on acquired attributes (education, political savvy, informal networks) than simply because they are women (Cannings, 1988).

Although we might like to wave a magic wand and make the use of stereotypes disappear, we cannot discount the level to which they effectively infiltrate our organizations. They are widely held and used by both men and women and consequently affect how individuals make decisions and evaluate others. Many of the stereotypes that have contributed to our beliefs and attitudes about men and women and the kinds of positions they should hold in the workplace have been built upon traditional and cultural roles that we have learned to play. It is far easier to identify and define these characterizations than it is to alter how men and women are viewed in the workplace by society. Changing these views requires a more far-reaching agenda that provides women with challenging situations to demonstrate their ability to succeed and provides others in the organization with the opportunity to observe women who are functioning as effective managers or administrators. Only when it becomes apparent to all that women in fact possess skills that are not defined by these stereotypical limitations, and that it is in the best interests of the organization to acknowledge this, will effective change occur. Instances of success will encourage us to see women's capabilities not in a negative light, as we have in the past, but in a positive and productive way (Catalyst, 1987).

In this chapter, we have discussed sex-role stereotypes and the implications of these stereotypes on organizational behavior. Cook and Mendleson (1984, p. 24), in their research on power dimensions for men and women managers, developed the following chart that illustrates stereotypical behavior and a correlation of these stereotypes to previous research findings.

SEX ROLE STEREOTYPES

Males are more:

adventurous	venturesome
aggressive	assertive
coarse	venturesome
confident	self-sufficient
forceful	assertive
independent	self-sufficient
stern	tough-minded
strong	tough-minded
tough	tough-minded
unemotional	tough-minded

Females are more:

affectionate	group-dependent
emotional	tender-minded
fickle	venturesome
fussy	proper
nagging	proper

sentimental	tender-minded
submissive	humble
whiny	humble

The following are the results of this study, which measured the power levels of managers in manufacturing concerns. Women scored higher in the categories labeled experimenting and venturesome, while men scored higher in tough-minded, assertive, and self-sufficient. Both groups scored equally in the category titled expedient. The conclusions emphasized no great difference in the power dimensions exhibited by the men or women surveyed. They did, however, point out that any power characteristic can in fact become a negative characteristic, depending on the situation and the outcome. In some cases, behaving in an appropriate manner may be more effective than using unexpected behavior; the opposite will hold true in different situations.

The stereotypical behavior that was used to identify male and female behavior in this study is very similar to the stereotypes that people use when making everyday decisions. In general, they are oversimplified characterizations that cannot begin to identify either individual strengths and weaknesses or personalities. What remains quite apparent is the fact that a woman manager always risks having her gender overshadow her management performance. If we could objectively assess individual capabilities, unaffected by gender-based stereotypes, we might recognize that men and women exhibit both masculine and feminine characteristics (Bushardt et al., 1987). Furthermore, the androgynous manager may possess qualities superior to the traditional male model (Denhardt and Perkins, 1976). The possibility that many effective managers may possess androgynous skills is one that has been well publicized, yet for the most part it has not been accepted in most work cultures.

Interestingly, masculine or feminine images embedded in work roles derive neither from the task at hand nor from the characteristics of individual personalities. Rather, all positions within the organization carry gender typing, depending heavily on the dominant group that traditionally occupies that position. For example, secretarial jobs carry feminine sex-role norms, attitudes, and behaviors. One must then ask whether secretaries are powerless because they tend to be women or because of the low hierarchical status of their jobs. Addressing this question, Kanter identifies job structure rather than gender as the critical variable in determining access to power and opportunities. In turn, job structure explains differential achievement (productivity, motivation, and career success), which further contributes to shaping the subordinate status of women in an organization (Kanter, 1977). One can see the development of a vicious cycle that has relegated women to support positions where they have little chance for advancement and of a job structure that encourages keeping women in these roles (Denhardt and Perkins, 1976).

Ten years later Kanter reiterates this philosophy, stating that differences in behavior and success can be attributed to what the individual was handed by the organization rather than to any inherent differences in ability or drive (Kanter, 1987). To overcome this trend, one must go beyond changing women's individual behavior and address an agenda for identifying systematic changes that release women from subordinate status. Therefore, organizations can begin by altering structure, as opposed to attempting to change individual attitudes. Ferguson lends support to this option with the following design:

As long as women are subordinate to men, the virtues of female experience will be turned to the requirements of surviving subordination: the capacity to listen, to empathize, to hear and appreciate the voice of the other, and so forth, will be used as strategies for successful impression management (1984, p. 168).

It is clear from reviewing this literature that little attempt has been made to examine how particular work cultures interpret these stereotypes in action. The result, however, is the underutilization and devaluation of women in the workplace (Ruble and Ruble, 1982).

Perhaps of greatest importance is the realization that individuals will behave differently in a variety of organizations. In addition, if women are in fact different from each other and from men, the benefits from their inclusion in an organization may far outweigh the costs. "Very few studies have considered that women may in fact behave differently as managers in ways that enhance their performance" (Statham, 1987, p. 412). Sameness and predictability need not be the cornerstones of effective management.

For a more personal perspective, women pay the price for negatively valued feminine traits. The devaluation of feminine traits contributes to a woman's feeling of lack of self-worth and will affect her behavior (Bhatnagar, 1988). Many women, rather than risking failure to attain a management position, will continue to work in support-type positions and exhibit traditional, stereotypical behavior. If by some chance, they should venture or end up in nontraditional positions, women may mask some of their personal vitality and creativity in fear that their behavior be perceived as nonrational. They will copy male behavior and hide their emotional, sensitive, and so-called feminine qualities.

Encouraging individuals to exhibit behavior that contradicts traditional stereotypes does not come without a personal and organizational cost. Many times women who in fact exhibit masculine behavior are placed in a double bind because of the negative sanctions against women "imitating" male management styles (Haccoun et al., 1978). This can be attributed to the perception that, on assuming the role of manager, a woman has violated the traditional standards of feminine behavior; consequently, her behavior becomes suspect. Therefore, dealing with this modification of traditional roles is difficult not only for the individual initiating change, but also for those adapting to the results of these changes. The altered behavior of one party usually assumes a reciprocal response on the part of others. These assumptions are based upon generalizations that have proved to be true in a limited way; when expanded, they lose their validity.

Stereotypes have evolved from the traditional roles that we have played for centuries. Therefore, changing them is not easy. Here are some pragmatic suggestions for gaining the most effective performance from employees.

1. Do not generalize about people; though individuals may belong to a group, their beliefs, actions, and responses are determined by more than just group membership.
2. Throw out stereotypes. They have not proved to be accurate and have added to the management hurdle that women or minorities have had to overcome.
3. Different situations will require different behavior. An effective manager is able to choose his or her management style to best meet the performance goals of the organization (Cook and Mendleson, 1984, p. 27).

The ability to change how we look at ourselves and at others in the organization is becoming less of an option and more of a necessity. As we move into the twenty-first century, organizational reality will dictate that we assess individuals on performance rather than on stereotypical assumptions.

SEX STEREOTYPES AND THE FORMAL AND INFORMAL ORGANIZATION

The ability of women to tackle the system in many cases reflects the degree to which they have advanced or are perceived to have advanced within their particular environment. The success of individuals will vary according to their own abilities and the degree to which the organization in which they work relates to them. Many factors, such as the number of women working in nontraditional female positions or reinforcement for accomplishments in male-dominated areas, can mitigate the impact of stereotypical assumptions in an organization. Organizations, like people, will determine the extent to which stereotypes are used in making decisions. It is then in the best interest of women to seek employment where they are seen as individuals and where their evaluations and promotions are a function of productivity, not of preconceived notions of their capabilities.

In one organization, a woman who is extremely competent, well-organized, and productive is turned down for a promotion because her immediate supervisor does not want to cope with the loss of this employee in his area. Those in the organization's upper management tolerate the supervisor's short-sighted behavior because they are ambivalent about whether they are ready for a woman at a higher level of the hierarchy. Because of the lost opportunity, the employee moves to another organization where the hierarchy is flatter. Though her position title and salary have not changed, her responsibilities have increased, and she has the opportunity for professional advancement. Clearly one can see that the primary motivation in her decision to seek other employment is based on a need to be considered for promotions and advancements within the organization. The ability to move up the ladder will encourage her productivity because she feels rewarded for her efforts, but also her efforts will serve to benefit the organization. The employer's willingness to entrust decision-making to women and to reward them for their efforts will encourage other women to seek employment with them. The first organization described above not only lost a productive employee but is also perceived as an organization that does not treat women in an equitable fashion and will find it increasingly more difficult to attract qualified employees.

With the disintegration of a stereotypical basis for decision-making, women and men will not be evaluated by gender-based standards, but be held accountable for their actions and the subsequent implications of these actions for that particular organization. In doing so, individual workers will realize that the potential for long-term and continued success in any organization requires a reasonable understanding of the internal and external components that affect the organization. To maximize their impact in the decision-making process, both the formal and informal hierarchy must be clearly understood and used to the individual's advantage. They cannot ignore the implications of this dual structure and the need to navigate strategically between the two.

The formal structure can be typified as the backbone of the organization, providing clear lines of authority, distribution of formal power, methods for communication, incentives, and leadership (Sharkansky, 1982). The formal organization is seen as being fairly stable and consistent. Through its policies and practices, it is able to further the career effectiveness of its employees and in turn to attain the overall goals of the organization. To achieve these goals organizations encourage employees to serve as links in the hierarchical chain, providing those in subordinate positions with direction, support, and guidance, and those in higher positions their support and initiative.

To realize one's potential through formal channels, one must in fact have not only an accurate perception of individual capabilities, but also a commensurate level of self-confidence that allows the person to attempt new assignments, assume additional responsibilities, or take a more visible role in the organization. Women have been stereotyped as expressing lower levels of self-confidence than men, thereby hindering their chances for success (Lenney, 1977). This, however, can be overcome with sufficient levels of feedback to moderate women's tendency of inadequacy. The use of externally mediated feedback will equalize the level of self-confidence for men and women (McCarty, 1986). Therefore, as part of the formal organization, programs must be developed to allow and encourage individuals to take risks and attempt that which goes beyond the responsibilities that the individual is comfortable performing. To support individual efforts, formal organizations must establish and use a method of communication that clearly identifies the potential rewards for individual efforts and elevates women's levels of self-confidence (McCarty, 1986). Indeed, this will foster greater integration in the system and will increase the availability of information.

Organizations cannot be captured solely through the formal context described above. The informal organization usually shapes how formal policies are implemented. Informal organizations and networks are not as clearly defined as the formal structure associated with an organization, and they will never be identified on an organizational chart, yet they exist simultaneously side by side and in many ways provide an opportunity for implementing what needs to be accomplished. On the whole, the informal organization operates using a different set of variables than the formal structure. In many cases, the informal structure will cope with the inflexibility of a traditional management and provide opportunities for individual expression and information that would otherwise not be available. Informal networks can also assist in the promotion of an employee by teaching an employee the right way to act, arranging sponsorships, and providing other forms of peer support (DiPrete and Soule, 1988).

Because of the wide range of opportunities for accessing and using the informal organization, many of the constraints and legal strictures that inhibit the formal structure have been removed. But with this flexibility comes a different set of rules and accepted behavior. Inclusion within an informal network then becomes a function of an individual's perceived fit with those who already have access to these channels of communication.

Although the nature of the informal organization is unique in each organization, exclusion of individuals of the opposite gender, from formal interactions, is common across organizations. In general the opposite gender is comprised of women, consequently they do not as a rule enjoy equal access to informal interactions and communications (Bartol, 1978; Hendrick, 1981; Kanter, 1977). It is impossible to determine whether people of the other gender are actively excluded from a group or whether members of each gender exclude themselves from ties with members of the opposite gender (Brass, 1985). Social comfort may provide a key to unlock this puzzle. In most work organizations, white males enjoy the advantage of being of the same race and gender as the members of the predominant and most powerful group. On a superficial level, they are acceptable to informal groups in ways that women are not. Some refer to this unconscious selection process as the "cloning effect" in organizations: we tend to be most comfortable with those like ourselves and assume that those similar to us will be acceptable. To white male work cultures, however, women and minorities appear to be different, may behave differently, and unintentionally can cause psychic discomfort and tension. The entry of women into a work group represents a threat to the integrity of the existing work culture by challenging the unconscious meta-views of how things are done in that particular organization.

For women and minorities to be accepted in the informal network, they often must pass spontaneous and informal "tests" concerning their behavior, attitudes, and values. For example, women frequently carry with them the image of being the standard-bearer representing the ideal of how people generally ought to behave. Consequently, when involved with a new group, a woman may find that she is closely scrutinized by men to determine whether she is acceptable as a group member. This scrutiny may take the form of an unconscious agenda: Will she fit in? Will she question or criticize the way we do things? Is she a take-charge type or afraid to take the initiative? Is she like "one of the guys" or one of "them" (just a woman)? When she speaks, she will be carefully evaluated as to what she says, how she says it, and the effect she has on others. Is she perceived as a force to be reckoned with, a woman who persuades others to her point of view, and consequently possesses the capability to reshape existing power connections?

In comparison, it is more frequently assumed that a man, if examined concerning these same questions, would pass inspection. He is as a result not tested. Since men assume that others like them are relatively "safe" prospects, not until a man openly and consistently begins to violate the group's norms is he excluded from informal networks. As a result, in order to be accepted in a group, women must be approved through informal means that the majority of men do not often encounter.

Brass reports from his research that in reality, once access to the organization's interaction network is open, women are found more successful at building informal networks, especially with other women, than are men (Brass, 1985). When women have the opportunity to become integrated into the workplace, they are perceived as being more central to the interaction network than men. Exclusion based solely on gender may reflect attempts by those in positions of dominance to continue previous levels of comfort or an active tactic of discrimination, rather than biological differences that would inhibit women's ability to interact within the informal arena. Limited access to networks not only limits the woman's ability to function in the organization, but lessens the organization's ability to maximize the effectiveness of all its employees.

The number of contacts with others is not in itself sufficient to guarantee access to an informal group. Rather, it is necessary that contacts be with individuals who are in positions of authority or have information or status that would be advantageous in an informal network (Campbell, 1988). The difficulty arises not only in getting to know people of high enough status, but in being able to ask them to provide the boost an individual desperately needs. Campbell et al. (1986) reinforce this finding by stating that the traits of personal networks are potential predictors of occupational outcomes and that the use of networks in jobs will affect occupational outcomes. Those with high levels of education and socio-economic status will have wider-ranging networks. Because men have historically dominated high-level hierarchical positions, women are less likely to be included in these informal high-level interactions.

In many instances, women's networks are less well-suited to job searches and subsequent occupational outcomes because none of the contacts hold high enough positions to be perceived as useful (Campbell, 1988). Only recently have women begun to have access to higher level administrative positions that would put them into contact with people who could help them develop support networks. Consequently, without access to higher placed networks, women have depended on others in similar situations as their safety nets. By depending on this lateral support, networks cannot be used to enable the female employee to have equal access to information and other invaluable assets when attempting to climb the hierarchical ladder.

As described above, the nature of informal networks and the inability to access those that can provide general or job-related information will hinder women's movement up the ladder. Limited access to such informal groups and means can be exacerbated by child-rearing responsibilities and mobility. In turn, the omission of these women from networks affects the quality of resources those groups can provide to members (Campbell, 1988).

Understanding the dynamics of formal and informal organizations, managers can better appreciate the need to encourage women to be influential in both arenas and to reinforce and reward them for maximizing their impact accordingly. It is quite apparent that women have had greater success in using formal strategies for redressing gender discrimination at work. Formal grievances, complaints, and lawsuits have been used successfully in addressing issues of discrimination. It is also quite obvious that the informal relationships that develop on the job are the most difficult to regulate and change. Later, in chapters 5 and 6, these subjects will be discussed in greater depth and with illustrations. Ultimately, women are hampered if they depend only on the formal mechanisms to further their career development rather than using informal levers for the same purpose. This is particularly deleterious if they perceive that the formal network can help develop their careers while they ignore developing the informal support system (Pazy, 1987).

Limited use of informal networks may be in part a function of ignorance as to their importance or the inability to participate in them. Various rationales for this behavior have been presented, ranging from statements that imply that women cannot differentiate between the formal and informal as men can (Reif et al., 1975) to those that state that men are uncomfortable communicating with women or that men want to maintain their dominance by excluding women from informal interactions (Kanter, 1977). For whatever reason, women are less central to informal interaction networks and consequently will suffer from a lack of valuable information resources and support that accompany inclusion into the network.

Often when avenues of approach are not available, alternative approaches must be found that utilize the resources that are at hand. The individual who does not possess equal access for whatever reason must develop the ability to attain similar results using different means or by using different approaches to access the same channels. Finding alternative means may become less difficult if the inclusion of women in informal networks is considered to be beneficial for members of the network and the organization.

Some of our traditionally held values regarding gender-based stereotypes may go by the wayside, not so much because of a desire to behave in an equitable manner but rather as a result of a need to access adequately trained, skilled employees who are capable of filling managerial positions. The need to expand the pool from which we draw our professional employees will be the impetus needed to encourage integrated work groups and will provide women with equal access to currently male coalitions and male networks.

REFERENCES

Bartol, K. M. 1978. "The Sex Structuring of Organizations: A Search for Possible Causes." *Academy of Management Review*, Vol. 3, 805–815.
Basil, D. C. 1973. *Women in Management*. New York: McGraw-Hill.

Bhatnagar, D. 1988. "Professional Women in Organizations: New Paradigms for Research and Action." *Sex Roles*, Vol. 18, Nos. 5 and 6, 343–355.

Boverman, I. K., S. R. Vogel, F. E. Clarkson, and P. S. Rosenkranz. 1972. "Sex Role Stereotypes: A Current Appraisal." *Journal of Social Issues*, Vol. 28, No. 2, 59–78.

Brass, D. J. 1985. "Men's and Women's Networks: A Study of Interaction Patterns and Influence in an Organization." *Academy of Management Journal*, Vol. 28, No. 2, June, 327–343.

Bushardt, S. C., A. Fowler, and R. Caveny. 1987. "Sex Role Behavior and Leadership: An Empirical Investigation." *Leadership and Organization Development Journal*, Vol. 8, No. 5, 11–16.

Campbell, K. E. 1988. "Gender Differences in Job-Related Networks." *Work and Occupations*, Vol. 15, No. 2, May, 179–200.

———, P. V. Marsden, and J. S. Hurlbert. 1986. "Social Resources and Socio-economic Status." *Social Networks*, Vol. 8, 97–117.

Cannings, K. 1988. "Managerial Promotion: The Effects of Socialization, Specialization, and Gender." *Industrial and Labor Relations Review*, Vol. 42, October, 77–87.

Canter, R. 1982. "Achievement in Women: Implications for Equal Employment Opportunity Policy." In *Sex Role Stereotyping and Affirmative Action Policy*, ed. by B. Guteck. Los Angeles: University of California, Institute of Industrial Relations.

Catalyst. 1987. "A Matter of Personal Ability, Not Gender." *Management Solutions*, November, 38–45.

Cohen, A., and D. L. Bradford. 1989. "Influence Without Authority: The Use of Alliances, Reciprocity, and Exchange to Accomplish Work." *Organizational Dynamics*, Vol. 17, No. 3, Winter, 5–17.

Cook, S. H. and J. L. Mendleson. 1984. "The Power Wielders: Men and/or Women Managers." *Industrial Management*, Vol. 226, No. 2, March–April, 22–27.

Denhardt, R., and J. Perkins. 1976. "The Coming Death of the Administrative Man." *Women in Public Administration*, Vol. 36, July/August, 379–84.

DiPrete, T. A., and W. T. Soule. 1988. "Gender and Promotion in Segmented Job Ladder Systems." *American Sociological Review*, Vol. 53, February, 26–40.

Dobbins, G. H., and S. J. Platz. 1986. "Sex Differences in Leadership: How Real Are They?" *Academy of Management Review*, Vol. 11, No. 1, 118–127.

Ferguson, K. 1984. *The Feminist Case Against Bureaucracy*. Philadelphia: Temple University Press.

Goldberg, P. 1968. "Are Women Prejudiced Against Women?" *Trans-Action*, Vol. 5, 28–30.

Goleman, D. 1989. "Research Looks at Fighting Racism." *Miami Herald*, September 13, 2-E.

Haccoun, D. M., G. Sallay, and R. R. Haccoun. 1978. "Sex Differences in the Appropriateness of Supervisory Style: A Nonmangement View." *Journal of Applied Psychology*, Vol. 63, 124–127.

Harragan, B. L. 1977. *Games Mother Never Taught You*. New York: Rawson Associates.

Haskell, J. R. 1985. "Women Blocked by Corporate Politics." *Management World*,
    Vol. 14, No. 9, October, 12–15.
  Heilman, M. E., M. C. Simon, and D. P. Repper. 1987. "Intentionally Fa-
    vored, Unintentionally Harmed? Impact of Sex-Based Preferential Selec-
    tion on Self-Perceptions and Self-Evaluations." *Journal of Applied
    Psychology*, Vol. 72, No. 1, 62–68.
Hendrick, S. S. 1981. "Why Women Don't Succeed." *National Business Employ-
    ment Weekly*, October 18, 9–11.
Hennig, M., and A. Jardim. 1977. *The Managerial Woman*. Garden City, N.Y.:
    Doubleday, Anchor Books.
Instone, D., B. Major, and B. B. Bunker. 1983. "Gender, Self-Confidence, and
    Social Influence Strategies: An Organizational Simulation." *Journal of Per-
    sonality and Social Psychology*, Vol. 44, No. 2, February, 322–333.
Kanter, R. M. 1977. *Men and Women of the Corporation*. New York: Basic Books.
———. 1987. "Men and Women of the Corporation Revised." *Management Re-
    view*, March, 14–16.
Kiesler, S. B. 1975. "Actuarial Prejudice toward Women and Its Implications."
    Journal of Applied Social Psychology, Vol. 5, No. 3, 201–206.
Kipnis, D., and J. Cosentino. 1969. "Use of Leadership Powers in Industry."
    Journal of Applied Research, Vol. 53, 460–466.
Lenney, E. 1977. "Women's Self-Confidence in Achievement Settings." *Psycho-
    logical Bulletin*, Vol. 84, 1–13.
Lott, B. 1985. "The Devaluation of Women's Competence." *Journal of Social Issues*,
    Vol. 41, No. 4, 43–60.
McCarty, P. 1986. "Effects of Feedback on the Self-Confidence of Men and
    Women." *Academy of Management Journal*, Vol. 29, No. 4, 840–847.
McGregor, D. 1967. *The Professional Manager*. New York: McGraw-Hill.
Osborn, R. N., and W. M. Vicars. 1976. "Sex Stereotypes: An Artifact in Leader
    Behavior and Subordinate Satisfaction for Male and Female Leaders."
    Academy of Management Journal, Vol. 19, No. 3, 439–449.
Pazy, A. 1987. "Sex Differences in Responsiveness to Organizational Career
    Management." *Human Resource Management*, Vol. 26, No. 2, Summer, 243–
    256.
Reif, W. E., J. W. Newstrom, and R. M. Monczka. 1975. "Exploding Some
    Myths about Women Managers." *California Management Review*, Vol. 27,
    No. 4, 72–79.
Ruble, D. N., and T. N. Ruble. 1982. "Sex Stereotypes." In *In the Eye of the
    Beholder: Contemporary Issues in Stereotyping*, ed. by A. G. Miller. New York:
    Praeger.
Schein, V. E. 1973. "The Relationship between Sex Role Stereotypes and Req-
    uisite Management Characteristics." *Journal of Applied Psychology*, Vol. 57,
    95–100.
———. 1975. "Relationships between Sex Roles Stereotypes and Requisite Man-
    agement Characteristics, among Female Managers. *Journal of Applied Psy-
    chology*, Vol. 60, 340–344.
Sharkansky, I. 1982. *Public Administration, Agencies, Policies, and Politics*. San
    Francisco: W. H. Freeman.

Shepard, H. A. 1977. "Men in Organizations: Some Reflections." *Beyond Sex Roles*, ed. by A. G. Sargent. New York: West.

Statham, A. 1987. "The Gender Model Revisited." *Sex Roles*, Vol. 16, Nos. 7 and 8, 409–429.

Trempe, J., A. J. Rigny, and R. R. Haccoun. 1985. "Subordinate Satisfaction With Male and Female Managers: Role of Perceived Supervisory Influence." *Journal of Applied Psychology*. Vol. 70, No. 1, February, 44–47.

Chapter 2 ———————————————

Demystifying the Status of Women

Access to atypical careers, though more of a reality for women today than in the past, is still for the most part fairly elusive. Women employees are concentrated in lower-level positions with lower pay and also fewer opportunities for advancement. Clerical positions have replaced factory employment as the single largest occupational category in the United States, with most of those positions filled by women. Currently, 20 percent of the total workforce, or one out of every three women who works for pay, holds a clerical position (Blum and Smith, 1988). In the past, the clerical position was seen as the first step in ascending the organizational ladder or the way to gain entrance into management. This, however, no longer holds true. Women who currently occupy management positions are younger recent hires with college degrees, and not experienced office workers (Rosenbaum, 1985).

Women's attendance at institutions of higher education is seen as a good predictor of their ability to have access to professional employment opportunities. In many cases, women who attend college and have completed higher levels of education will have a greater tendency to work and exhibit the drive, ambition, and capacity to set goals that reflect upward mobility and leadership capabilities (Nickles and Ashcraft, 1981). College provides the academic knowledge and technological skills that are perceived by administrators and managers as necessary requirements for advancement in an organization. But college also offers the opportunity to integrate information and develop interpersonal skills. Only part of the learning experience takes place in the college classroom itself; many of the basic management and people skills are learned from others when living together. Urban universities with many working students provide a place for students from a variety of backgrounds to meet and discuss life from different perspectives. In many ways, this is a protected environment where it is expected that one experiments with new ways of thinking and behaving, questions ideas taken for granted, and develops a personal style and image. This is particularly important for women who have grown up with little exposure to many of the opportunities for development that are characteristic of college campuses.

Colleges and universities attempt to reinforce individuals for setting and reaching goals, experimenting with creative ways to solve problems, and tackling difficult situations. Through this academic process, the acknowledgment of accomplishment becomes expected. The move to the workplace can be difficult because of the limits placed on individuals and the degrees and levels of rewards that are available as reinforcement. The transition to the work environment will require that a woman stretch her traditional framework to maximize opportunities for advancement and develop a strategy for integrating creative ideas with the operational needs of the organization. Though this transition may come at some personal cost, women who have not attended college and have entered the job market after high school will find themselves facing greater difficulties in overcoming the transition from entry-level employment to mid- to higher-level management positions than are faced by their better-educated sisters.

Clerical positions, though in reality they often lack advancement possibilities, are demanding and extremely stressful. Many offices would cease to operate without the qualified staff who provide support to middle and upper managers. In many cases, staffers are the backbone of the organization and are the only employees who have a clear understanding of the basic operations of the office. Though the clerical staff plays an important role in these operations, they as individuals stand little chance of rising above their support status. Chapman and Luthans (1972) reinforce this by stating that there has been an increased emphasis on equal opportunity, improved education and training for women, and change in values and stereotypes, yet in general most women have not successfully moved from the organizations' lower ranks into management positions. This is not to say that a college education is the only way to reach upper management; through intensive retooling, women are able to develop expertise and earn credentials that will allow them to be promoted into positions of greater responsibility with higher levels of compensation. However, access to upper management will be closed to most women, especially to those who do not enter the workplace with the requisite degrees.

This limited access to all occupations has been highlighted in the study of 290 organizations that reaffirms the level of job segregation found in the workplace. After careful review of the organizations in question and the goal of reaching gender balance in all positions, it was determined that 86 percent of the women employed by these organizations would have to be transferred to attain job position parity (Bielby and Baron, 1986). This reflects the degree to which women are relegated to female positions and the amount of change necessary to balance hiring practices. In general, organizational structures that include highly differentiated jobs and rigid personnel systems will have the greatest level of job segregation and consequently more difficulty in changing to a system of greater parity in job access. The general plight of women in organizations may not improve dramatically even with an increase in the number of women employed, if they have no opportunity for developing individual levels of success and receiving recognition for their efforts.

Considering the status of women prior to the beginning of this century, the role of women in the workplace has undergone substantial change. Women today enjoy greater and continued opportunities in diversified employment than in the past. Historically, women were afforded access to nontraditional employment during periods of labor scarcity. Due to cyclical economic demands for an increased workforce, women were tolerated in traditionally male-linked occupations. Of particular note is the role that women played during World Wars I and II, when they held positions that were vital in supporting wartime production. These hiring trends were temporary, and the employment of women was seen as a necessity in which they were filling in until men were able to resume their normal responsibilities. Currently we are experiencing a similar and more permanent trend in expanding employment options that reflects a different set of causes and needs. The opportunity for gainful employment is becoming less of a myth and more of a reality, if only for a minority of women in our society. This can be attributed in part to the gradually dwindling numbers of exclusive male preserves that have been found in the traditional male-dominated workplace (Kanter, 1987). Women are no longer restricted by custom and prejudice to clerical or operative positions (Bushardt, et al., 1987). Therefore, the opportunity for employment in areas that have been filled traditionally by men has been widened to include women as a viable part of the workforce. These opportunities have been possible in part because of the dedicated and concentrated individual efforts being made by women in developing the requisite skills and technological competence that effectively ensure chances for advancement in the marketplace.

From a societal perspective, possibilities for advancement can be attributed to the long-term social, economic, and technological shifts that are transforming our work environment. This transformation from a manufacturing-based economy to a service-driven society has not only encouraged our use of a diverse labor force, but has also altered our perceptions as to the nature of work. With a decreasing ability to compete in international manufacturing, the need for highly-paid, semi- or unskilled, unionized workers will decline. There will be little incentive to continue high-wage, low-skill jobs. To compete within a service-driven market and receive above-average compensation will require less initiative and luck, and more education and skills (Johnston and Packer, 1987).

As part of this transformation comes a reassessment of many of the beliefs and norms that have held constant historically. The aging of our current workforce and its anticipated retirement, coupled with a population growth rate that is to remain constant except for immigration, will allow entry for individuals who were traditionally excluded from the market. Women are benefiting from this change not only because they are seen as viable participants in management but because the dependence on stereotypical characterizations of individual capabilities is decreasing (Catalyst, 1987). Women will be seen not as necessary evils, but rather as assets for an organization.

Though competence and skill have provided access to previously closed professions, one cannot discount the impact of the sheer numbers of women in the labor force as a major factor in the diversification of employment possibilities. The rise of female-headed households, the need for additional income, a desire for self-fulfillment, and a society that accepts women working outside the home have contributed to the advance of women in the workplace (Bushardt et al., 1987). It is not anticipated that the trends that have effectively widened the employment market will change in the foreseeable future. By the year 2000, it is projected that 47 percent of the workforce will be female and that 61 percent of all women will be working outside the home for pay (Johnston and Packer, 1987). These statistics reflect a decline in the growth of our population and anticipated changes in our workforce that will include an increase in older, female, disadvantaged workers. These factors, coupled with an increase in demand for higher skill levels, would support an increase in access for women with the needed education and training in atypical careers (Johnston and Packer, 1987). Whether the availability of positions will be in middle or upper management remains to be seen; however, one can anticipate a greater emphasis on a more highly educated workforce who will play an increasingly large role in organizational decision-making.

The relative numbers of women in the workplace increase the possibility of women making an impact on the organization and playing a role in the decision-making process. But numbers in themselves are not significant indicators of the ability to influence. Kanter (1977) has asserted that it is the position, not the person, that exerts influence in the organization. Women, for the most part, occupy positions that are routine and highly standardized, and, because of the nature of these support positions, it is almost impossible to have an impact on decision-making or to be given credit for individual input.

Though women as a group have made inroads in lower and upper management positions, few women occupy upper management. The rationale for these small numbers in part can be attributed to the length of time required to attain upper-level positions. Most female managers are still too young in years and training to have reached the upper echelons (Williams, 1988). However, if one agrees with this analysis, one can anticipate a noticeable increase in numbers over time. Women who currently hold middle-management jobs have the requisite education and technical knowledge and are developing the skills and techniques that are often learned on the job. How far women actually will progress in the organization will depend on the political savvy that directs the individual woman in successfully navigating within the organization, as well as the corporate structure's willingness to support change.

Though managers and administrators would like to think that their operations are based on a rational and planned process, much of what occurs is actually crisis management or "putting out fires." Often constraints will force managers to make decisions that may not serve the best interest of the unit in the long run but are necessary to continue the day-to-day operations. Decisions that are made in this manner may not reflect the best interests of women and of how they are treated. If women are not visible and not consulted when crisis management decisions are being made, their overall impact on the organization will be decreased.

Often women feel that they are being shortchanged on promotions or raises because they perceive that they are working harder yet receiving less recognition or compensation than their male counterparts. This can occur if the female employee expects to be evaluated solely on job competence and ignores the politics that are present in every organization. Women must also be aware that their gender may predetermine how others evaluate their efforts (Haskell, 1985). Efforts to break down preconceived notions may require that women work twice as hard as men to receive the same level of recognition.

These obstacles that inhibit women's advancement trace their origins to the internal dynamics that control the organization. Organizations by definition must be self-perpetuating and are designed to ensure their continued existence. Ironically, although all systems must change, a proposed change in an organization is perceived as threatening and will be met with resistance by those who feel they have the most to lose. Change, particularly that which has long-term pay-off instead of short-term gain, will be difficult to justify. Consequently, managers will be less motivated to attempt change when the degree of risk is uncertain and the possible implications remain unclear (Blum and Smith, 1988).

To ensure their long-term viability, organizations protect their assets not only in terms of maintaining and expanding physical structures but in retaining and developing upper-level employees. These well-paid employees represent a sizable investment in terms of both dollars invested and the costs associated with personnel replacement (Glinow, 1982). Organizations commonly become wedded to the manner in which they operate and to the individuals who have been placed in positions of power and authority. This close alliance is reinforced by those in power who, based upon their self-interest, want to continue as they have in the past. Much of how we behave in an organization as a result of these factors is referred to as job politics.

Dubrin (1978) observes that individuals will depend upon subtle maneuvers to gain attention and ultimately to receive rewards for their efforts. Competition for power, lack of objective standards, and emotional insecurity motivate otherwise rational employees to behave politically. Competition for power assumes a zero-sum game in which there is a limited amount of power to be divided among an ever-growing number of employees. Those who seek power will find it in their best interest to acquire as much as possible and to nurture what they control. Organizations that have little at stake will find themselves besieged by office politics; with very little turf to divide, there is greater desire to control that which is available. An example of the desire to control is described below:

The company existed as a one-store operation; there were three salespeople and the owner/manager. When the manager was away from the office, it was up to the three employees to share the responsibility for running the store. Joe, the most outspoken of the three salespeople, felt that one of them should be named Assistant Manager who in the absence of the manager would be responsible for making sure all went well. As part of his efforts to document his case, Joe took it upon himself to make note of any problem or loss of sales that occurred during the manager's absences and to inform him of them upon his return. If customers made comments about the manager's absence, Joe encouraged them to inform the manager about some of the problems they experienced because of the leaderless sales staff. After a particularly slow week, Joe decided to confront the manager about the long-term implications of not promoting a sales-person to the position of assistant manager. Based upon the political campaign waged by Joe, one can only question how long it would take before the manager decided to reward a particularly concerned and supportive employee by promoting him to Assistant Manager.

Setting standards, though a goal for many organizations, can become a living nightmare when implementation is attempted. It is easy to assess productivity that results in numerical calculations or the bottom line. But in organizations whose reputations and productivity are measured in terms of the ability to provide services to the public, less emphasis is placed on the numbers and more on a concern for meeting the needs of the client or customer. Consequently, when standards are based on individual strengths and personal interactions, less consistency in measurement is possible. Greater latitude is afforded, and those with an eye for personal aggrandizement may feel it is in their interest to promote themselves first and be concerned with others second. In the scenario that follows, personality, rather than accomplishment is perceived to be the basis for success.

It wasn't real clear how salaries were determined or how raises were distributed. The whole process appeared to be dictated by chance. In general, the employees felt content and had little desire to question the process until a rather aggressive employee was brought into the regional office. Pat, the new employee, revolutionized their vision of management and how they distributed benefits and rewards. The position that Pat occupied was never clearly defined but one could always find Pat smiling and reassuring management with comments about their effectiveness and sensitivity. Even though Pat was considered the office joke, no one seemed overly concerned, at least until raise time. Pat was not only moved to a window office closer to the executive suite but provided with a parking space near the main door. Rumors throughout the office were indicating that the reason for the low salary increases for the group were to compensate for a major increase for Pat.

Emotional insecurity, whether it reflects a factual appraisal of an individual's worth on the job or not, will determine how he or she approaches the job and others in the organization. In some cases, employees who feel inadequate will ingratiate themselves with their superiors in hopes that their performance will not be reviewed as critically or completely, based on their job-related responsibilities. Subordinates who are seen as supportive and part of a team effort will be given the benefit of the doubt, at least initially.

Flattery also can be used effectively in bolstering the ego of an insecure or uncertain supervisor. A manager who feels personally vulnerable due to lack of experience or previous criticism may surround himself/herself with individuals who portray themselves as supportive, available, and trustworthy, but who in reality are simply "yes-men/women." This dependence on playing the political game and being surrounded by those who make the supervisor feel better can be extremely dangerous, not only for the supervisor but for the well-being of the organization. As described in the following paragraph the opposite can also hold true:

Jane was extremely hard working; she spent her spare moments learning about the organization and reading trade journals. Whether called upon for advice or not, she would give critical reviews of current problems and well-thought-out suggestions. Unfortunately, she had never learned to do this quietly or out of the hearing range of others. Had she learned to make her supervisors appear more in control and knowledgeable, she would have been perceived to be an asset rather than a thorn in the side of administration. Jane, though one of the brightest and hardest-working employees in her area, had little chance of receiving recognition for her efforts, and possible hopes for promotion were limited.

Success clearly requires an understanding of office politics and an individual's maneuverability within the organization (Dubrin, 1978). Organizations as they exist and function reflect the years of accumulated investments on the part of management and individual employees, the perceived requirements for individual success, and the desire to continue operations. Change, though we would like to think of it as an automatic reflex in response to a problem or difficult situation, can result in hard-fought battles that will test the very structure of a unit.

Historically, management has supported policies that have excluded both women and minorities from the mainstream of decision-making and have limited their access to positions of authority. Cross (1986) reinforces this statement when he contends that successful individuals and groups advance their economic and political status by joining special-interest groups, making connections, building alliances, erecting barriers against others, establishing exclusive turfs, camouflaging the locus of power, and blocking competition from possible rivals. Change that has occurred in organizations has been both conventional and incremental by definition and therefore has not threatened the power brokers or those who will personally lose the most by radical change. To ensure greater access to all, organizations must go beyond the granting of special dispensations for selected females and minorities and open the door to opportunity for all those who are talented and qualified. Economic necessity may be the major determinant in implementing changes that would result in an environment that facilitates equal access to opportunity based on merit.

Organizational change that provides equal access to the fast track must be accompanied by conscientious efforts on the part of those traditionally excluded to develop the necessary reputation and clout that evolve into a personal power base. Good management skills are developed both formally and informally, with individuals reaching different levels of facility in areas that reflect their personal goals, needs, and abilities. The opportunity to use and develop strategies or techniques to attain a specific goal or goals will vary depending on what is successful for the individual and what is within the individual's own range of behavior.

When one examines carefully the definition of good management, it is apparent that the ability to manage automatically implies that the individual not only possesses knowledge and information but has the power to implement. McMurray states that "the most important and unyielding necessity of organizational life is not better communications, human relations, or employee participation but power" (1973, p. 140). The ability to exercise power reflects one's status within the organization, control over resources, level of expertise, and confidence (Stechert, 1986). Power, or the ability to control others' behavior despite their opposition, is often the bottom line of organizational behavior and ranges in scope from "controlling scarce resources, negotiating agreements, establishing professional and personal goals, and directing others' energies toward those goals" (Fairholm, 1985, p. 45). This theme is further discussed in chapter 5, which includes a descriptive case analysis.

Traditionally, women have lacked acknowledged power within organizations. Even in situations where women hold administrative positions, they are often responsible for units that are predominantly female. Two examples are found in the nursing and teaching professions. A greater proportion of female principals is found at the elementary school level than at the high school level. In Dade County, the fourth largest school district in the United States, four of the county's high school principals are female (less than 15 percent), while a majority of the county's elementary school principals (57 percent) are women (Listing of Dade County Schools, 1989–90). Nursing units in hospitals will often be headed by the only woman holding a top-level administrative position.

To attribute this differing access to power solely to women's recent entry into the workplace ignores the masculine components of organizational life. This status quo has been developed based on interactions between men and women who play subordinate or powerless roles.

Men acquire a lot of power through default; just because they're male we expect them to hold the reins. Women, on the other hand, have to earn—and often fight for—whatever power they get. All other factors being equal, a woman, simply by being female, is less powerful than a man. (Stechert, 1986, p. 173)

Men traditionally have been powerful in organizations because of the status of their positions, their control over resources, their levels of expertise, and their overall confidence in their abilities. In some situations, though, minimal levels of power could be held by women, if their supervisor held a powerful position and was willing to allow this empowerment. Historically, women's limited empowerment reflected the power wielded by their supervisors and to some degree their own ability to control others.

We have stated in general terms how power is defined, but it is important to include in this discussion an understanding of the different forms of power, be it expert, perceived, referent, or coercive (Stechert, 1986). Expert power relies on an individual's ability to demonstrate a sufficient level of knowledge or skill that others feel is necessary and important in the operation of the organization. The required level of skill must exceed that which is considered a standard requisite of the organization. In the days prior to the integration of personal computers in the workplace, individuals who were able to work on the main-frame and provide data runs and cost analysis with what appeared to be little effort were considered invaluable to the organization. They not only were able to produce needed information but they had the ability to control the distribution of resources. An understanding of computer capabilities, purchasing requirements, and future trends provided them with information that others did not quite understand but were afraid to avoid. In order to maintain this power base, the computer expert of pre-PC days has had to expand his or her capabilities into areas that now exceed those of the computer literate masses.

Perceived power, or the imagined existence of power, can be most effective. How a person is perceived often has more impact than what he or she actually may know or be capable of doing. Perceptions, though based on particles of reality, will often be an illusion of capabilities that make others feel that their support is justified. In many ways, a charismatic leader will generate the support of his or her followers based not so much on substance as on an emotional or nonrational dimension. It would be difficult to change others' opinion of the boyish, good-looking executive, who always remembers and makes reference to his staff's personal needs and goals when making any decisions that affect their jobs. In reality, that personal veneer may cover a cold and calculating interior that is run not by a concern for others but for a desire to get what he wants, at any cost.

Referent power, or the clone effect, may be a powerful source of influence. If an appeal can be made to an individual based upon either a real or perceived similarity, the desired response may result because of this feeling of sameness. It is difficult to ignore the request of one's friend; it is easier to dismiss the problems of someone with whom you feel no ties or attachments. Consequently, the sole female manager in the office who can discuss the coming football game or is capable of playing a challenging game of tennis or golf may have an easier time being seen as one of the guys and increase her chances of being effective and getting things done.

Coercive power is the ability to force others to take action or behave in a way that is not of their choosing. Coercion can be physical, but in the organizational setting it more often controls through fear and anxiety. Coercive power may range in significance from a minor comment or remark that embarrasses or diminishes one's reputation to the with-holding of a reward or a punitive action that may have long-term financial and emotional implications. In the short-run, coercive power, though extremely effective in getting another's attention, can demoralize not only the subordinate who is the recipient of this coercive act but others who fear that they could be next. A quick turnover of staff can result, if employees feel that it is in their best interest to relocate professionally. However, one should not underestimate the impact of coercive power when dealing with a situation that is destructive to the unit and needs immediate remedy.

Power in itself is neither positive or negative: "How the manager copes with the situation is the test. . . . What works for a man manager may not work for a woman manager and vice versa" (Cook and Mendleson, 1984, p. 27). Individuals should choose their behavior and modify their actions based upon their own preferences and the probability of using the most effective method, not because a specific behavior is acceptable for their gender. Doing the unexpected may in fact produce the desired results.

There are rules to be followed that can assist women in gaining or increasing their power in an environment that has been successfully operated by men who follow a traditional gender-based division of labor. A woman must:

• take her career seriously
• be exceptionally competent at her job
• act as if she is important enough to her organization to move up
• develop credibility by getting things done and getting results
• develop connections with people who have power
• have a strong ego
• be able to take criticism and implement suggestions (Haskell, 1985, p. 13–14).

By including the preceding rules in her behavioral repertoire, others in the organization will regard the female manager as an individual and not limit their perception of her role to one that has been defined by stereotypical views of what is expected of women. The woman manager will be seen as a member of a team, who brings to the group specific skills and expertise and provides additional resources that will enhance the efforts of all. This must be balanced against the competitive spirit that encourages us to strive for acknowledgment and rewards for having accomplished a task because of one's individual efforts. Morrison et al. (1987a) have described the following four variables that need to be in balance to ensure professional success: to take risks, but be consistently outstanding; to be tough, yet not be macho; to be ambitious, but not expect equal treatment; and to take responsibility, but listen to the advice of others.

To achieve this balance requires not only intelligence but a highly developed level of confidence in oneself and one's abilities. The female manager who has attained this balance will have the ability to apply pressure to make things happen in other places (Wyse, 1987) and concomitantly be respected for this ability. Empowerment then becomes a reality, if only for a few.

Being successful requires more than simply having access to positions within the organization. Some may attribute success to "being at the right place at the right time" or simply luck, but realistically, individual efforts cannot be minimized. The inability to adapt, wanting too much, and performance problems are the three common and deadly causes for failing to live up to one's potential (Morrison et al., June 1987b). The inability to adapt reflects a woman executive's inability to understand the organization, consistently misreading others and not understanding how things work. Because she cannot adjust, her behavior will be at odds with that of her fellow employees and management. Lacking a sense of common ground, her behavior will reflect these misperceptions, and she will be judged ineffective and nonproductive.

If she is seen as wanting too much, being overly concerned with amassing an empire, or having all the perks of the job, she will gain a reputation for being over-ambitious. Being seen as selfish and demanding, with no apparent pay-off to others and the organization as a whole, will isolate the offender and leave her basically alone with no allies or support.

Finally, if the woman does not have the ability to perform at the required level, she will be unable to develop the necessary skills. Others soon tire of having to help carry her weight and will leave her to her own devices. In addition, her lack of effectiveness will cause embarrassment to the organization, and it will have little choice but either to render her harmless (limit her responsibilities) or relieve her of her position.

When attempting to gain power and to legitimize their place in the organization, women must realize that they will face unique burdens, differing from men in similar situations. The competitive spirit that drives men in the workplace (Hennig and Jardim, 1977) can become personally destructive for women who are not prepared or capable to compete and exert power from within. Some men will find it difficult even to anticipate losing to a woman and consequently will strive to keep her out of the race completely. On the other hand, male counterparts can provide the needed support and critical evaluations that women require in developing a power base. Though women mentors and role models can play an important part in facilitating the empowerment of a female player, because of their limited numbers and lower positions, women may often find themselves in situations where they are the sole female participants. (The final chapter includes specific methods to assist in the implementing of mentoring programs and the development of networking skills.)

To gain the greatest impact, plan an approach that not only deals with the technical aspects involved in reaching solution but takes into consideration alternative approaches to gaining power (Wagner and Swanson, 1979). Wagner and Swanson have stated that men and women express power differently. There is a tendency on the part of men to express power by direct aggression, while women tend to build power bases through a network of interdependent relationships and indirect contact. These strategies in many ways reflect the traditional roles that men and women have played in organizations, men being more aware of the competitive nature of the game because they have held the positions longer, with more at stake, and women depending upon the skills developed while serving in support positions. These skills may not be sufficient when reaching upper management and the zero-sum game of power politics takes over.

One would like to assume that women could depend upon other women who have made it to the top to be supportive and helpful to those still striving to succeed. Research has shown that women are not necessarily supportive of other women simply because of gender. Those who have been promoted and are no longer part of the network that helped them get where they are can be seen as overachievers, having violated the existing norms of behavior. Since they no longer are part of the network, they must now make it on their own. Consequently, the successful female manager may feel that she has made it on her own and will not provide support to other women on the way up. She substantiates this with the justification that women have to play by the same rules as men and be given no special privileges to gain the respect of their peers. Other women, feeling that there may be few positions at the top, would like to minimize the competition from other women and adopt very traditional positions regarding women in the workplace (Miller et al., 1975).

What becomes increasingly apparent is the implicit need for strategic planning on the part of the female manager. Dluhy and Chen (1986, pp. XIII–XIV), in their description of planning perspectives, have provided five points that are integral to the planning process. These points provide insight not only for organizations but for individuals intent on developing personal strategies for success.

1. Planning is action research and requires knowledge and information in making decisions.

2. Planning is knowledge-driven and requires the ability to communicate using technological advances (computer technology, languages, profession-specific information, etc.)

3. Planning is both process- and technique-oriented, and the individual should pay attention to problem-solving while utilizing effective analytical techniques.

4. Planning is interdisciplinary and requires attention to both theoretical and practical issues.

5. Planning is adaptive to emerging concerns, responding to a broad and ever-changing set of circumstances.

This five-step overview of strategic planning provides women with the opportunity to individualize their planning approach and to maximize their impact on the organization. As part of this process, an individual must go beyond what she assumes to be true and investigate both the organization and the field to be firmly in control of information. This research serves a dual purpose, first to benefit the organization and second to inform the individual of what is relevant in both the formal and informal arenas. Next, the need to maintain a level of competence in the technical areas becomes more important as technological changes occur more quickly and are absorbed into the organizational process. These must be balanced with a clear sense of what is realistically possible within the organization and blend both the theoretical, or what ought to work, with the pragmatic, or what is actually possible. And lastly, be ready to adapt personal goals to fit within the realities of the organization and individual needs. Change is as important for individuals as it is for organizations.

There is no cookbook approach to succeed in the corporate world. Rather, a woman must develop an individual strategy that takes full advantage of her skills, abilities, and personality and that includes a careful assessment of what actually works in her organization, as well as a clear understanding of her professional goals. (See chapter 5 for different strategies that can be used to maximize one's impact as a subordinate, co-worker, and manager.)

The ultimate balance requires a certain level of political game-playing with a strong commitment to professional behavior. The cost to be paid for compromising one's personal and professional integrity can extend throughout one's career. When playing the game requires behaving in a way that is personally unacceptable or places greater importance on personal success than fulfilling responsibilities, one must question whether the ends can realistically justify the means. We cannot assume that women are any more or less willing than men to compromise their beliefs. They simply have not had the same opportunity to test their commitments.

REFERENCES

Bielby, W., and J. Baron. 1986. "Men and Women at Work: Job Segregation and Statistical Discrimination." *American Journal of Sociology*, Vol. 91, No. 4, 759–99.

Blum, L., and V. Smith. 1988. "Women's Mobility in the Corporation: A Critique of the Politics of Optimism." *Journal of Women in Culture and Society*, Vol. 13, No. 3, Spring, 528–545.

Bushardt, S. C., A. Fowler, and R. Caveny. 1987. "Sex Role Behaviour and Leadership: An Empirical Investigation." *Leadership and Organization Development Journal*, Vol. 8, No. 5, 10–16.

Catalyst. 1987. "A Matter of Personal Ability, Not Gender." *Management Solutions*, Vol. 32, November, 38–45.

Chapman, J. B., and F. Luthans. 1972. "The Female Leadership Dilemma." *Public Personnel Management*, May–June, 173–179.

Cook, S. H., and J. L. Mendleson. 1984. "The Power Wielders: Men and/or Women Managers?" *Industrial Management*, Vol. 26, No. 2, March–April, 22–27.

Cross, T. 1986. *The Black Power Imperative: Racial Inequality and the Politics of Non-Violence.* New York: Faulkner Books.

Dluhy, M. J. and K. Chen (Eds.). 1986. *Interdisciplinary Planning: A Perspective for the Future.* New Brunswick, NJ: Rutgers.

Dubrin, A. 1978. *Human Relations: A Job Oriented Approach*, Reston, VA: Prentice-Hall.

Fairholm, G. W. 1985. "Power Tactics on the Job." *Personnel*, May, 45–50.

Glinow, M. A. V. 1982. "Career Concepts and Human Resources Management: The Case of the Dual Career Couple." *Sex Role Stereotyping and Affirmative Action Policy*, ed. by B. Gutek. Los Angeles: University of California, Institute of Industrial Relations.

Haskell, J. R. 1985. "Women Blocked by Corporate Politics." *Management World*, Vol. 14, No. 9, October, 12–15.

Hennig, M., and A. Jardim. 1977. *The Managerial Woman*. Garden City, NY: Doubleday, Anchor Books.

Johnston, W., and A. Packer. 1987. *Workforce 2000: Work and Workers for the Twenty-First Century.* Indianapolis: Hudson Institute.

Kanter, R. M. 1977. *Men and Women of the Corporation*. New York: Basic.

———. 1987. "Men and Women of the Corporation Revisited." *Management Review*, Vol. 76, No. 3, March, 14–15.

Listing of Dade County Public Schools, Dade County, Florida, 1989–90.

McMurry, R. N. 1973. "Power and the Ambitious Executive." *Harvard Business Review*, November–December, 140–145.

Miller, J., S. Labovitz, and L. Fry. 1975. "Inquiries in the Organizational Experiences of Women and Men." *Social Forces*, Vol. 54, 365–381.

Morrison, A. M., R. P. White, and E. Van Velsor. 1987a. "Executive Women: Substance Plus Style," *Psychology Today*, August, 18–25.

Morrison, A. M., R. P. White, and E. Van Velsor, and Center for Creative Leadership. 1987b. "Women With Promise: Who Succeeds, Who Fails?" *Working Woman*, June, 79–82.

Nickles, E., and L. Ashcraft. 1981. *The Coming Matriarchy: How Women Will Gain the Balance of Power.* New York: Seaview.

Rosenbaum, J. 1985. "Jobs, Job Status and Women's Gains from Affirmative Action: Implications for Comparable Worth." In *Comparable Worth: New Directions for Research,* ed. by H. Hartmann. Washington, DC: National Academy Press.

Stechert, K. B. 1986. *Sweet Success: How to Understand the Men in Your Business Life and Win with Your Own Rules.* New York: Macmillan.

Wagner, K., and C. Swanson. 1979. "From Machiavelli to Ms: Differences in Male-Female Power Styles." *Public Administration Review,* Vol. 39, 66–72.

Williams, M. J. 1988. "Women Beat the Corporate Game." *Fortune,* Vol. 118, September 12, 128–138.

Wyse, L. 1987. "The Finer Points of Building Power." *Working Woman,* January, 79–80.

PART II

Integrating Women into Organizational Life: Perspectives on Gender and Work

For most people involved in human resource development (HRD), organizational integration is interpreted as making people "fit" into existing work cultures. While this state of affairs is neither ideal nor preferred, this dilemma is further complicated by knowing that at present women are treated as a special case. Because of women's marginal status, it is assumed that their integration will require extra measures not needed by men. Part II tries to come to terms with whether this premise is accurate or must be revised. On that basis, what implications does this premise have for those considering organizational change programs?

In this section, chapter 3 will review theories and perspectives about women's thought and behavior. In this field of study, many pages have been devoted to the debate over whether women's experience is an extension of or similar to men's. Recently, more attention has been paid to the question, if research has determined that women do differ in specific and unique ways, whether these specific behaviors and attitudes significantly affect the conduct of the workplace.

After coming to terms with these issues, chapter 4 applies what we know about women to the question of involving them in organizational life. Definitions of organizational integration are presented that relate to work culture, socialization, and indoctrination. Most instances of integrated organizations are the outcome of informal efforts that, whether by fortuitous circumstance or design, result in productive, harmonious working relationships, forging a cohesive unit in the process. Chapter 4 describes essential components for a formal program to accomplish those ends.

Chapter 3 _____

Views of Women: Gender Comparisons and Feminist Perspectives

Since the world is full of a number of things, . . . we must categorize and simplify in order to comprehend. But the reduction of complexity entails a great danger, since the line between enlightening epitome and vulgarized distortion is so fine. Dichotomy is the usual pathway to vulgarization.

Stephen Jay Gould, 1984

This chapter looks at several approaches that attempt to explain how women think and behave and why. We are interested in how women and men have symbolically come to represent polar aspects of life as well as the inadequacies of this perspective. We also discuss how thinking about women has changed in recent decades. Some research and writing are cited that explain women's behavior, attitudes, and performance as comparable to men's; other studies treat women and men as dissimilar. We also explore feminist perspectives, which argue that women possess special or unique qualities that are equal or superior to men's. Finally, we address several provocative questions in this field of study: How does what we think we know about women influence their behavior at work? Can the feminist perspective offer fresh insights to illuminate the reflexive relationship between the individual and the organization?

GENDER AND DUALISM

There are several ways to interpret the nature of women's involvement in work organizations. In many ways, genuine concern for women in the workplace may signify a major shift as to which values institutions and society consider important. Symbolically, increasing women's participation in organizational life means to some that the "softer" side of human nature is becoming a legitimate concern commanding attention from management. At the same time, it may be no coincidence that labor experts predict that American business and industry will devote increasing attention to women workers and their interests. As the American economy begins to recognize shrinking labor pools for workers, qualified, trained women become valued members of the workforce. Issues previously labeled "women's concerns"—affordable day care, flex-time, job sharing—become priorities for institutional and executive agendas.

Examined from another perspective, many cultures share views of women and men as complementary personalities, two sides of a coin, a duality. Both sides need to be represented within the complete personality, or the one-sided personality at least requires a significant relationship with another who serves to complement him or her. Without a blending of masculine and feminine, the human being is considered incomplete. Following this reasoning, men have represented the classic notion of *homo faber* . . . man the "doer," the instrumental, task-oriented side of human nature. Women, on the other hand, have been regarded as complementing men by fulfilling the role of helpmate, the perpetuator of culture, and have represented the expressive, emotional side. Hence, a popular form of expressing this dualism is to say that women are supportive, passive, dependent, other-oriented, and emotional, while men are analytic, assertive, independent, rational, and self-directed (Glennon, 1979).

Along these same lines, Harding (1981) distinguishes between men and women in terms of the public-private distinction. As Ferguson observes, "The equation of women's experience with the private realm and men's with the public is a useful vehicle for capturing the two distinct world views," especially since, as she continues, "members of each gender carry the world view of their own domain with them into the other realm, and must consciously put it aside to 'succeed' in the other world on its terms" (1984, p. 27). The notion that each gender carries an opposing world view predominantly influenced by the respective gender's sense of identity raises the concern that each "side" is by itself inadequate or insufficient. If we are to bring both halves of the human personality into organizations, we must allow for the expressive and nonrational side to be acknowledged and dealt with, for all members of the organization. Therefore, sincere efforts to understand how women's introduction into the workplace influences work culture not only force reexamination of these cultural stereotypes but also raise the question of human-centered concerns, such as balance in the individual personality.

In any form, the dualist perspective is capable of provoking thought and insight. However, we question whether it is adequate simply to declare that the "halves" are equal irrespective of cultural ascriptions of masculine or feminine behavior. As a case in point, refer to the arguments that, in the American West of the the nineteenth century, female and male homesteaders were equal by virtue of the importance of their respective complementary roles. Since that time, this argument proceeds, women's work that was originally valued (housekeeping, home schooling, and the general transmission of key cultural components) has been assumed by other institutions. Women's current role in performing these functions has been drastically reduced or, at least in the case of transmitting cultural values, radically transformed. Public education, organized religion, and the mass media have contributed to reshaping how children and recent immigrants become socialized in American society. Viewed in this light, we can trace the devolution of homemaker as a label and as a career: generally, jobs exclusive to women are devalued in our culture. This is the reasoning behind comparable worth proposals: in exclusively female preserves such as child care, employers translate women's social inequality into lack of worth and lower salary scales. Consequently, women's work systematically pays less than men's work. Even to use the term "woman's work" carries cultural ascriptions of weakness; to be compared to a woman or a girl is tantamount to insult. Through the use of such examples, we can begin to see that women's "half" in a supposedly equal dualism has been discredited solely because of their gender.

Finally, we can reframe the idea that the greater involvement of women can mean that integration of all members, despite their gender or background, becomes a high priority in the workplace. Epstein (1988) holds that if given a little incentive, people can change their behavior and take charge of their lives. A Civil Rights Act can serve to motivate members of minority groups to attend colleges and universities, opening doors for professional careers and social advancement. Affirmative action legislation can help to propel women's advancement in situations where previously they dared only hope. If such incentives become so influential in facilitating social change even on a small scale, then organizations should provide similar incentives for the benefit of individuals. The difficult challenge is how to move employers to do so. We will address some of these issues in changing organizational culture in chapter 4. But first, it will be helpful to present arguments based on the elucidation of gender differences. We begin with a feminist argument that women's behavior differs from men's in important ways.

THE FEMINIST CRITIQUE

The power and potential of the feminist argument generally rest on several assumptions: 1) that outsiders to circles of power, or "marginal people," are capable of seeing most clearly where change is needed; 2) that the dualism of male-female worlds and public-private domains must be challenged so that the basic values upon which society rests can be revised (Glennon, 1979); and 3) perhaps most fundamentally, that the broadest area where dominance and subordination are experienced in modern cultures is not race, ethnic, or age-based, but occurs along lines of gender. All cultures make sex-role distinctions that typically assign women to the subordinate role. The universality of this phenomenon does not make it natural, inevitable, or morally correct; it does, however, make it extremely resistant to change. Feminist theory is about women's views of the world, how women make sense of the way the world works. It offers an original approach to critiquing and changing that world. This literature also asserts that women's experience is in and of itself a subject meriting serious attention.

Formerly, social science literature assumed women's experience was the same as or similar to men's. Instead of investigating gender questions, writers have too often framed their research agendas by assuming that women's experience is comparable to men's. Basing epistemological concerns upon a male standard has drawbacks, however, if the investigator's approach has not first validated whether women do make sense of their world in a similar fashion.

Millman and Kanter (1975) present six themes as part of the feminist critique of sociology of which we cite the following:

1. Conventional topics studied by sociologists lead us to ignore issues that would further illuminate women's lives.
2. Sociology, by focusing on public roles and behaviors, ignores the areas where women's experience is more likely revealed.
3. Sociology tends to depict society as a single generalizable entity.
4. Gender is seldom considered by sociologists to be a significant factor that influences behavior (Andersen, 1983, p. 16).

These criticisms can be extended to organizational research as well. Surprisingly little research has investigated the nature of gender differences in organizational life and a related question: If women and men behave and think differently, does this influence organizational behavior and performance? Most of the recent literature that has been completed deals with women in management; women in nonmanagerial or staff positions remain relatively neglected subjects of study. Later in this volume, research into the subject of gender differences will be summarized, centering on comparisons of men's and women's managerial behavior. As is apparent from the rapidly increasing volume of literature on this subject, we are now beginning to see the extent of any gender differences and, based on these empirical findings, can make informed generalizations concerning the probability that any differences have genuine impact on the workplace. We still however lack a complete, clear picture of women employees at all levels in public- and private-sector organizations. Consequently, generalizations based on this research remain purely speculative.

From the foregoing discussion, it should be apparent that generally speaking, feminist theory has much to offer for purposes of critique, asking fundamental epistemological questions concerning why we think as we do about social behavior and organizational life. As one example, writers examining current work practices have observed that the predominant values and norms in any given organization are much more likely to support bureaucratic action and protect the "organization's stake" in events than to choose human-centered values. As is widely known, the bureaucratic form of organization values functions over interaction, technique over social norms, the role over the person, control over effectiveness, means over ends (Hummel, 1982). Partly because of its routinization of domination and its emphasis upon control and efficiency, bureaucratic forms are pervasive in modern society, crossing ideological boundaries and extending the example of bureaucratic structure and process into the far corners of the earth (Gouldner, 1977/78). From a bureaucratic perspective, integration would be defined as the process of facilitating the individual's identification with organizational goals, but always with the subversion of personal goals implied. If the individual's effectiveness is enhanced, this outcome is not valued as an end unto itself but only insofar as individual effectiveness serves the overall needs and goals of the organization. In their analysis of bureaucratic structures, Denhardt and Perkins have stated that feminism challenges the crux of modern organizational life. They find that feminism "argues that superior domination through hierarchical patterns of authority is not essential to the achievement of important goals but in fact is restrictive of the growth of the group and its individual members" (1976, p. 382). As a critique of bureaucracy and its influence on modern life, feminism provides a useful vantage point on taken-for-granted ways of seeing things.

The next section will be devoted to the role that gender plays in creating personal identity to lay the foundation for how men and women proceed to identify with and belong to larger associations.

THE QUESTION OF GENDER

We begin this section on gender influences with an anecdote. It is the kind of story that may be familiar to many readers since they may have witnessed incidents like it.

A married couple, let's call them Susan and Sam, invites another married couple, Andrea and Paul, for dinner. During the evening, they banter, they laugh, they share topics of common interest and enjoy the rare opportunity to catch up on events in their lives. After their friends leave, Susan casually speculates about how their friends are doing. Sam responds, "They seem to be getting along. They seemed a little tired. I guess they needed this chance to unwind. I think they enjoyed themselves tonight." Susan's curiosity is piqued. She says, "That's interesting you felt that. I felt tension somewhere between the two of them. I wouldn't be surprised if something's going on." Challenged, Sam probes Susan's remarks. Susan counters, "It's not anything specific, just the way they avoided looking each other in the eye sometimes, like they just had a fight. How they looked when they did connect, like they were unsure of themselves. How they talked more to us than each other. Did you notice: they hardly ever said 'we'?" Sam dismissed Susan's observations as "reading too much into things. Even if what you say is accurate, it doesn't necessarily mean anything." Roughly three weeks later, Andrea phones Susan to say that she and Paul have decided on a trial separation.

What has happened here? Are women and men so far apart that they inhabit separate worlds? Do they see the events so differently that their interpretations appear diametrically opposed to one another? Is this the dualist perspective lived in everyday life? For the moment, assume that dualism is the most accurate way to explain what has occurred. Sam and Susan might represent polar extremes on a continuum. Susan represents the private dimension: the socially sensitive woman who "reads" people and relationships well. As Sam might counter, perhaps not too seriously, perhaps she's using her "woman's intuition." He, on the other hand, portrays the public side, discounting Susan's ideas unless she can produce the facts and evidence to back up her feelings.

While this explanation may satisfy some readers, others will prefer a less adversarial view, a perspective that stresses that because Sam's and Susan's differences are so extreme, they fail to represent men and women in general. Polar opposites support stereotypes that elevate superficial differences to something meaningful and have the capacity to stimulate generalizations. Nevertheless, the fact that basic physiology separates women and men means that many people expect that behavioral differences, important ones, must exist as well. These observers typically conclude that biological and behavioral differences are influential. Following this reasoning, we must explore the effects and extent of those differences, and, if the differences cannot be explained solely by genetics, determine what precisely accounts for them. Because the treatment of these questions fills volumes and is so full of contradiction, much has been written concerning the accuracy of the literature itself (Epstein, 1988). While we will address the question of accuracy in later chapters, the next section will present treatments of sex-role socialization and its influence on work roles.

SEX ROLE SOCIALIZATION AS PREPARATION FOR WORKLIFE

To advocates of the dualist perspective, the worlds of women and men resemble parallel tracks within the same culture due to different socialization practices for each gender. In particular, the kind of identity fostered in males is quite different from that for females. In American culture, manhood is defined in terms of separation, independence, and autonomy. A boy becomes a man through severing his connectedness to his family and pursuing his personal goals. In summarizing Chodorow's influential work (1976), Ferguson states:

Male self-identity is founded largely on the repression of affect, the denial of relational needs, and the rupture of connection. Men tend to judge themselves and others by standards of achievement and competency, and to draw moral judgments on the basis of the application of abstract and universal notions of individual rights. (1984, p. 159).

In such a world, phenomena are viewed as "physically and socially disembodied 'things,' governed by ultimately predictable laws or rules that can be rationally perceived and controlled" (pp. 159–60).

Girls are raised with a different set of expectations. A girl's identity is grounded in social relationships and a sense of connectedness with others. Girls are raised to value the interdependence of self and others and, because affiliation is valued for its own sake, learn to judge themselves by standards of responsibility and care toward others. Generally, women's moral judgments tend to be based upon feelings of empathy and compassion for others. Rather than search for objective rules that can govern a class of circumstances, most women will try to explore approaches to accommodate diverse interests fairly in ways satisfying to those affected. Rather than viewing the world as objectively composed, women tend to see "physically and socially embodied 'things' which are concrete, particularistic, and continuous with one another" (Ferguson, 1984, p. 160). These things are treated as wants and needs that resist control, almost as if they had interests of their own.

Just as revealing are the differences between the types of games played by boys and girls. Boys tend to choose competitive games that involve the use and interpretation of rules and procedures for resolving conflicts. Girls choose turn-taking or noncompetitive games. When conflict is not dealt with successfully, the game is terminated to preserve relational ties (Gilligan, 1979).

Boys' games teach skills that entail organizing and coordinating the efforts of relatively large numbers of people, dealing directly with conflict and competition. . . . Girls' games continue the intimate and dyadic patterns of interaction characteristic of the earlier infant-mother relation, and encourage the learning of cooperative skills and the empathetic ability to take the experience of others as one's own. (Ferguson, 1984, p. 163).

For girls, games and their attendant rules can be dispensed with if relationships are at stake. Conflict is dealt with less from a win-lose stance than from an orientation of fairness and a balancing of everyone's interests and feelings. Women sometimes point out that even when boys dislike one another, they will seek each other in order to play a particular game (Hennig and Jardim, 1977). The game must be played, preserved with rules intact, no matter what the individual interests involved.

In later life, these early competitive and accommodative experiences with play will form the background upon which political games involving competition, dominance, and subordination are engaged. Clearly, boys advance to manhood with skills and attitudes for fitting into bureaucratic life and with preparation in gamesmanship that permits them to cope with its rigorous requirements. As Ferguson (1984, p. 46) so eloquently states, schools train children for a "lifetime of hierarchy and domination," depending on their social class, race, and gender. Girls are prepared for social relationships particularly within the family; at work, girls' play experience is translated into support roles and maintenance functions. Traditional socialization prepares girls to accept, or at least perform, subordinate roles. It does not teach them the fundamentals of political games. Femininity is consequently a response to the requirements of subordination; it reflects, but does not cause, women's powerlessness (Ferguson, 1984, p. 95). Because women are powerless in the work domain particularly, passivity, compliance, and the "spectator" role are endorsed as ways to remain non-threatening workers while maintaining their traditional female identification and upbringing.

Beginning with their respective identities, men and women bring their different views of politics and the world into play in organizations. Drawing on the imagery found in men's and women's fantasies and thoughts, Gilligan (1982, p. 62) has chosen the symbols of web and hierarchy to convey the different ways men and women structure relationships. The web signifies the connectedness through which women articulate their identities; the hierarchy, with its attention to dominance and subordination, communicates the power of position, rules, and gamesmanship. These images also convey some of the differences in how men and women view politics and questions of ethics.

But these images create a problem in understanding because each distorts the other's representation. As the top of the hierarchy becomes the edge of the web and as the center of a network of connection becomes the middle of a hierarchical progression, each image marks as dangerous the place which the other defines as safe. Thus the images of hierarchy and web inform different modes of assertion and response: the wish to be alone at the top and the consequent fear that others will get too close; and the wish to be at the center of connection and the consequent fear of being too far out on the edge. These disparate fears of being stranded and being caught give rise to different portrayals of achievement and affiliation, leading to different modes of action and different ways of assessing the consequences of choice (Gilligan, 1982, p. 62).

The metaphors of web and hierarchy illustrate the structures and domains with which women and men are expected to feel secure, as judged by the strictures of traditional sex-role socialization. Although sex-role socialization fosters these images and elaborates biologically based differences into full-scale social differentiation, it should be mentioned that individuals of each gender can and do operate with views of relationships and work that deviate from traditional sex roles.

GENDER AND INTELLECTUAL DEVELOPMENT

Women Are Similar

According to some accounts, men and women share more similarities than differences in their ways of developing intellectually and ethically. Perry's classic study in the field of epistemological development (1970) investigates how men and women conceptualize their intellectual development. He describes how (Belenky et al., 1986, p. 9) "students' conceptions of the nature and origins of knowledge evolve and how their understanding of themselves as knowers changes over time." He bases his findings on a sample of male and a small number of female college students. He reports that both proceed through progressively more comprehensive stages of intellectual development called positions (Perry, 1970):

Basic Dualism The world is viewed in terms of opposites (right/wrong, black/white, good/bad). Dualist thinkers are passive learners who depend on experts or authorities for knowledge and understanding. Gradually, however, they begin to see holes in these views and begin to notice and entertain diverse perspectives which challenge this position's simplistic ways of making meaning.

Multiplicity: Less dependent on authorities and outside sources of knowledge, the individual attempts to develop his own views which are now regarded with greater confidence and a sense of worth. However, teachers will challenge these perspectives for logic, evidence, and support. This position then gives way to Relativism Subordinate.

Relativism Subordinate: Here, the student internalizes the lessons and standards of objective evaluation which may have begun during the last stage. Analysis, at least in one's major field at college, becomes standardized and operationalized.

Relativism: The individual begins to appreciate that (Belenky et al., 1986, p. 10): "truth is relative, that the meaning of an event depends on its context and on the framework that the knower uses to understand that event, and that relativism pervades all aspects of life, not just the academic world. Only then is the student able to understand that knowledge is constructed, not given; contextual, not absolute; mutable, not fixed. It is within relativism that Perry believes that affirmation of personal identity and commitment evolves."

Women as Special Cases

The power of Perry's schema is such that educators have endorsed it as the pre-eminent framework to guide their practice. While conceding that Perry's map appears to depict men's progression through these intellectual positions accurately, Belenky et al. (1986) have commented that only a few women were included in Perry's study. In particular, only the men's interviews were used to develop his schema for categorizing both groups' stages of development. As a result, when the results for women are assessed, women are found to conform with the patterns found for men. Belenky continues, "while this strategy enabled the researchers to see what women might have in common with men, it was poorly designed to uncover those themes that might be more prominent among women" (1986, p. 9). Therefore, Belenky's work probes for additional themes that may have been missed through Perry's research protocol.

In an attempt to discover how women view the nature and origins of knowledge, Belenky and colleagues interviewed 135 subjects in depth. Participants were informed that the interviewers wanted to hear what they considered important about life and learning from their own points of view, allowing the patterns indicating certain epistemological categories to emerge from the interview data. As Belenky describes the interviews, each:

began with the question, "Looking back, what stands out for you over the past few years?" and proceeded gradually at the woman's own pace to questions concerning self-image, relationships of importance, education and learning, real-life decision-making and moral dilemmas, accounts of personal changes and growth, perceived catalysts for change and impediments to growth, and visions of the future (Belenky et al., 1986, p. 11).

Building upon Perry's findings, the authors categorized women's perspectives into five epistemological categories (p. 15).

Silence: Women experience themselves as lacking voices and minds of their own. Silent women deny a sense of self. They are passive recipients, subject to the actions of external authorities. They are extremely dependent upon external authority for direction. Due to the extreme voicelessness of this position, this category is rare. In other words, not all women begin viewing the world from this position. When found, this position typically characterizes younger women. If their self-esteem and confidence improve, silent women can progress to the next higher position.

Received Knowledge: Women consider themselves capable of receiving and even repeating knowledge acquired from experts but cannot author knowledge themselves. They "take knowledge in" through listening in order to understand. Women classified in this group feel more comfortable promoting themselves than the Silents but justify self-advancement primarily as a means of helping others. As they rely on others for knowledge, direction, and care, they explain that they "should devote themselves to the care and empowerment of others." Their altruism in this context is viewed as "self-less." For some, however, authorities and experts fail to guide, and these women realize that they must develop their own voices and understanding.

Subjective Knowledge: Truth and knowledge are viewed as "personal, private, and subjectively known and intuited" (Belenky et al., 1986, p. 15). Here women begin listening to an inner voice that informs them about the world. This posture is, however, anti-rationalist; while these women describe truth as personal, this justification does not hold up to the tests of rational thinkers (e.g., academic life). After seeing for themselves the logical flaws and deficiencies in subjectively-based arguments, some Subjectives may be compelled to explore the merits of the next position.

Procedural Knowledge: These women want to learn approaches to obtain and communicate knowledge that are "objective" and thoroughly reasoned. They believe that rational procedures will enable them to know how to think, how to criticize, and how to analyze. Proceduralists understand that the world is more complex than they might have originally thought and appreciate the value of perspective-taking. By understanding others' ways of forming opinions and ideas, they can see the world through their eyes.

Within this group lie two epistemological sub-categories: separate knowing and connected knowing. Separate knowing is based on the acquisition of impersonal rules. The earlier account of boys' play and games illustrates separate knowing: in order to win, players must know the rules and be able to apply them to their advantage. Applied to the work world, such women choose to play games of impersonal reason or politics, games that have traditionally been part of the male preserve.

Connected knowing, as implied by its name, is based on relationships. Connected knowers, like separate knowers, also develop procedures for apprehending others' knowledge. However, the content of their procedures differs. Frequently, they use empathy and conversing. To these women, deep relationships offer a lens onto another world, another way of knowing. Their ultimate purpose is not to evaluate these views according to impersonal rules, but to understand. Unlike the differences between girls' and boys' play, however, some women can and do alternate between both perspectives.

Constructed Knowledge: These women appreciate that people who need to understand the world in great depth need to invent and thereby discover their own voices. Constructed thinkers view all knowledge as context-based. They are authors, originators of knowledge, and frequently radical thinkers. Not only do they "value both subjective and objective strategies for knowing," they can integrate the two domains. Observers might describe these individuals as "frame breakers," for they persist in seeing things in their own unique ways (Belenky et al., 1986, p. 133). They move beyond standard explanations of events, disciplines, or systems of thought and make connections that relate "pockets of knowledge" (p. 140). They possess great sensitivity and perceptiveness in the ways they understand how others come to know the world and, starting with that perspective, are capable of thinking at a higher level, building to a new frame of reference. In this manner, constructed knowers can create original perspectives for themselves and help others to do the same. They are capable of proposing ideas that define the nature of work problems in novel ways and can foster creative solutions for organizational problems.

One way that constructivists acquire new knowledge and understanding is to connect with others through "real talk." Elshtain describes it like this: "Speech that simultaneously taps and touches our inner and outer worlds within a community of others with whom we share deeply felt, largely inarticulate, but daily renewed inter-subjective reality" (1982, p. 620). Those who engage in real talk find problem-centered conversation and small talk ultimately dissatisfying. Their interest is in understanding their own and others' experience from their perspectives. Building upon what connected knowers do well, relating to others, Constructivists apply what they learn through "real talk." Not only can they integrate what has been discussed, they can invent original explanations that serve to crystallize the meaning in that conversation.

The authors of this typology are the first to acknowledge its possible application to men (Belenky et al., 1986, p. 15). It can also describe, supplement, or expand Perry's notions of epistemological development. Using a similar research protocol, Perry might have arrived at the same categories of intellectual development. In any case, we can speculate that Perry's relativist thinkers end where Belenky's constructed knowers begin, while Belenky's group of voiceless women precedes Perry's basic dualists. Following this reasoning, Belenky's typology could be used to illuminate the intellectual development patterns of men as well as women. The application of this typology raises once again the question of how or if men and women differ.

MEN AND WOMEN: ARE WE BOUND BY SIMILARITIES OR DIVIDED BY DIFFERENCES?

The accumulating feminist literature concerning women's perspectives provides some evidence that women may indeed possess different views, attitudes, and experience than was previously thought. Observable, measurable differences between men and women appear in research about communication styles, language, ethics, and epistemology. The important question to answer, however, is are these differences influential at work? In research examining language and interaction, Marshall (Marshall and Rossman, 1989) reports that women use fewer examples of power and control language and consequently can be *interpreted* as being less suitable prospects for leadership positions. Of course, much in this equation depends on how much power and control language is in fact related to effective leadership. It would appear that those valuing power and control prefer that leaders express themselves in compatible language in order to be judged as competent, independent of whether they perform effectively. Epstein (1988) observes that to assume that women are different from the male standard frequently means that the extent and nature of that difference become magnified. This elaboration contributes to gender divergence arguments when, in truth, the genders share more similarities than differences. For many women managers who, according to research, are comparable to men in terms of commitment, risk-taking, leadership, and influence (if not power and communications), their special background in intellectual development or ethics may not greatly impinge on their day-to-day behavior in the workplace.

As support for this point of view, Bruning and Snyder's discussion of gender and organizational commitment proposes that programs exclusively for women possess hidden pitfalls. These programs:

may actually facilitate sexism or lead to perceived sex differences where none had existed. That is, management practices based on assumed differences between men and women may actually help to create such differences through self-fulfilling prophecy or may magnify differences that otherwise would not have had serious detrimental consequences (1983, p. 485).

By this reasoning, the question of whether women in some organizations require different approaches or strategies than men becomes problematic. Much depends on the individuals in question on the one hand, and on the change agent's assumptions about what integration means and involves and the best approach for determining the needs of employee groups on the other. Bruning and Snyder continue, "sex differences in commitment may not occur in every organization and . . . managers, therefore, should not assume that such differences exist." They conclude, "Managers need to verify the existence of potential sex differences [to be distinguished from differences flowing from positions held exclusively or predominantly by women]before initiating programs that treat men and women differently" (p. 490). We would pose the question about how to plan for organizational integration in different terms. Given the broad sense of mission consensually agreed upon by organizational members, what do employees generally require in order to exercise greater control over their environment? In addressing this question, we should discover how employees prefer to belong.

In summary, the Belenky formulation contributes some powerful insights for understanding epistemological views in the workplace. In specific terms, the typology may be most useful in explaining how various employees attempt to make sense of a seemingly chaotic environment. While Perry's typology charts the progression of intellectual development in stages and is to be credited for setting a solid foundation for further study, Belenky's typology advances Perry's typology through the authors' emphasis on the human-centeredness of their connected and constructed thinkers. In the authors' attempt to understand the mechanisms or tools people use to progress through these stages, the Belenky typology can be used to create orientations toward organizational life and understand how people invent their work worlds.

ORIENTATIONS TOWARD ORGANIZATIONAL LIFE

Referring to Table 3.1, the ends of the continuum are similar to Belenky's extremes, silence at one end and constructed knowledge at the other. From these extremes, we have derived two opposing orientations, the passive on the left and the centered on the right.

The passive posture toward organizations resembles Argyris' notion of bureaucracies treating individuals as "children," passive recipients of management decisions, and victims of routinized domination (1954). This contrasts with the employees' preferred role, in which they are treated as adults with rights and influence over their own work. Passive employees are managed or controlled through external authority or means of control. Bureaucracies prefer rational-legal means of control and authority as the most reliable way to ensure the predictability of

Table 3.1
A Comparison of Orientations Toward Understanding Organizational Life

Passive	Centered
child	adult
victim	agent
reactive	proactive
externally motivated	self-directed
views organizations as:	views organization as:
chaotic, anarchic or elitist	penetrable, discoverable and alterable
content with others'	prefers to develop own
explanations; relies on experts for views	point of view
uses categorical rules to	prefers progressively more
develop plans for action	comprehensive approaches
fragmented, compartmentalized	views driven by a need to
view of organizational life	integrate, synthesize

workers' performance and, therefore, efficiency and productivity. At the same time, employees are socialized according to these expectations, and obedience, loyalty, and performance only to management-set quotas or standards become the norm. Under this system, employees can suffer exploitation and alienation.

While these negative consequences are destructive in and of themselves, their influence extends beyond the workplace (Pateman, 1970). More central to our purposes, individuals' work experience carries over to political life through its power in shaping how they think. Workers in strongly bureaucratic, dehumanizing cultures tend to perceive themselves with little value or worth. Their sense of efficacy or perceived ability to influence suffers as a result. They tend to see their world as beyond their power to affect it, too complex to understand, and they find few opportunities to make meaningful decisions. Such experience provides a relatively limited foundation for learning, so the ensuing interpretation of organizational events is consequently narrow, proceeds incrementally or in spurts initiated by crisis events, and offers a generally unarticulated, undeveloped view of the organization, accompanied by feelings of fatalism and determinism. Finally, the generalizations that are likely to be derived from crisis experiences revolve around self- and co-worker-fashioned rules that attempt to make sense of the nature of these crises and generate recommendations for avoiding events of this kind in the future. These guidelines center around specific classes of events: "If Joe was docked for returning to work from lunch ten minutes late, then we can probably afford to be no later than five minutes." Rules in this sense are narrowly defined, created in response to crises, and regarded as outside personal control.

The centered orientation is based upon expectations that employees are "adults" and deserve to be treated as such. Independent of how these employees have been socialized and treated by work organizations and other institutions, somehow those with a centered view have cultivated a proactive, self-directed approach toward their work roles and careers. Where passives are externally driven and subject to control, centered employees are self-starters, take initiative in solving what they see as problems, and enjoy learning more about why things are the way they are. These individuals are driven to understand and strive to develop a personal, and thus original, view of organizational life that is validated, confirmed, or checked out by other means. While passives rely on specific rules dealing with classes of events to guide their behavior, centered workers have greater internal resources for guiding ethical, behavioral, and work decisions. They are driven toward progressively comprehensive and inclusive approaches to capturing the essence of events; they want to understand fully. To serve that purpose, they must invoke creative means to integrate what they hear, observe, and reflect upon, even to the extent of using metaphors to link or associate ideas and promote insights (Isenberg, 1984).

There should be no doubt that centered workers enjoy greater independence, autonomy, and feelings of accomplishment concerning their performance as well as their place in the organization. They also enjoy other advantages. We speculate, not coincidentally, that when faced with an ethical or moral dilemma, centered workers will also tend to apply personally grounded if divergent standards to an ethical problem and behave as they think is ethically correct, rather than succumb to social pressures to conform. Some writers feel that a premier problem in administrative and managerial ethnics is that people know what is ethical but feel restrained to put into action what they believe (Bowman, 1976). In comparison, centered individuals are more likely to follow through where others fail to act. For all these reasons, centered orientations are to be encouraged.

We will revisit the concept of centered orientations in the next chapter. At this juncture, a few comments regarding our assumptions about employee development are in order. It should be apparent from the foregoing that, in our view, the supervisor's or HRD manager's role in organizational integration is based on a developmental, employee-centered model. This model assumes that the change agent becomes sufficiently involved with each individual to address personal needs and goals to the employee's satisfaction—within reason, of course. Advocating this model means that women and men are treated as unique or special individuals. While gender identification may help to categorize people initially, thereby rendering a complex world more understandable, we cannot determine whether a given set of women subordinates will require more emotional support than their male counterparts. Nor can we assume that the men will, following cultural prescriptions, be greater risk-takers or better entrepreneurs. Those hoping to understand what motives their people must begin with where the individual stands, so that human relations strategies are driven by subordinate needs and interests.

Thus, no short cuts or recipes serve to guide our understanding of how to manage people. The art (by some considered a science) of human relations at work must be acquired and passed on much the same way we apprehend foreign cultures: creatively, spontaneously, informally, and guided by the learner at his or her own pace. There are benefits to this developmental approach for employees that are not obvious at first. Putting employee need-driven strategies into practice means that, over the long run, a manager reduces the likelihood that some subordinates' needs and interests will be neglected or overlooked, or that others will be treated as marginal or deviant employees. With these strategies in place, the woman with a superior performance record should less frequently encounter a stacked deck in performance appraisal, being evaluated with unconscious prejudices or biases shaping a supervisor's assumptions. The woman who stands out from the group, because of either her feminism or her individualism, will tend to be judged more by her performance rather than by her behavior, while the complacent or passive employee should be judged by her capacity to solve problems rather than her ability to "fit in" with the group. After all, even while under contract to an employer, she ultimately remains her own person.

From the individual and group realm, we need to move to a grander scale, namely how managers need to guide their actions through continually revisiting the question of what makes for successful public and private organizations. Many studies explore what accounts for instances of organizational success and have searched for the answer(s) in economic resources, grand strategies, organizational structure, and technology, as well as other factors. But in his study of schools, armies, and prisons, DiIulio (1989) states that what distinguishes the successful has to do largely with their stock of managerial/organizational ability as well as the influence of management upon the cohesiveness of personnel.

While many volumes consider how best to manage and organize, relatively few explore how we integrate people into organizations. Most of this writing approaches the subject from the point of view of informal, unplanned socialization but, as we shall see in chapter 4, something more is required if we are to work on personnel cohesiveness. Following that reasoning, we turn our attention to the issue of organizational integration.

REFERENCES

Andersen, M. 1983. *Thinking about Women: Sociological and Feminist Perspectives*. New York: Macmillan.

Argyris, C. 1954. *Human Behavior in Organizations*. New York: Harper & Row.

Belenky, M., B. Clinchy, N. Goldberger, and J. Tarule. 1986. *Women's Ways of Knowing: The Development of Self, Voice, and Mind*. New York: Basic Books.

Bowman, J. 1976. "Managerial Ethics in Business and Government." *Business Horizons*, 19 October, 48–54.

Bruning, N., and R. Snyder. 1983. "Sex and Position as Predictors of Organizational Commitment." *Academy of Management Journal*, Vol. 26, No. 3, 485–491.

Denhardt, R., and J. Perkins. 1976. "The Coming Death of Administrative Man." *Women in Public Administration*, 36 July/August, 379–84.

DiIulio, J. 1989. "Recovering the Public Management Variable: Lessons from Schools, Prisons, and Armies." *Public Administration Review*, Vol. 49, No. 2, March/April, 127–33.

Elshtain, J. 1982. "Feminist Discourse and Its Discontents: Language, Power and Meaning." *Signs*, Vol. 7, 603–621.

Epstein, C. Fuchs. 1988. *Deceptive Distinctions: Sex, Gender and the Social Order*. New Haven: Yale.

Ferguson, K. 1984. *The Feminist Case Against Bureaucracy*. Philadelphia: Temple University.

Gilligan, C. 1982. *In a Different Voice: Psychological Theory and Women's Development* Cambridge, MA: Harvard University Press.

———. 1979. "Woman's Place in Man's Life Cycle." *Harvard Educational Review*, Vol. 49, November, 431–46.

Glennon, L. 1979. *Women and Dualism*. New York: Longman.

Gould S. J. 1984. "Triumph of a Naturalist." Review of *A Feeling for the Organism: The Life and Work of Barbara McClintock*, by Evelyn Fox Keller. *New York Review of Books*, March 29, 58–71.

Gouldner, A. 1977/78. "Stalinism: A Study of Internal Colonialism." *Telos*. Vol. 34, Winter, 5–48.

Harding, S. 1981. "Toward a Strong Program for Epistemology: Clues From Feminist Inquiry." Paper presented to the American Political Science Association, New York. September.

Hennig, M., and A. Jardim. 1977. *The Managerial Woman*. Garden City, NY: Doubleday, Anchor Books.

Hummel, R. 1982. *The Bureaucratic Experience*. 2nd ed. New York: St. Martin's.

Isenberg, D. 1984. "How Senior Managers Think." *Harvard Business Review*, November–December, Vol. 62, No. 6, 80–90.

Marshall, C., and G. Rossman. 1989. *Designing Qualitative Research*. Newbury Park, CA: Sage.

Millman, M., and R. Kanter (Eds.). 1975. *Another Voice*. Garden City, NY: Doubleday, Anchor Books.

Pateman, C. 1970. *Participation and Democratic Theory*. New York: Cambridge University Press.

Perry, W. 1970. *Forms of Intellectual and Ethical Development in the College Years*. New York: Holt, Rinehart and Winston.

Chapter 4 _____

Organizational Integration in a Culturally Diverse Society

> This chapter reviews definitions organizational integration and various approaches toward involving personnel in work cultures. Proceeding with the premise that all organizations need to work to balance pressures from individual interests for creative expression on the one hand, and institutional demands for cohesive, collective efforts on the other, the authors invent a descriptive model for the purpose of guiding integration efforts.

In tracing the origins of how people learn—or fail to learn—how to work together cooperatively, we can begin with Barnard's formal–informal organization distinction (1987). While formal organizations may purposely set out to orient, indoctrinate, train, and effectively socialize their employees, integration usually depends on more informal methods, such as spontaneous, unplanned events. Most work organizations do not choose to work on integration problems, perhaps because the benefits of an integrated workforce are not well articulated. Compounding this, the drawbacks of applying known, successful techniques, such as communications workshops and team building, are many. One such problem is the widely-held notion that integration amounts to idealizing uniform thinking and practice. In American culture, such views raise the specter of totalitarian ways of organizing work, centralized planning, and ideals of extreme conformism. As Edgar Schein so presciently observed in 1961, for some work organizations attempting to change employees' values, the indoctrination and socialization practices can resemble "coercive persuasion" or "thought control" as practiced in Korean P.O.W. camps. From another angle, most executives in government and business expect professionals and managers to join organizations already equipped to work with people and practicing adequate human relations skills. When public managers fail to possess these skills, a common argument is invoked: We can't ask the taxpayers or elected officials to foot the bill for retraining. Similar reasoning prevails in the business and nonprofit worlds: Human relations training is not our raison d'etre. Knowing how to work with others, how to behave as a member of a team, constitutes a basic component of a manager's pre-existing repertoire. While human relations skills are regarded as essential when a manager is found deficient in them, organized efforts to remedy the situation are at the same time, paradoxically, usually considered a luxury that most organizations can do without.

WORK CULTURES AND ORGANIZATIONAL INTEGRATION

These arguments notwithstanding, integration is essential to an effectively functioning workforce. As Argyris describes it, tomorrow's organizations require employees who:

1. do not fear stating their complete views,
2. are capable of creating groups that maximize the unique contributions of each individual,
3. value and seek to integrate their contributions into a creative, total, final contribution,
4. do not need to be individually rewarded for their contributions, thus
5. find the search for valid knowledge and the development of the best possible solution intrinsically satisfying. (1969, p. 216)

These individuals not only know how to work with others but examine and critique their own assumptions to correct their thinking and discover the problems that really need resolution. Such people are invaluable assets to a work organization. To respond in a summary fashion to some critics: integration is not the same as indoctrination, although some components of indoctrination, such as reinforcement of new behaviors and attitudes, may be used during the integration process. Integration is also not synonymous with adaptation, in which employees must strive to learn the existing culture's ways and mores without hope of imprinting their own goals, values, beliefs, and preferences upon the organization. In situations where only adaptation or obedience is expected, organizations cannot be influenced. Integration also involves more than meshing the individual's needs with the organization's goals.

Organizational integration can be interpreted as the two-way process of involving members: in the best of a range of scenarios, individuals can have influence over others and upon organizational activities such as goal setting. In other words, they can be agents who initiate, are capable of leading, and contribute to significant events. For their part, those representing the institution are sensitive and responsive to workers' needs because they value individual rights and human dignity. Integration is the label used to describe what most people see as the outcome of a cohesive culture. In this respect, integration is not planned or part of a conscious design; integration is a sign of a productive, harmonious and dedicated employees. In order to do justice to the complexities and subtleties accompanying organizational integration, its relationship to work culture should be discussed.

To begin, the aspects of organizations observable to most outsiders are typically those signs or symbols of culture that represent the proverbial tip of the iceberg. This is the artifactual level of culture that cannot be fully understood without penetrating deeper into organizational dynamics. Beneath that layer are the beliefs and values that form the "glue" of culture. This can be found wherever people find reasons to hold together; they share the same sense of the way things are and of what is meaningful, genuine, and true for themselves and each other. They are aware and appreciate how they as individuals and as groups fit within the larger context of the organization. In the best form of organization, members encounter an environment that supports efforts to clarify the meaning of their mutual experience (Moore and Anderson, 1969). The least visible level of culture concerns members' basic assumptions about human nature, their relationship to their environment, and so on. Usually preconscious, this is the level of analysis least accessible to researchers (Schein, 1986). It is at the level of beliefs, values, and assumptions that any thorough analysis of culture must begin. Interpreting culture in these terms means that when integration is discovered, understanding the factors and dynamics that contributed to an integrated culture entails seeing how an organization works from the inside. Since each organization is unique, the lessons learned do not normally apply universally because they are bound by specific people in particular relationships. This kind of "personal knowledge" (Polanyi, 1962) is crucial to disclosing the often mysterious reasons why one work culture serves to bond people together and another fails to connect. Acquisition of this knowledge then will help us to diagnose our own work cultures in a more meaningful manner.

With this foundation, we can turn our attention to how a managerial or work culture tends to develop (Ott, 1989; Sathe, 1986). First, we can begin with how the members' (or founders') belief and value systems and behavior connect in constructing a culture. This association is two-way and interactive: people's beliefs and values influence their own behaviors, and their behavior influences the expectations and mindsets of others. Under certain conditions, changing people's behavior can stimulate internal changes as well. New ways of thinking may result in order to reduce the dissonance between beliefs or values and observable bahavior. Frequently, however, even when their behavior or performance changes, people persist in holding on to old beliefs and values. They tend to rationalize their new behavior by reasoning that it is required or has been ordered by authorities. *Unless they are able to see the intrinsic worth of new ways of work, the change will be cosmetic and short-lived.* For change agents, this means that their primary efforts must emphasize how to have people identify and "buy into" new ways to work. How, in short, can they enable people to discover the intrinsic worth of new behavior? Consequently, a problem for those concerned about organizational and professional effectiveness is how to support and reinforce the kinds of performance and dedicated behavior that will lead to reaching long-term goals.

Whether new behaviors are desirable or current practices are reinforced, the means through which a new culture is initiated or existing culture is communicated remain the same. People's values and beliefs are communicated through implicit methods, such as rituals, customs, ceremonies, dress, and more explicit forms, such as announcements, memos, and procedures. While perpetuating a culture rests upon the habitual transactions between values, beliefs, and culture expression in a more or less "natural" flow, those interested in authoring behavioral change need to ensure that the new values and beliefs are communicated clearly and successfully. At each point in the socialization process, however, entrenchment and intransigent behavior can occur. When executives and managers face the problem of adding or replacing workers, their choice usually articulates an image of who they believe will have the best chance of "fitting in" with cultural constraints. Depending upon the kind of organizational culture, interpretations of fitness can vary. The managerial perspective, for example, focuses on informal aspects. Those who do not fit in, fail to comply, or deviate from the norm are often removed, isolated, or sanctioned until many choose to leave. The ramifications of this view of fitness and the varied aspects it raises warrant some discussion.

As we shall see in later chapters, informal and "loose" perceptions of fitness usually revolve around issues tangential to the work itself: behaviors, values, beliefs, and personality types, as well as demeanor, style, and appearances that approximate the image set by the predominant group in the organization. This homosocial reproduction, or "cloning," of executives and managers stems from deeply-rooted issues of trust and power. People tend to trust and grant power to those they see as like themselves. This also means that all too often, those not fitting the desired mold are gradually excluded, resulting in an informal, sometimes preconscious, form of discrimination against women and minorities. Therefore, the managerial perspective views integration as a quantity to be achieved in the simplest fashion: that is, staff the organization with homogeneous employees, modeled after those in authority. As Burrell and Morgan observe, most views of the informal organization—and, by extension, integration—are often "implicitly informed by a managerial perspective which regards 'informal' as 'deviant' " (1985, p. 194). From the vantage point of "culturally disadvantaged" groups and the powerless, those responsible for personnel policy should broaden their definitions of member acceptability to include diverse groups. For managers willing to learn, marginal members and the noncompliant can offer some valuable lessons.

According to this view, noncompliance with prevailing cultural norms should not be summarily criticized or negated out of hand; so much depends upon the object of noncompliance and its means of expression. To explore the latter first, individuals who are psychologically unstable or emotionally disturbed to the point where their mental competencies and behavior are questionable are extreme examples. Such cases are thankfully rare in most work settings. More common are those who choose not to comply with cultural norms when they see the latter as unethical, inappropriate, or contributing to ineffective performance. Employees who voice their comments in a reasonable manner in appropriate settings may have messages worth listening to. As to the object of noncompliance, what is the nature of their behavior or attitude that causes tension in the culture? What are their intentions? Are their comments related to the fundamental mission, the raison d'etre, of the organization? If so, they may want to choose another line of work. But if their divergent thinking or behavior raises questions concerning untested assumptions and the process by which people reach conclusions and make decisions, they may have valuable insights to offer.

Using the latter interpretation of this behavior, more venturesome managers have recognized that many noncompliants, or what Kilmann (1984) calls objectors, can offer productive questions as to why things do not work or could work better, even creating ideas for new product lines and services, thus providing compelling reasons to understand how some maverick and original thinkers manage to thrive. Peters and Waterman (1982) suggest that in some companies and public sector organizations, it is the creativity and radical ideas of such mavericks that sustain the collective effort to innovate. Similarly, Hickman and Silva (1986, p. 70) include two core skills in their road map to creating excellent workplaces: one is the need to be a culture builder. This skill involves the careful and rigorous hiring of staff so that candidates will possess the high commitment and competence needed. Conant Associates is

cited for its rigorous employee selection procedures. The company focuses on the question of whether a particular candidate can "fit" a highly
creative culture where the essence of competence rests on employees'
abilities to see, analyze, and resolve even the most minute problems.
Another requirement is that supervisors be sensitive to human needs
and individual differences. As one illustration of Conant's seriousness
of purpose concerning this requirement, Hickman and Silva warn:

Even if you have successfully crawled into another person's head, you have to
be constantly on guard against projecting your own ideas onto that person's
decision or solution to a problem. Fortunately, if an employee's decision concerns
the organization's commitment, competence, or consistency, a strong corporate
culture will narrow the range of acceptable courses of action, but many decisions
do not concern cultural factors. Some executives push so hard for conformance
to a cultural model that they thwart innovative, independent thinking, creating
'yes' people instead. Such people do not support strong cultures. To remove
this block you must avoid projecting your own skills or style when you evaluate
employees' actions. Detach yourself and rely on the tenets of your organization's
culture rather than letting your biases determine your judgment. (Hickman and
Silva, 1986, p. 136; emphasis added)

In our view, every effectively functioning organization can be depicted
as experiencing the "push-pull" between bringing people together in
the pursuit of common purpose without expecting conformity and obedience, and at the same time encouraging creativity, individual expression, and original thinking. Unfortunately, the companies successful in
blending the two in appropriate measures are the exception, not the
rule. As demonstrated in the above works and related literature, most
work organizations are far more bureaucratic than a Nordstrom or Conant Associates. Most readers are aware that, insofar as they fit the bureaucratic form, too many work cultures can be described as expecting
uniform, compliant behavior, conventional thinking, and cautious approaches to questions of change. To frame how managers may use the
lessons of noncompliants and deviants, we suggest the concept of subculture. Turner enlightens us as to the essential components in a subculture:

A subculture is a distinctive set of meanings shared by a group of people whose
forms of behavior differ to some extent from those of [the larger organization].
The distinctive nature of the set of meanings is maintained by ensuring that
newcomers to the group undergo a process of learning or socialization. The
process links the individual to the values of the group and generates common
motives, common reaction patterns, and common perceptual habits. (1971, p. 1)

Distinctiveness is also maintained by the use of sanctions that operate
against those who do not behave in appropriate ways.

Note that while the "weeding out" process referred to earlier is often used to strengthen cultures and enhance the cohesion of those who do fit, divergent subcultures distinguish themselves through their thorough and comprehensive efforts to reinforce individual identification with the group, as well as the quality of attention given to how meaning is communicated and shared. Following this logic, change agents can learn some valuable lessons from how subculture identification is forged among members.

From this discussion, it should be apparent that in American society, heterogeneity and diversity of people, personalities, and cultures are considered part of our democratic heritage. If we are to promote the meaningful participation of diverse groups and peoples, we need to explore some of the individual characteristics worth cultivating in the workplace. Building on what we have learned about how women and men progress intellectually, the next few pages describe the view of human nature that undergirds our model of organizational integration.

THE CHANGE AGENT/MANAGER AS CULTURE BUILDER

Earlier we mentioned that essential to any cultural change effort is the problem of how to get people to see the intrinsic worth of behaving or performing differently. In our view, this is an extremely subtle and complex problem. In all cultural change efforts, we believe that managers or trainers can encourage, aspire to, and work at fostering an integrative climate; they cannot arrange for one to occur. More than with most organizational dynamics (performance appraisal, goal-setting), integration is not a feature that can be *caused*. Clearly, much depends on participants choosing to commit to change in the same direction. There are consequently real limits to how much a change agent can be held responsible for outcomes. Like motivation, integration can be hoped for only when individuals respond and are responsive, when they identify with the organization's purposes or sense of mission, because they own their place as part of the organization. Genuine integration involves the identification and commitment of individuals with group or organizational goals because they share the meaning of those goals. The emphasis here is on building with the people you have, working with their problems and needs, as opposed to wholesale "weeding out" and replacement. Time and effort must be spent on how they view the current state of affairs, what can be done and, what, if enabled, they could accomplish. In this process, managers or change agents can serve as catalysts and role models. What Smircich and Morgan say about leaders can be extended to change agents:

because of their role in framing experience in a way that provides a viable basis for action, e.g., by mobilizing meaning, articulating and defining what has previously remained implicit or unsaid, by inventing images and meaning that provide a focus for new attentions, and by consolidating, confronting, or changing prevailing wisdom. . . . [They can generate] a point of reference, against which a feeling of organization and direction can emerge. (1982, p. 258)

In relating her experiences studying a research and development corporation, Smircich (1983) explains what such a "point of reference" looks like. She states that the employees differed concerning how they saw their collective self-image. This was further played out in their

confusion and disagreement about roles and responsibilities. . . . The underlying pattern of conflict regarding the image of the organization in the world was a unifying framework for understanding life in this organization. (p. 169)

Although change agents can and should employ their leadership skills to pull together a frame of reference or a more comprehensive interpretation of, let's say, a problem voiced by trainees, they cannot authoritatively define or choose which frames best represent a group's approach. This onus must fall on group members. Smircich's clients needed to understand these issues in their own words, using their own language, metaphors, myths, and symbols. Because only individuals can create culture, only they can author cultural change. It is only their successful efforts that produce integrated organizations. Therefore, change efforts must be directed at individuals and their development in order to enjoy the best prospects for cultural enhancement. To accomplish this, change agents must rely solely upon indirect strategies, which have the capability of fostering certain attitudes and behaviors, skills and competencies. Several levels of analysis must be targeted, however, for cultural change to occur system-wide. Change agents may need to use some strategies to augment the individual's identification with department goals; other approaches would be required to address the needs and goals of groups and the total system. In such an effort, it is important to bear in mind that the yardstick by which to measure success in such a venture can be fairly applied only after much trial and error, preferably in the long run. First, let us consider one set of qualities that are largely within the individual employee's control and that concern personal mindsets or cosmologies.

DEVELOPING CENTERED EMPLOYEES

In offering a framework for organizational integration, our purpose is to consider how people in organizations can be brought together to cooperate effectively, contributing their talents and expertise freely without sacrificing individual integrity and stifling creativity. Considering our purpose, we must first make certain assumptions and qualifications about the framework. To begin, all cultures can be considered as dynamic, changing enterprises; they are in the process of becoming. Culture is not a static concept that is material, concretized, or struck in a certain space and time. The same is also true of work cultures. We assume that, due to the concerns raised by women entering the workplace or to the subject of integration generally, those in authority must prefer another end state, no matter how vague. Perhaps they want to move the organization toward "excellence," more effective accomplishment of goals, or possibly even greater worker satisfaction.

Finally, in order to integrate people into this kind of culture, we will need to consider, among other things, individuals' perspectives toward their workplace: their openness to change, their viewpoints, their preferences, as well as other aspects of their cosmologies. In terms of our earlier discussion of passive and centered orientations it should be apparent that centered individuals possess an adequate sense of independence of judgment and autonomy. Centered employees are flexible, confident, not threatened by change, and can therefore afford a receptivity to cultural change. Their willingness to change and capacity to experiment can in turn contribute to constructive transformations at the collective or systemic level. We state this not to advise that trainers first concentrate their efforts on transforming workers into centered people and then turn their attention to encouraging bonds between them; trainers pursuing this course of action rarely find the time and energy left to tackle the interpersonal level. Rather, we merely suggest that in our experience, the more that people tend to fit the Centered profile, the easier it is for ties and constructive efforts to build.

Efforts to integrate an organization, in our view, should include interventions that cultivate employees' centered postures toward their organization as one basis of an action plan. Moving people from passive stances to a more "proactive" stance will involve the cultivation of at least six traits. We describe these traits as follows:

1. possessing confidence and trust in their own judgment*;
2. having empathy for others and the capacity to assume other points of view;
3. preferring to understand rather than judge or evaluate, inspired by a need to break frames and construct new ways of seeing problems and events;
4. using "real talk" that is directed toward connected behavior; understanding the other's point of view and in the process being able to make sense of one's own context;
5. possessing the ability to engage in critical thinking, which can in turn encompass some or all of the following qualities:

a) the use of varied formats for solving problems as opposed to standardized formats and institutional procedures*,

b) the use of multiple perspectives, including a willingness to experiment with alternative approaches*,

c) seeing knowledge as context-based, not absolute*, and therefore open to question, and

d) an interest in original, even radical thinking for potential insights; and

6. being receptive to change for its developmental opportunities* rather than regarding change primarily as a threatening prospect. [Asterisked items are from Pierce and Dechant, 1989.]

Centered qualities are difficult to achieve. Accounts of individuals holding constructivist intellectual positions (Belenky et. al., 1986) or of those reaching some measure of self-actualization (Maslow, 1964) indicate their relatively minuscule representation in the general population. Similarly, centered traits converge with Bernstein's participatory-democratic consciousness (1976): self-reliance; ownership of problems, issues, and events; "a facility for compromise and receptivity to the needs of others" (Bernstein, 1976, p. 97); curiosity about one's context; ability to think critically, which is comprised of a need to clarify, avoiding distortions and preconceptions; a facility for synthetical thinking, borrowing from many diverse sources; a tendency to analyze in depth; a conception of longer time frames; and an active, take-charge stance toward organizational life. This list appears lengthy because Bernstein believes that the democratic mentality or mindset is central to the process of democratization. This mindset is one of six minimally necessary prerequisites for creating and maintaining democratic workplaces. This list of mental traits supplements what we call centered organizational postures with one important difference. Bernstein observes that a participatory-democratic consciousness is critical in efforts to democratize the workplace. Without such a mindset, such experiments inevitably fail. In efforts to enhance organizational integration, however, we feel that although a wide distribution of people already possessing centered traits is most conducive (for a program of innovation would be welcomed and advanced by such people), it cannot be depended upon as a prerequisite for an experiment to proceed. Provided with a program designed for a particular organization, with the needs and goals of those individuals as its foundation, we expect that after a lengthy period of time, changed behaviors will generate centered traits.

The reader might inquire as to how those entering organizational life already in possession of centered traits acquired them? We venture to say that an unusual or at least special combination of circumstances must occur for individuals to progress to this level of thought. Some of these circumstances might include: having parents and family who foster self-confidence and engender trust; possessing a security of identity that comes from being well cared for; being taught the value of caring for and respecting others; being surrounded by people who genuinely think that what a child, or any person, has to say is important and worth responding to; being taught the value of understanding other points of view; and experiencing the presence of influential role models who assert themselves, take risks, and encourage and reward risk-taking in others. Drawing from this partial list, the explanations for why these individuals are rarely found probably lie more in the area of environmental conditions during primary socialization than in any inherent, inborn personal traits. But what if, as for overwhelming numbers of Americans, some of these features were lacking in our backgrounds? Then how can these qualities be cultivated in the workplace, where arguably even the best examples offer an inadequate substitute for these conditions?

Some involve simple techniques: for example, assignment to situations that provide new vantage points and as a result encourage the use of different perspectives, reward risk-taking behavior, reinforce self-worth, model alternative ways of thinking, and show care for employees so that they can in turn care for and respect others. A key to the success of these techniques is that they must be practiced with everyone on a regular basis. Other strategies involve more complex approaches and techniques, such as critical thinking skills that rest on interest and prior knowledge (Pierce and Dechant, 1989). While we have not experimented with techniques for all six characteristics, some have been developed for training programs as keys to empowerment. Experiences with some of these techniques are described in chapters 6 and 7.

While the initiative for becoming centered rests with the employee, another set of characteristics are external to the individual and are therefore appropriate for a change agent's attention. The remainder of this chapter will be dedicated to outlining the features common to integrated cultures. In culling characteristics from the literature on organizational culture and change, we were interested in their commonalities. But focusing on commonalities had certain drawbacks. It meant that we necessarily omitted some of the most interesting information about certain cultures: interpretations of how each organization was special or unique. Each organization's members enact their own culture, a process which in some fashion, however circuitous or misguided, reflects or responds to their efforts. In so doing, employees create a unique history which, when institutionalized, becomes a point of reckoning for future actions (Berger and Luckmann, 1967). We think that however idiosyncratic cultures are, culture builders attending to the continuous process of employee development need to start with a kind of road map with signposts indicating what to look for on the way. Although a particular organization will translate a characteristic in a manner unique or special to that work culture, the labels remain the same.

Our signposts will cover eight necessary components to which change agents can attend so that certain desirable behaviors will be encouraged in employees. These features represent what can be targeted on an individual, group, and system level. While we list eight characteristics, we cannot be sure that they are sufficient; that is, we make no claim that the components listed are exhaustive or comprehensive. Nevertheless, they provide a rudimentary map that managers, supervisors, and HRD officers can use to guide their efforts. These qualifications notwithstanding, it is wise to bear in mind that this is not a fail-safe proposal or recipe. This framework represents instead our proposal for change.

EIGHT CONDITIONS FOR FOSTERING INTEGRATION

1. Endorsing Individual Worth and Diagnosing Individual Needs

Integration has thus far been described as depending upon the commitment, as opposed to compliance or obedience, of members to shared and jointly created group goals. Or to put it another way, as Fibich notes, "obedience is achieved more by internalization of norms than by threat of negative sanctions" (quoted in Bernstein, 1976, p. 100). A compatible view of human nature endorses the worth of the individual. For decades, the students of scientific management have advised managers to treat all subordinates the same. Their logic says that treating subordinates individually with different incentives for those at different levels or with different needs can raise the dilemma of equitable treatment or, at the very least, makes the supervisor's job too complex.

Motivation literature teaches, however, that this flies in the face of effective supervisory practice. The fact that supervisors spend far too much of their time dealing with aberrant behavior and human problems could be grounds for recommending that so much time and effort would be more wisely spent on the front end. If you treat workers as individuals with different personalities, different needs and interests, and different perceptions of appropriate rewards at the outset, these problems might be circumvented. A side benefit of diagnosing employee needs and planning around them is that supervisors can begin to distinguish high-performing prospects from objectors (well-intentioned deviants) and troublemakers (destructive individuals) (Kilmann, 1984). Good supervisory practice advises that, in order to target incentives appropriately, we must first address individual needs, and this will involve sensitivity to human relations. As Hickman and Silva (1986) propose, sensitivity motivates people—at least those with positive intentions—and initiates strong cultures.

2. The Importance of Reward Systems

In determining what can be done to integrate members into a work culture, much depends upon the strategies and resources available to set new patterns of behavior in motion. Rewards can influence culture directly by selectively reinforcing certain beliefs and values, and compelling them to become the dominant patterns of behavior and standards to emulate. Indirectly, reward systems contribute to culture by influencing the quality of human resources. Knowing that rewards offer supervisors the most direct key to creating a culture, what kind of culture do we aim for?

Depending upon whether cultures and reward systems demonstrate high or low concern for people or production, Sethia and Glinow (1985) arrived at a typology that labels human resource cultures as apathetic (low on both dimensions), caring (high on people, low on performance), exacting (low on people, high on performance), and integrative (high on both dimensions). The apathetic culture corresponds with our passive posture discussed earlier, although an exacting culture, with its low concern for people, can contribute to fostering this posture as well. Where concern for people is uniformly high, as in caring and integrative cultures, those with centered postures will gravitate. While caring cultures may not offer sufficient cues to the nature of performance standards or tie rewards to performance in a direct fashion, they focus attention on human values and transmit messages of concern for workers' well-being and dignity. The typical reading of these signs is that this culture will tolerate, perhaps will encourage, a variety of personalities, leadership styles, and behaviors. Tolerance for diversity of personalities and human vagaries extends beyond the homogeneous "mold" so frequently found in most bureaucratic systems (exacting and apathetic cultures) that value performance alone. As a result, the creativity, proactivity, and autonomy that distinguish centered workers are not likely to be lost or stifled in a caring or integrative culture. Creativity and proactive stances will, on the contrary, be prized.

In a comparison of only the two polar types on their typology, exacting cultures tend to possess a range of financial rewards, good job content, average career challenge, and moderate status differentiation. Integrative cultures enjoy superior financial rewards, are superior in both job content and career challenge, and are low in status distinctions. The criteria for rewards differ for both cultures; exacting cultures emphasize individual short-term success and value efficiency and competition, while integrative cultures prize group/company success and the long term, as well as valuing innovation and independence.

It should be apparent from earlier discussion that for an organization to foster centered employees, management should aspire to emulate the integrative culture. But what if broader issues, such as the nature of financial rewards, job content, career challenges, and status distinctions are beyond the manager's scope to define? Are there other strategies that can help? We think that these exist, although they are less direct than reinforcement of appropriate behavior via rewards. They are therefore less controllable in predicting how they might shape individual responses.

3. The Work Itself: The Key to Commitment

So much of employees' job satisfaction is crystallized in the concept of commitment. If an individual identifies system goals as her own and is dedicated to realizing them, she is said to be highly committed. According to Walton's investigation of innovative work cultures, these systems are marked by their dependence on high worker commitment (1986). Indeed, high commitment by workers is presumed in the basic design of work. The system cannot thrive without this level of dedication. High-commitment work cultures can be described as those "designed to *generate* high commitment, to fully *utilize* high commitment for gains (human and business), and to *depend* upon high commitment for its effectiveness" (Walton, 1986, p. 209, italics in original). The justification for choosing this particular culture is that it is usually accompanied by motivational energy, by responsiveness to the organization's needs and those of fellow employees, by identification with work group members and their goals and with the overall quality of work life (Walton, 1986, p. 211). The level of commitment also depends partly on whether opportunities for participation in management activities are available to employees and whether mutual trust and open communication describe the work culture.

From the abundance of literature following the Herzberg et al. classic study of job enrichment (1959) as well as the quality of work life research, we find more than adequate evidence to suggest that work tasks frequently require reorganization, enlargement, and enrichment to provide the kind of challenge and learning prospects employees prefer.

A special kind of learning is intended here, which differs from traditional notions:

• Learning, rather than being solely confined to special training courses or seminars, becomes an everyday part of the job and is built into routine tasks.

- Employees are expected to learn not only skills related to their own jobs but also the skills of others in their work unit and are also required to understand how their work unit relates to the operation and goals of the business.
- Employees are expected to teach, as well as learn from, their co-workers. In short, the entire work environment is geared toward and supports the learning of new skills. (Casner-Lotto, 1988, p. 114)

She further states that continuous learning can be fostered by structures and methods, such as learning by objectives, train-the-trainer programs, semiautonomous work teams, and the Scandinavian-inspired pay-for-knowledge incentive schemes. Most if not all of these ideas will appear novel to many American employers; until recently, most employers were reluctant to consider broadening the narrow scope of most workers' jobs. Until popular management literature began disseminating the lessons of Japanese companies, employers failed to see the value of a worker learning how what he does contributes to and is shaped by how the larger organization operates. This was typically read as beyond what was essential for the worker to know. Perhaps with new economic constraints and the competitive nature of a global economy, literature connecting learning to empowerment will be taken seriously (Casner-Lotto, 1988).

4. The Importance of Trust

Returning to the earlier metaphor of organizations as webs, Handy (1978) uses this metaphor to describe the power culture of small entrepreneurial firms. In his version, power spreads from the center outward, with those at the periphery being strong or influential only if they enjoy direct ties to the center. The way we use the web to depict an integrated organizational culture rests upon a substantially different interpretation of the metaphor. Webs, first of all, communicate interconnectedness: what impinges upon one part of the web resonates throughout the system. So it is with effectively functioning work teams: what affects one member is perceived as having the potential of affecting all. Typically, the extent of commitment to the group is high. Apart from group identification, individual well-being and respect have a high priority. Members' self-preservation is a concern of the group; feelings are respected. Control issues, which may be resolved or unresolved, at least do not inhibit group members' abilities to resist control from others.

Like most of the factors we will consider, trust builds gradually over time. It cannot be created in the way that rewards may be manipulated to reinforce selected behaviors. Nevertheless, the change agent can go a long way toward building trust by modeling the appropriate behavior and making sure that related issues, such as effective conflict resolution techniques and open communications, are skills not only learned but practiced in work units. As Eddy describes it:

Developing trust requires clear statements on the part of top management regarding the values that the organization seeks to achieve. No retribution for speaking the truth, encouragement of risk taking, no sacred cows, team development sessions involving frank communication across levels, and evaluation based on long-term goal achievement rather than image are some typical ingredients. (1981, p. 93)

5. The Role of Creative Conflict: The Right Measure

Conflicts and tensions occur in all but perhaps the most passive groups; nevertheless, in the most effectively functioning teams, conflict plays a more creative role. It serves to air disagreements or different views that might threaten or challenge the status quo. However, in the context of joint problem-solving, conflict is treated as grounds to work out a resolution or possibly arrive at a consensus (Eddy, 1981). In this approach, the functional aspects of conflict are stressed: disagreements as to procedure or content are regarded as ways to stimulate creative thought and possible innovation. This way of approaching conflict helps to stem group think (Janis, 1972), by means of which the group has developed over time such a high degree of cohesiveness and homogeneous outlook that conformity in thinking colors group performance. As a result, the group becomes hampered in its ability to read the environment, perceive problems accurately, or make effective decisions. Interestingly, effective work teams are thus typically characterized by some conflict. Too little conflict, and we may find a "group think" phenomenon; too much, and the unit's functioning is paralyzed. If the conflict is geared to the right issues—that is, the conflicts do not revolve around control of the group but emphasize problem-solving—and there is the right level of conflict, the only question that remains is whether the group has developed adequate skills to manage conflict. If it has, over time it will see a level of trust that has grown out of the members' ability and willingness to risk.

Most teams have worked long and diligently to cultivate these qualities. Many may have enjoyed the additional advantage of coming from the same or similar backgrounds so that trust is expedited from the earliest formation of the team. But what if the work group is comprised of women and men, or of people from a variety of backgrounds? How does a manager go about developing trust in that situation?

6. Free and Open Communications: the Search for The Ideal Speech Situation

One approach is to plan communication workshops to focus on the quality of relationships between men and women in the organization. If the reasons for men preferring men as co-workers are rooted in trust and comfort, workshops targeted toward:

reducing mistrust between men and women and at exploring the fear, discomforts, and hostilities men and women have toward each other are a very important step in building relationships. Such workshops can be very valuable, because they provide a place where men and women can try out new behavior appropriate to the collegial relationship that they have so little experience with. (Meltzer and Nord, 1981, p. 230)

Meltzer and Nord believe that with time, women and men working together can gradually learn to accommodate each other. Structured activities that devote attention to gender-based issues can not only expedite mutual adjustment but also enhance the overall quality of working relationships. This essentially involves replacing views in which women are perceived as inferior with views in which women (and feminine qualities in general) are positively regarded and are characterized by competency and worth. In this way, women and men can learn to trust and respect others. One benefit to this approach is that we can begin to make inroads into the chronic devaluation of women and things feminine described earlier. More central to organizational needs, helping workers to uncover common ground for social interaction "will improve the ease of relating to each other, allowing women more access to informally transmitted information and to the political channels that are often critical to their careers" (Meltzer and Nord, 1981, p. 231).

Working on the processes and dynamics of communications is essential to effectively functioning work teams. And we do not quibble about the view that communication for the purpose of improving perceptions and enhancing self-concepts is worth doing. This notwithstanding, there are some loftier goals that cut across individual identity and gender issues, namely, the pursuit of the truth. Schutz (1984) places great faith in the power of truthful communications. An atmosphere of truth can release energy and creativity, as well as contribute to change and productivity, yet aspiring to a truthful climate is often blocked by job politics, turf protection, self-interest, and bad faith, to cite only a few obstacles.

In describing a parallel track to the truth, Habermas introduces readers to the ideal speech situation that he feels should constitute the goals for communications. An ideal speech situation refers to "a situation of absolutely uncoerced and unlimited discussion between completely free and equal human agents" (quoted in Geuss, 1981). All evidence would be considered, all conflicting rightness claims would be debated freely, checking and/or justification would be carried out without manipulation or resort to influencing opinion (Forester, 1983, p. 238). In many if not most work cultures, communications fail to adhere to these rules. Members, especially those without power or authority, have no protected recourse toward discovering the "truth" about things. Normally, the "right way" to look at problems or situations is that which is perceived as serving the organization's interests. When seeking to further integration, some redefinition of the organization's interests, as well as employees', may need to take place within a particular group for members to be able to clarify their place in the organization.

7. Interconnectedness: Working on Work Relationships Amidst Cultural Diversity

Webs are also masterpieces of connections: connections are made from center to periphery, across radials, in a variety of directions. Organizations where women and men feel free to converse and choose to talk easily and frequently with others are likely to be places where trust issues have been worked through. These are also places where people have worked through dependency problems; having experienced independence, they have progressed to a point of comfort with interdependence. The resulting associations, ranging from the spontaneous and short-lived to those that endure, have the capacity to form around problems and concerns. Insights can be shared and can in turn spark creative ideas. Too frequently in work organizations, we witness the opposite: employees communicating as required or speaking only about superficial topics. In these situations, the only "real talk" usually occurs between those of similar backgrounds where trust is not questioned. If most human beings avoid the unfamiliar because they are discomfited by what is strange and "different" to them, then, depending upon your own target of anxiety, look at what you might have to avoid:

- If you are disabled, avoid the able;
- If you are elderly, fear the young;
- Women avoid men;
- Black people mistrust white people, as may Hispanics and Anglos;
- Refugees from political repression mistrust those in authority.

And, of course, fear, mistrust, and discomfort can proceed in the reverse direction as well: an Anglo's discomfort with foreign speakers, youth's resentment of the old, and so on. All these typifications add up to an impressive list—so many for those embracing homogeneity to avoid! As American culture becomes more diverse, the number of labels and categories grows, so that the stereotypes and prejudices of the Archie Bunkers of the world could conceivably multiply. It would be much less stressful to learn to appreciate "the meaning and the value of difference" (Janeway, 1989).

From another vantage point, if an increasingly technological, complex society requires people with highly specialized skills to work together effectively, the difficulties posed by poor working relationships may become critical. In large measure, people in work units need to dedicate themselves to establishing interdependencies—perhaps learning each other's jobs through cross-training—out of necessity. Since communications workshops geared toward these issues were described earlier, other mechanisms to engender high-quality, cohesive, and productive working relationships should be mentioned.

Bennett discusses social contracting as one team-building technique that "is based on the idea that workers have tacit agreements with each other on what is and is not acceptable behavior" (1980, p. 205). Social contracting is one way that work teams form the basis for cooperative relationships. Under Bennett's formulation, members begin by stating in writing what they want to receive from the group, what they do not want, what they want to contribute, and what they don't want to contribute.

Team-building programs are often conducted by having existed work unit members identify the needs, issues, and problems which, if resolved, could improve the unit's performance. The topics can range from issues such as dependency and control to intimacy and distance.

The team then analyzes the ways in which members work together in their daily operations. The consultant plays the roles of helping individuals understand the interpersonal and group process problems that hinder their ability to work together and gain satisfaction and assists them to devise solutions to the problems that they identify. (Eddy, 1981, p. 186)

As described here, team-building might implicitly involve asking people to confront what they choose to repress or avoid in a variety of relationships. As just one example, expecting team members to practice consultation, work together, and appreciate their interdependencies means that the isolated individual who prefers working alone can experience real and perceived pressures to change his style. His private and reserved demeanor may be interpreted differently by those expecting a freely communicating, disclosing, and inclusive teammate. It should be apparent at this point that a team's emphasis must be placed on work-related behaviors; we add to this the importance of preserving individual identity.

For those interested in evaluating the level of effectiveness of a team, Kilmann provides some guidance. This checklist should suggest some directions to pursue.

- Is the group clear about its objectives and the overall organizational mission?
- Does the group feel it is accomplishing its objectives?
- Can the group identify in what area it excels?
- Can the group identify obstacles hampering its performance or growth?
- Does the group judge that members are spending the right amount of time on appropriate tasks with at least an adequate standard of performance?
- Do members feel that their work hours are not spent in the most productive manner? Can they identify how their time is diverted from reaching objectives?
- Do members feel that their talents and abilities are being fully utilized? How could they be used more effectively?
- Are all relevant issues and problems discussed publicly and openly, or are some avoided?
- Do members feel solutions "work" or do some problems persistently recur?
- Are members satisfied or dissatisfied with the quality of group decision-making?

8. Participation in Decision-Making

With this last component, we have in a sense come full circle. Beginning with a centered mindset, which is similar in many ways to a democratic consciousness, we arrive at a cornerstone of workplace democratization efforts: participation in decision-making. Affording employees opportunities to make choices about significant issues or events affecting them can serve as a catalyst for the bonding process, especially in workplace democratization efforts reinforced by executives and managers implementing most decisions. Two dimensions to participation are key here: the degree of employee influence over decisions and the types of issues over which control may be exercised, ranging from physical working conditions at one extreme to raising capital on the other. From a systemic perspective, the organization benefits. First, employee feedback can contribute to organizational innovation; second, feedback helps to monitor and correct the system's performance (Bernstein, 1976). On a personal level, employees begin to realize that over time, authorities consistently back employee decisions and encourage even greater employee involvement. This in time may mean that employees begin to experience psychic ownership of the organization, thus fostering many of the qualities discussed as centered or democratic traits: self-reliance, critical thinking, an active stance, facility for taking multiple perspectives, and so on.

In comparison to the other seven components, participation can involve the most risk. While manipulation of rewards is relatively self-contained and can directly intervene in the performance and evaluation cycle, participation is much less predictable and controllable. If management begins offering employees opportunities to participate in making decisions about things that matter, such offers must be sincere, enacted in a spirit of learning together, mutual respect, trust, and two-way communication. If an employee's decision cannot be supported and executed, the rationale must be thoroughly presented and discussed with decision-makers. Failing in this will jeopardize any further attempts to experiment and innovate; employees will probably read management's intentions as dishonorable and believe that only "mock" democracy is possible. If participation is introduced suddenly, without preparation or the benefit of supporting mechanisms, troublemakers or "difficult" people can control the decision-making process. Many of us have witnessed the terrible influence of destructive individuals who in effect (if not by intention) prevent those with the necessary information or opinions from being heard. For this reason, participation efforts require careful and gradual introduction throughout the organization, preferably with supporting mechanisms such as employee assistance programs in place to identify and help those who might short-circuit group decision-making processes. The consequences of failure are sufficiently grave that they should serve as adequate counsel to prospective change agents.

It should be apparent from the presentation of these eight components that they reinforce each other to create high-quality associations and forge links and cohesive units within an organization. Many features could be added to reinforce this foundation. Kilmann (1984) suggests counseling and interteam building to get at the individual problems, deficiencies, or inadequacies of interlocking groups not addressed here; we will address supplementary approaches like these in the final chapter. Nevertheless, whether you consider our basic eight or another model, it should be apparent that genuine efforts to involve women in organizational life, given our definition of integration, means that integration of all employees becomes a top priority for management. With the organization development and change literature of the 1960s and 1970s, we witnessed the first wave of enthusiasm and popularity for employee-centered experiments and democratic approaches to the organization of work. Perhaps now, with economic and fiscal pressures brought to bear, these experiments will begin to take root in the American workplace.

REFERENCES

Argyris, C. 1969. "Today's Problems with Tomorrow's Organizations." In *Behavioral Science and the Manager's Role*, ed. by W. Eddy, W. Burke, V. Dupré, and O. South. Washington, DC: NTL.

Barnard, C. 1987. "Informal Organizations and Their Relation to Formal Organizations." In *Classics of Public Administration*, 2nd ed., ed. by J. Shafriz and A. Hyde. Chicago: Dorsey.

Belenky, M., B. Clinchy, N. Goldberger, and J. Tarule. 1986. *Women's Ways of Knowing: The Development of Self, Voice and Mind*. New York: Basic Books.

Bennett, D. 1980. *Successful Team Building Through Transactional Analysis*. New York: AMACOM.

Berger, P., and T. Luckmann. 1967. *The Social Construction of Reality*. Garden City, NY: Anchor.

Bernstein, P. 1976. *Workplace Democratization: Its Internal Dynamics*. Kent, OH: Kent State University Press.

Burrell, G., and G. Morgan. 1985. *Sociological Paradigms and Organizational Analysis*. Portsmouth, NH: Heinemann.

Casner-Lotto, J., and Associates. 1988. *Successful Training Strategies: Twenty-Six Innovative Corporate Models*. San Francisco: Jossey-Bass.

Chodorow, N. 1976. "Oedipal Asymmetries and Heterosexual Knots." *Social Problems*, Vol. 23, April, 454–68.

Eddy, W. 1981. *Public Organization Behavior and Development*. Cambridge, MA: Winthrop.

Forester, J. 1983. "Critical Theory and Organizational Analysis." G. Morgan (Ed.). *Beyond Method: Strategies for Social Research*. Beverly Hills: Sage, 234–246.

Geuss, R. 1981. *The Idea of a Critical Theory: Habermas and the Frankfurt School*. New York: Cambridge University Press.

Gould, S. 1984. "Triumph of a Naturalist. Review of a Feeling for the Organism: The Life and Work of Barbara McClintock, by Evelyn Fox Keller." As cited in C. F. Epstein. 1988. *Deceptive Distinctions: Sex, Gender, and the Social Order*. New Haven: Yale University Press, ix.

Handy, C. 1978. *Understanding Organizations*. New York: Penguin.

Herzberg, F., B. Mauser and B. Snyderman. 1959. *The Motivation to Work*. New York: Wiley.

Hickman, C. and M. Silva. 1986. *Creating Excellence: Managing Corporate Culture, Strategy, and Change in the New Age*. New York: New American Library (Plume).

Janeway, E. 1989. "Strange Creatures Among Us." *The New York Times Book Review*. October 1, Vol. XCIV, No. 40, 13.

Janis, I. 1972. *Victims of Groupthink: A Psychological Study of Foreign Policy Decisions and Fiascos*. Boston: Houghton Mifflin.

Kilmann, R. 1984. *Beyond the Quick Fix: Managing Five Tracks to Organizational Success*. San Francisco: Jossey-Bass.

———, M. Saxton, R. Serpa, and Associates. 1986. *Gaining Control of the Corporate Culture*. San Francisco: Jossey-Bass.

Maslow, A. 1964. *Eupsychian Management*. Homewood, IL: Irwin-Dorsey.

Meltzer, H., and W. Nord. 1981. *Making Organizations Humane and Productive*. New York: Wiley.

Moore, O., and A. Anderson. 1969. "Some Principles for the Design of Clarifying Environments." In *Handbook of Socialization Theory and Research*, ed. by D. Goslin. Chicago: Rand McNally.

Ott, J. 1989. *The Organizational Culture Perspective*. Pacific Grove, CA: Brooks/Cole.

Peters, T., and R. Waterman. 1982. *In Search of Excellence*. New York: Harper & Row.

Pierce, G., and K. Dechant. 1989. "The Manager-Learner: Developing Critical Thinking in Managers." Paper Presented to The Second Annual National Conference for Management Development Professionals in Industry, Government and Health Care. Boston, MA.

Polanyi, M. 1962. *Personal Knowledge: Toward a Post-Critical Philosophy*. Chicago: University of Chicago Press.

Sathe, V. 1986. "How to Decipher and Change Corporate Culture." In R. Kilmann et al. *Gaining Control of Corporate Culture*.

Schein, E. 1961. *Coercive Persuasion*. New York: W. W. Norton.

Schein, E. 1986. "How Culture Forms, Develops, and Changes." In R. Kilmann et al. *Gaining Control of Corporate Culture*.

Schutz, W. 1984. *The Truth Option: A Practical Technology for Human Affairs*. Berkeley, CA: Ten Speed Press.

Sethia, N., and M. Glinow. 1985. "Arriving at Four Cultures by Managing the Reward System." In Kilmann et al. *Gaining Control of Corporate Culture*.

Smircich, L. 1983. "Studying Organizations as Cultures." In *Beyond Method: Strategies for Social Research*, ed. by G. Morgan. Beverly Hills, CA: Sage, 160–173.

————, and G. Morgan. 1982. "Leadership: The Management of Meaning." *Journal of Applied Behavioral Studies*, Vol. 18, 257–273.

Turner, B. 1971. *Exploring the Industrial Subculture*. London: Macmillan.

Walton, R. 1986. "Establishing and Maintaining High Commitment Work Teams." In *The Organizational Life Cycle*, ed. by J. R. Kimberly and R. H. Miles. San Francisco: Jossey-Bass.

PART III _____

Women Managers and Influence Strategies: Changing Conceptualizations and Actions

In this section, we examine how women managers attempt to negotiate the work world, and on what the literature reports regarding how they do behave and how they might be empowered. Chapter 5 focuses on how women managers choose strategies to influence others at work. Through use of a case study, we demonstrate ways of interpreting and analyzing a supervisor's dilemma ranging from dependent and reciprocal power to organizational influence strategies.

Chapter 6 discusses the concept of action training and empowerment of managers. Empowerment is described not only as a means to acquiring power and stature but also as a way to reflect upon organizational events to generate critical insights about the dynamics of power. Concepts borrowed from action theory, critical theory, and dialectical analysis are worked into a training program designed for women managers. Throughout the program activities, trainers ask participants how they understand their work, strategize, act, and contribute to the overall functioning of their work organizations.

Chapter 5 _____

How Women Influence Organizations: Strategies and Approaches

Chapter 5 revisits the subject of gender, this time in relation to how women influence others at work. A case study describing a manager's quandary about how to influence her secretary is provided. Next, we analyze the effectiveness of the strategies she employs as opposed to those she fails to consider. Finally, the concepts of dependent and reciprocal power are examined, including related organizational influence strategies. We propose several factors to consider in choosing influence strategies for particular situations.

GENDER AND THE POLITICAL PERSPECTIVE

Much of the early research and writing concerning women managers shared the fundamental premise that women, due to their differential primary and secondary socialization, would transfer these behaviors, values, and attitudes to the work setting. Nevertheless, as previous chapters have demonstrated, more recent literature reflects a subtle shift in the assumptions concerning gender differences in managerial behavior. Once women and men reach middle and upper managerial levels, differences in behaviors, values, and attitudes tend to diminish or begin to disappear altogether. Whether this convergence between men and women managers is due to indoctrination, work culture influence, professional socialization, or a combination of influences is not clear. Nevertheless, it is clear that as research continues to accumulate, writers report greater convergence between male and female managers' behavior.

It is important, however, to note that although convergence trends appear in the literature, widespread discrimination and bias concerning women's prospects for advancement to upper-level positions continue to be reported. Martin et al. (1983) analyze research and writing using a five-level framework of social organization. The five levels reviewed range from societal, institutional, and organizational to role and individual. As one would expect, the authors conclude that fundamental change is required in all five levels for women's status to improve but, more centrally to our purposes, since each level incorporates pockets of resistance to change, these pockets may reinforce each other and act to block women's prospects for upward mobility in a systematic manner. Discrimination, like most contradictions that we shall explore in chapter 6, is rooted deeply in formal and informal structures, dispersed widely throughout organizational culture, and consequently cannot be removed simply by addressing one segment of organizational life. Martin and many others indict this lamentable state of affairs in society, institutions, and organizations for perpetuating serious societal and structural obstacles and continually giving new life to antiquated biases and discriminatory attitudes.

When aspirations for career advancement have been raised and at the same time fail to be realized, we may witness the beginning of a self-defeating cycle. As women rise through organizational hierarchies and as legal barriers continue to fall thereby assisting women, many women begin to believe that they can enjoy the same advancement opportunities as men. Some will plausibly argue that since important barriers to women's advancement are falling, only some women encounter discrimination and that the legal system protects most women adequately. However, bias and discrimination persist in more subtle, deep structural, and extralegal forms (Rizzo and Brosnan, 1990). When barriers to women's advancement do appear, a common explanation is that, since legal protections are adequate, the fault lies with the victim; more precisely, we can justifiably "blame the dead-end manager." She should have learned the right skills or management strategies.

The reader will find some of these strategies and tactics in the following pages. Types of power, kinds of influence strategies, and issues to consider when deciding which strategy or tactic to use will be explored. There is, as we shall see, a rapidly growing volume of research and writing on the subject of women's use of organizational influence. The essentials are summarized in this chapter for the purpose of describing how women attempt to influence others, as well as to examine some approaches that managers may want to consider in broadening their repertoire of influence strategies. Considering the publicity and exposure given to the "right skills" in popular publications such as *Working Woman* and *Savvy*, we present these strategies, skills, and knowledge cautiously and with reservations. We feel that a special caveat should be attached to them: learning and practicing these strategies will not by themselves guarantee success. As we shall see in this chapter as well as the next, there is more involved in ensuring equality and the integration of women into work organizations that can be addressed by using power or political strategies alone. Nevertheless, the ability to recognize and employ power and influence strategies when needed is central to a manager's perceived effectiveness by most organizations' standards, and for this reason alone, the following pages may appeal to some readers.

To introduce approaches to power and influence, we begin with a case study based on a local government manager's real-life dilemma.

EVELYN AND THE SECRETARY

A Case of Influence: Appropriate Kinds, Inappropriate Kinds, and Powerlessness

Evelyn is a relatively experienced first-line supervisor in a metropolitan urban development authority. She has worked in the agency for seventeen years in a range of capacities and is widely regarded as hardworking, knowledgeable, able to follow through on details and stick with a project. She is generally seen as the kind of person you would want to have on your team because of her dedication and persistence. In the past year, however, she has encountered an obstacle that she readily acknowledges she cannot manage: her own secretary.

Evelyn's secretary was appointed to her office because others have refused to deal with her. She was assigned to Evelyn's office in a way that gave Evelyn no choice. Evelyn had to take her. The reason for the heavy-handed manner of assignment is that Tammy is less than competent as a secretary and, as is a frequent topic of discussion around the water cooler, retains her job only through her close—some would say intimate—acquaintance with a political appointee in the mayor's office.

Over the years, she has developed a talent for blocking supervisors and is notoriously clever at manipulating her way out of unwanted assignments. She lets it be known, frequently and vociferously, that she is nobody's lackey and that, if she is crossed, there will be recriminations and penalties to pay. She delivers on her promises. Tammy has a diverse repertoire of skills to draw upon to get what she wants: she has engaged in psychological blackmail, has verbally assassinated more than a few characters in her time, is reputed to be talented in setting people up, and has taken credit for other secretaries' work. She has successfully divided her opponents so that she can maintain the upper hand. In one situation, the opposition was comprised of other secretaries complaining about uneven workloads since Tammy failed to pull her weight; in another, a formal complaint lodged against her for inadequate performance

brought informal censure against two superiors. The power of her connections reaches far and wide. She is not above using temper tantrums
to get her way, can behave irrationally, and is generally feared for her
unpredictability. No previous supervisor in the agency has attempted
to terminate her.

But this account would mislead the reader to focus primarily on Tammy's style of influencing a situation; we are more concerned about what
Evelyn does or can do about Tammy. As a student in a graduate public
administration class, Evelyn reported on Tammy and her relationship
as part of a case study of Evelyn's ineffective supervision. After a brief
description of general dealings with Tammy, she wrote that she was
stymied in terms of tactics to supervise her effectively or even to work
with her cooperatively. Most often, Evelyn avoided Tammy, assigning
her few tasks, certain that if she did complete the work, a questionable
prospect at best, it would be substandard anyway.

At first, when examining this case study, most of Evelyn's classmates
advised her to take control of the situation in as direct a manner as she
could muster: "Be assertive!", "Take charge! Let her know that you're
the boss." Or, after we discussed behavioral interventions, "at least air
the conflict and [talk about discussing the undiscussible!] confront her
with your feelings."

As one might suppose, Evelyn had already experimented with various
forms of assertive and authoritative behavior, all of which were met with
resistance or worse, no response. She had even gone to her superior
and found her complaint answered with, "That's the way it is. Learn
to work with her or leave." Considering that Tammy's transfer into her
unit was conducted in a manner that successfully undermined Evelyn's
authority and discredited her importance to the agency, Evelyn had long
ago concluded that avoidance was her best option. At the time of this
writing, the problem appears too complex and deeply embedded in
institutional memory, agency history, and the web of everyday work
patterns to be easily resolved.

VIEWING EVELYN'S DILEMMA FROM A POLITICAL PERSPECTIVE

Issues of Power and Dependency

Many different kinds of influence are represented by Tammy and
Evelyn's behavior in this case. Tammy's behavior includes many of the
games that popular management literature counsels managers to recognize but not to practice: blackmail, character assassination, removing
the opposition (Evelyn?), divide and rule, setups, and receiving undue
credit. Her repertoire also includes several of the more constructive

approaches to acquiring power that Dubrin (1978) recommends in certain situations: identify and win support of influentials, bore from within (otherwise known as "plant an ally"), acquire seniority, be distinctive and formidable (or, in Tammy's case, disagreeable), and acquire power in a step-by-step manner (that is, "camel's head in the tent"). Like most employees, Tammy has probably learned these political skills and strategies and when to use them through informal means. Although she exhibits skill in employing these strategies, Tammy's motives are suspect.

Neither Tammy nor Evelyn uses constructive strategies that are generally recommended to broaden one's base of power. For example, Dubrin advises that managers should be able to recognize certain constructive strategies when they are employed and should utilize them when possible. These strategies include mutual back-scratching, developing expertise, sawing wood (working hard), making a quick showing, controlling vital information, helping your boss succeed, displaying loyalty, volunteering for assignments, making effective use of praise, and becoming a crucial subordinate. While we may criticize Tammy for resorting to destructive game-playing, many would admire her general skill at gamesmanship and political strategizing. Evelyn, on the other hand, mostly avoids game-playing or the use of any strategy that puts herself on the line. It is clear she is not a risk-taker. When pressed, she uses a formal strategy—complaining to a higher authority—without success. She uses the control of vital information with colleagues and superiors, but perhaps this approach is serendipitous and not the product of conscious choice. In either case, she does not try to use the control of vital information with Tammy. Since that is her only base of strength, she can be criticized for her lack of adaptability. Managers more politically adept than Evelyn would zero in on her limited repertoire as well as her incomplete use of official channels, informal power, and influence strategies. Thus, a commonly invoked perspective on Evelyn's situation would begin here, with the adequacy of her power base.

The general perspective commonly used to describe Tammy and Evelyn's behavior has been called the political frame because it concerns the exchange of favors and competition over power. According to this view (Bolman and Deal, 1984), organizations are political arenas where the powerful and aspirants to power compete over scarce resources with those who succeed in shaping the configuration of influence and power. While this power arrangement is an artifact, a kind of cultural byproduct that is not the result of anyone's intentional action—due to the complex dynamics of social and political interaction, no one can ever ensure that any particular group will hold power—, the resulting pecking order at any particular point in time represents the net product of the participant's interplay. In a real sense, aspirants to power become the force to be reckoned with. Although scarce resources are most often pointed out as logical grounds for power struggles, control of boundaries, information, knowledge, decision-making rules, even differences in terms of values, beliefs, and perceptions of reality can serve as grounds for contest. The fundamental question is: Whose definition of the situation will prevail? The winner of a given battle or, judging from outcomes of previous conflicts, the likely winner in a continuing game is said to have power. This view of power and political games is founded upon dependency relationships where those without power must rely on the largess of the powerful to protect their interests. In a dependency scenario, notice that the power game is framed in win-lose terms so that power is an all or nothing possession; power is not normally described as shared.

Power in organizations is the capacity or potential to get people to do something that they would otherwise not do (Dahl, 1957). There are many bases of power, as French and Raven point out (1959). We can use Evelyn's situation to illustrate each. Legitimate power is granted by official organizational prerogatives. As a supervisor, Evelyn officially possesses legitimate power even though it is frequently undermined, an issue we will explore later. Reward and coercive power, used informally by those controlling critical resources, skills, or knowledge, is in certain ways an extension of legitimate power and, although not discussed in this case, the best guess is that Evelyn's reward and coercive power is undermined as well. In expert power, where technical skill or knowledge is critical, Evelyn has earned a reputation based on her expertise, but her reputation is not so distinguished as to be able to overcome the negative influence of a discredited formal power base. The net consequence is that she has little power over Tammy.

Referent power is found when one is respected as an organizationally knowledgeable and politically savvy player. Evelyn may know for example which strategy should be used in what situations. A long-time successful player will usually be seen as a winner at job politics and will gradually be credited with the important quality of charisma, the magical appeal that attracts followers. Referent power thus involves others wanting to identify with a winner and model themselves after him or her.

It is noteworthy that only those regarded as autonomous and independent are normally seen as having charisma. Those dependent upon others for their power, a derivative power if you will, are not admired for their magical qualities or appeal but for their connections to legitimate or coercive/reward power, or possibly for their expertise gained from continued acquaintance with the powerful. They are not powerful in their own right but are considered only as powerful as their original source. Due in part to her dependent status as well as her lack of self-confidence, the reader may feel that Evelyn probably lacks charisma.

The powerless, by virtue of their condition, generally lack the quality of magical appeal to followers (Mintzberg, 1983).

EXPLORING THE CONDITION OF POWERLESSNESS

Evelyn is probably more accurately depicted as powerless rather than powerful. We can reach this conclusion indirectly from the cumulative weight of case details. Although she has an unusual command of good information—she knows where to acquire information and, if it is unavailable, she knows whom to call—she has to date been unable to build on this foundation to be respected as a good decision-maker. Superiors and colleagues call her for technical information and respect her expertise at culling and supplying it; however, they do not consult her concerning how that information should be applied to a problem or how it translates into a decision. She also is not an astute diagnostician or strategist, which affects not only her reputation but hampers her ability to cope with Tammy. She is treated as a helpmate, an assistant to decision-makers, rather than as an autonomous player deserving of respect.

The most direct evidence of Evelyn's powerlessness, however, rests on her superiors' and colleagues' successful efforts to undermine her authority. As one example, assigning a secretary to her unit without consultation suggests that the powerless label had been attached to Evelyn earlier. Her expectation that those in authority will "do the right thing" on behalf of her unit's interests (she asks her supervisor to intervene with Tammy) illustrates her dependency. In her case, as is true for many women, obstacles faced while working her way up the rungs of organizational ladders may recall earlier feelings of powerlessness that women generally experience as part of their gender-specific primary socialization. Thus, dependency upon power and authority to protect employees is many women's only perceived recourse. They need something from the organization and can get it only from the few people who have it (Mintzberg, 1983). They are not psychologically prepared for autonomy and independence. Their dependency is further augmented if their prior training and socialization do not prepare them for the give-and-take, competitive, game-oriented world of job politics (Hennig and Jardim, 1977). Irrespective of the complex social causes of their dependent status, women managers and supervisors frequently find themselves without power for a confounding variety of workplace-specific reasons as well:

- they lack political clout;
- they lack powerful mentors or sponsors;
- for whatever reason, they are not viewed as upwardly mobile;

- they cannot command adequate resources for their units;
- they have little influence in decision-making;
- they are in situations where they are neither expected nor encouraged to take risks;
- their authority or positional power is undermined by their superiors;
- they feel insecure about their authority and communicate this insecurity to subordinates, who in turn resist their authority. In this way, they perpetuate a self-sustaining cycle that contributes to discounting their abilities. (Carr-Ruffino, 1985)

Evelyn is also not well-integrated into the organizational culture. She is not in touch with the right networks and cannot link with "people in the know" except for routine information. She may be on a dead-end career path, which will not change without her initiative or without a new sponsor or mentor appearing to support her. What can she do to have a voice in organizational life? Considering the volume of writing about power and influence that has accumulated over the years, are there skills she could learn, styles she could emulate, and attitudes she could practice?

FINDING WAYS OUT OF HER DILEMMA: FROM DEPENDENT TO RECIPROCAL POWER

Hirschman (1970) says all organization members have three basic choices when determining whether to engage people in their organization and on what terms they prefer to play the game:

- to stay and contribute as expected, which is called loyalty;
- to leave, which is referred to as exit;
- to stay and try to change the system, which is called voice. (Mintzberg, 1983, p. 23)

If the player chooses exit, he either seeks work elsewhere or prepares to leave. One who chooses loyalty prefers to obey directives and does not engage in the power game or try actively to influence others. Since our treatment of influence is inextricably tied to the voice option, the player choosing voice becomes an influencer as a matter of course.

To resort to voice, rather than exit, is for the customer or member to make an attempt at changing the practices, policies, and outputs of the firm from which one buys or of the organization to which one belongs. Voice is here defined as an attempt at all to change, rather than to escape from, an objectionable state of affairs. . . . (Hirschman, 1970, p. 30)

Those choosing voice require:

1. Some base of power such as the legitimate, expert, coercive/reward or referent foundations or a source of power (Carr-Ruffino, 1985, pp. 29–30) such as:
   a. influence on superiors in the decision-making process;
   b. the ability to get needed resources and information;
   c. the ability to reduce people's sense of dependency and uncertainty; perhaps even by defining a problem or issue and through clarifying it, enabling people to make sense of things;
   d. upward mobility.
2. energy to act and, we might add, the willingness to take risks;
3. political skill.

Drawing from the above, Evelyn could try to control a scarce commodity, resource, skill, or knowledge critical to the organization's functioning. Later in this chapter, we will identify another type of resource that, due to its abundant supply, wide dispersion, and two-way nature, is reciprocally exchanged between employees in contrast to what is described here. In the win-lose, have versus have-not scenario of dependency described thus far, however, a critical resource or skill would need to be concentrated in Evelyn's hands so that she would be virtually indispensable in order to shift the dependency from others in the organization to her. In deciding on this course of action, she should consider just two environmental constraints: she lives in an information-rich age in which many share information and knowledge, and in a highly competitive professional labor market where unique or special skills are difficult to own. As a result, attempting to put the organization in a dependent mode would probably be difficult if not costly to her career aspirations. She could also try to "play the game" of organizational politics and learn not only the strategies of acquiring power but also how to remain aloof, to stay morally and emotionally removed, to protect herself. In other words:

An employee with this perspective feels that organizations operate as systems or games and that one must know the rules or procedures to acquire a complete picture of events. Once she acquires a sense of the rules and clarifies the way the system works, she may feel more capable and play a greater role in organizational activities but will do so in keeping with 'the rules of the game.' . . . [T]his individual chooses to remain separate from events—'you must play the game whatever it is but the game player is not really you'—and can explain her behavior in terms of her varying role in the game. [See Chapter 7 for a complete survey.]

Would Evelyn be capable of such a posture? She is sufficiently intelligent to learn the mechanics of game-playing and organizational politics but like many women balks at treating people instrumentally, as a means to furthering her career aspirations (Hennig and Jardim, 1977). We should examine why this is so. Perhaps Evelyn is politically naive or she may frame issues in completely different terms. Gilligan's (1982) depiction of women as motivated by a different moral system than that held by men offers an alternative explanation. Gilligan argues that while men tend to view moral dilemmas from the perspective of what is an objectively fair or just resolution agreeable to all rational parties (Kohlberg, 1973), women tend to point out the limitations of any particular resolution and emphasize the conflicts that remain. Due to their care and responsibility orientation toward morality, women will adopt a different point of view toward existing social norms at work. They also order human experience in terms of different priorities (Gilligan, 1982). Consequently, women who fully understand the world of job politics and appreciate the necessity of game-playing within their organization may still focus upon the human consequences of game-playing and, valuing relationships as ends unto themselves, choose to avoid job politics. While this rationale neatly meshes with the requirements of empowerment strategies (discussed in the next chapter), it contradicts the assumptions of the political frame that governs norms, values, and culture, and in general describes mainstream thought concerning organization life.

In Evelyn's case, we suspect the reason for her avoidance of game-playing is that she is politically naive and plainly uncomfortable with taking action to change her behavior, even if, as the political frame asserts, such action could augment her effectiveness. She, like many women, may fear failure or success (Horner, 1968), either of which may derive from a more basic fear of taking risks. She may lack the self-confidence to experiment with game-playing. In any case, since forcing others in the organization into dependency has been ruled out as impractical (or, depending upon one's perspective, immoral), the remaining set of options emphasizes reciprocal power—the exchange of power and trading of favors in order to foster a system based on access through personal initiative. In this system, more subtle, long-term, and indirect influence transactions shape the configuration of power and the resulting balance of forces at any given point in time. We must then turn our attention to a discussion of reciprocal power, in particular, personal organizational influence strategies.

INFLUENCING IN ORGANIZATIONS

Power is often viewed as a capacity or potential for getting others to do what one wants, which may or may not be used or enacted toward others. Influence is frequently used to describe an individual who actively engages others politically. While some writers (McCall, 1979; Kanter, 1977; Mintzberg, 1983) argue that it is unrealistic to separate the power a person holds from the power she actually uses, our treatment will focus on influence as an informal activity or the absence of authoritative (that is, official or positional) power. In the following pages, influence will be used to describe those who actively seek to control, persuade, or otherwise affect the behavior of others. Regardless of the arguable subtleties in definitions of power and influence, our purpose is to describe how women attempt to influence others at work independent of the legitimate authority inherent in official managerial positions. By using this approach, we hope to explore how a manager like Evelyn, who possesses legitimate authority by virtue of her position but lacks both potential and real power, can overcome the obstacles of her own precedent and the negative impressions held in institutional memory to influence employees like Tammy effectively.

ARE WOMEN INFLUENCERS DIFFERENT?

Chodorow (1978) says that women's lives are embedded in social interaction and personal relationships while men's social orientation depends upon their position. This relational quality to women's lives ostensibly affords them greater opportunity to acquire the highly cultivated and subtle knowledge of persuasion and influence that allows them to get what they want in non-work settings, at least indirectly. This expectation is so deeply ingrained in Western culture that women are generally thought to possess great native cleverness and skill at manipulating people. Confined to the social (nonwork) realm, women's skill at persuasion and influencing is seen as posing a genuine threat to a man's well-being, power, and sense of self. This myth, which is integrally related to the stereotype of woman as seductive and possessing feminine wiles, is part of the reasoning behind the popular and nearly universal advice to managerial women to avoid even the appearance of using seductive (meaning sexual) charms at work or with fellow employees away from the job site. However, some (Carr-Ruffino, 1985) argue that the constructive side of this aspect of women's socialization, which can offer a foundation for influencing skills at work, has been lost in the process and must be rediscovered.

Are women more capable of "reading" people, understanding their needs, using their "native" intuition to be more creative in problem-solving, their social skills to resolve interpersonal conflict, and applying humanitarian approaches to management and supervision? The research offers ambiguous answers. At the Center for Creative Leadership (Morrison et al. 1987), an investigation into gender differences in managers found no differences between the sexes in, to cite a few areas, capacity to lead, influence, or motivate, humanitarian approaches, social sensitivity, or interpersonal skill. Vilkinas (1988) also reports few significant differences between men and women attempting to influence others at work. Our research with public and private sector managers, using the Profiles of Organizational Influence Strategies (Rizzo and Mendez, 1988), found that women differed only in their less frequently reported use of assertiveness. Thus, "Gender differences in management style may be mainly in the eye of the beholder" (Catalyst, 1986). While women's development of moral reasoning may be unique and their intellectual views may diverge from men's (Gilligan, 1982; Belenky, 1986), this curiously does not appear to influence their managerial behavior or, as yet, to enhance the functioning of organizations. Is this cleavage between women's unique psychological make-up and their male-standardized professional performance due to the overwhelming power of bureaucracy to shape work behavior? Since this separation between women's thought and action seems spurious, we must conclude that research into this territory has yet to clarify some important connections.

The following section is based on several assumptions. First, unlike men, women are powerless as a class and, if they are to be considered successful by most current standards of measurement, need to compensate by augmenting their skills in job politics. Second, like men, women need to learn how to influence and persuade others, especially if more direct power approaches, discussed earlier, are not successful or cannot be employed. Let us turn our attention to how influence is used and how it can be learned.

ORGANIZATIONAL INFLUENCE STRATEGIES

Organizations are, in one sense, systems of interaction and influence. We often limit our thinking about organizational influence to "leadership"—the influence of a manager over a subordinate—or perhaps to that and "politics," which could include all other forms of influence. However, these limits really are not appropriate. Throughout organizations, at all levels, across levels, up and down, people are trying to influence one another. (Kipnis and Schmidt, 1982, p. 1)

Some writers (Kaplan, 1984) feel that while popular conceptions of influence in organizations are founded upon power and authority, in the real world, successful managers find they must rely on informal networks of mutual exchange. In this light, the powerless condition of women can be seen as a more extreme and gender-specific version of the powerlessness experienced by all, or at least most, employees. Those managers who realize the limitations of legitimate authority may find that in order to persuade others to adopt their ideas or views, they require a wide variety of informal influence tactics and strategies. As one example, Kanter (1983) describes how managers accomplish major innovations through forging coalitions based on critical alliances built gradually and carefully over time. Cohen and Bradford (1989) observe that the successful manager must find ways to develop mutual influence without formal authority. Commanding colleagues, superiors, and, frequently, subordinates to adopt an idea or change a posture will not work.

Viewed in this light, Evelyn's case may be fairly commonplace. Since higher-ups refuse to support Evelyn's authority and instead undermine her power to sanction, Tammy enjoys the equivalent of colleague status and must be persuaded and influenced, rather than commanded, to perform up to standard. In situations such as these, Cohen and Bradford feel that informal strategies based on the notion of reciprocity are what is needed. Stated briefly, this is the belief that "people should be paid back for what they do, that one good (or bad) deed deserves another. . . . Because people expect that their actions will be paid back, influence is possible" (1989, pp. 7–8). The exchange between parties can involve tangible goods (equipment, staff support) or intangibles (enhanced reputation)—whatever it takes to influence the individual in terms of his particular needs and goals. Mutually satisfactory exchange may involve one or several forms of organizational "currency." Whatever commodity is traded, the transaction must be guided by certain assumptions, among them, that the target of influence is a potential ally, not an adversary, and that win-win outcomes will be assured (Cohen and Bradford; 1989).

When choosing which influence strategy or particular tactic to use in a given situation, Evelyn may benefit from considering four components that especially characterize the problem situation:

- *Target* of influence or, in other words, the target person. In this situation, Tammy's special qualities and idiosyncrasies should be reviewed as part of the case history in order to construct probable reactions to an particular strategy. At the same time, Evelyn would be wise to bear in mind that Tammy's general intransigence may mask some constructive qualities that have yet to manifest themselves. Consequently, past responses and behavior may not form complete and reliable predictors of her future responses.

  A separate concern warrants special attention: Evelyn needs to be aware of key goals and resources that are valued by Tammy (Cohen and Bradford, 1989). Since Evelyn lacks the information to answer this important question, her first task should be to explore with Tammy and others the nature of Tammy's goals as well as which currencies might be successful in redirecting Tammy's efforts.

- *Resources* available to or possessed by the influencer. As mentioned earlier, Evelyn enjoys some expert power and has a reputation as a diligent, reliable worker. We might add that after seventeen years, she is well acquainted with agency employees socially, although she does not know how to tap their resources in a manner that would be useful to her in resolving this dilemma. Clearly, Evelyn does not know how exchange operates.

Regarding Tammy, as already mentioned, Evelyn needs to know which resources she needs in order to influence her. Does she hold authority to allocate space, budget increases, or personnel? Does she have enough time and energy to provide personal and emotional backing to one who requires it? These are basic resource questions that require answers. Evelyn should then become familiar with commonly traded organizational currencies, ranging from inspirational (for example, involvement in realizing a "vision"), task-related (information, support), position-related (advancement), relationship-related (inclusion, understanding), and personal (enhances self-concept). No information is provided in the case concerning this important issue, yet discovering what is important to Tammy can indicate what helps to motivate her.

- *Adverse* reactions of the target person. Potential costs are attached to using any tactic or strategy to influence a situation. If you practice brinkmanship (or disrupt the balance of forces in any situation), that act may set a precedent with individuals witnessing your use of that tactic. Consequently, most organization members choose to be careful when considering their choice of the most direct, forceful, and therefore risky tactics. When Evelyn reviews each possible influence strategy one by one, she should try to probe with herself and others the answer to this question: What might be the worst behavior she could expect of Tammy? What is Tammy's most likely response? With a background of experience with Tammy to draw from, Evelyn should have a good grasp of the most extreme measures Tammy could take.

- *Purpose* of the use of influence. Would it be to contain Tammy for the time being or gradually build respect for Evelyn's interests and goals? In the best of all possible scenarios, how would she imagine Tammy at her best behavior? As a submissive subordinate, an obedient follower, a cooperative team player? Is it important to Evelyn to present herself as a take-charge, commanding supervisor? If so, part of her goal may be to alter her external reputation as well as her supervisory performance.

The overall purpose of influence is to involve Tammy in such ways that, over time, she would begin to feel obligated to reciprocate with Evelyn.

After reflecting on these considerations, (Kipnis and Schmidt, 1982, pp. 5–6) Evelyn might then determine which of these influence strategies could supplement her reciprocal strategy: reason, friendliness, bargaining, assertiveness, coalition, appeal to higher authority, and sanctions (Kipnis and Schmidt, 1982). Reason describes the strategy of influencing people by relying on data and information to support one's requests. It involves preparation and expertise, not spontaneous, unplanned arguments for one's position. Facts and logical arguments are used to persuade the target. Reason is the strategy most used in organizations. However, in Evelyn's case, she has abundant evidence that indicates that reason does not work well alone to influence Tammy. Tammy knows how to counter reasoned approaches, and she is prepared to be unreasonable.

Friendliness involves creating such a favorable impression of the influencer that Tammy will do what Evelyn wants. To achieve a referent base of power through friendliness, Evelyn's personality, interpersonal skills, and sensitivity to others would be factors here. If Evelyn possesses these social and empathic skills, they have not appeared or been utilized as yet. Perhaps she can maximize her real potential at using friendliness. She is probably aware at some level of its pervasiveness at work, if not appreciative of its usefulness. It is the second most commonly used strategy.

Bargaining is used to influence others through negotiation and the exchange of benefits or favors. Its power base relies on forming reciprocal relationships where if Evelyn performs a favor for Tammy, Tammy will be held accountable to do the same for Evelyn. Evelyn faces two challenges in establishing reciprocity: first, she must develop a plan to transform her relationship with Tammy toward one of mutual exchange, obligation, and good will; second, as discussed, she must know and be able to choose from an array of organizational "currencies" that will appeal to Tammy, and must be able to mobilize these currencies spontaneously to meet a given situation. Movement toward exchange transactions opens up a whole new territory for Evelyn; she is unskilled in this area and must begin small and gradually.

Coalitions that mobilize others to assist Evelyn in influencing Tammy are based on the premise that "there is power in numbers." Used less often with subordinates generally, it would probably be seldom effective with Tammy in particular. Higher authority is one strategy that Evelyn has used informally. She has appealed to the chain of command, which has authority over Tammy through both formal appeals and informal requests. Evelyn may, however, need to use higher authority outside the organization, perhaps through professional groups, to reach the ears that matter.

Assertiveness means using demands, setting deadlines, and generally the direct and forceful expression of the influencer's demands. While assertiveness has been used on isolated occasions, it has not been used consistently to reach Tammy. Similarly, Evelyn has not adopted a consistent program based on the use of sanctions. Sanctions rely on the rewards and punishments that accompany legitimate authority; while Evelyn is probably limited in the kinds of sanctions available to her, she has used existing sanctions incompletely. Her haphazard experimentation with these two influence strategies suggests that she may need to develop a consistent program of strategies to use in certain common situations. Evelyn wants to change from her current status as a bystander or avoider (Hirschman, 1970) who does not try to influence others, to a tactician, an organization member who possesses a repertoire with a solid core that has enough variety—three or four influence strategies—to be able to adapt to a range of situations. To accomplish this transformation, she may need to consider some additional factors.[1]

Any act of influence can be analyzed in terms of how it is transmitted to the receiver. The manager who understands and appreciates that overall influencing style is composed of small, seemingly isolated acts should be able to promote a new style by examining those components of her own. She could begin by analyzing previous acts of influence or an example that was highly successful, reviewing the act's qualities and recomposing them to reflect the influencer's needs and goals in a particular situation. Analysis may include the channel through which influence is communicated (formal or informal), the larger context of the act including its role in an overall pattern of events, its frequency over time, as well as its meaning in both sent and received interpretations. Any or all of these components is capable of transmitting influence to a greater or lesser degree. An act of influence may be:

- regular or episodic; frequent or haphazard;
- general, focused on the entire organization or range of decisions, or targeted to a unit, a person;
- detached or personal, where the personal dimension involves high personal stakes or investment;
- of an initiative or obstructive nature. Initiative means persuading a target to do something new; obstruction involves blocking an action or person;
- formal or informal, using official channels to stage an action or unofficial means to persuade others. (Mintzberg, 1983)

When moving from left to right on A Continuum of Influencing Behavior (see Figure 5.1), notice that behaviors listed on the left—the regular, general, and detached tactics such as social norms and to a lesser extent, formal constraints—are not as direct and forceful as those on the right— the episodic (or, depending upon the situation, regular), focused, or personal tactics.

PUTTING IT ALL TOGETHER: SOME FINAL CONSIDERATIONS

In developing a plan of intervention, Evelyn should consider:

- the consistency of her efforts. She needs to invoke certain strategies, such as assertiveness, appropriately and frequently;
- when and how to offer general criticisms or focused feedback;

Figure 5.1
A Continuum of Influencing Behavior

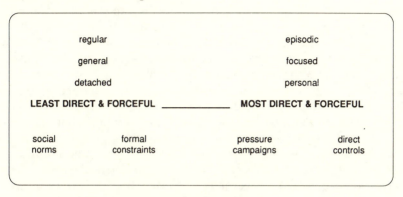

Source: Adapted from Mintzberg, 1983, pp. 47–48.

• when to remain detached, when to be personal;
• when to initiate, when to obstruct, and how;
• when to use formal means of persuasion (formal constraints), when to use informal means (social norms), and how.

If a manager like Evelyn is serious about resolving a problem situation, she needs to develop a contingency plan to be prepared to support positive behavior and block and/or sanction negative behavior through varying her use of currencies, resources, tactics, and overall organizational influence strategies. For the plan to succeed, additional conditions and qualifications should be mentioned, and these will demand a great deal of Evelyn. She will need to cultivate what many call the "intuitive" aspects of management (Isenberg, 1984). In a management setting, intuitive knowledge includes diagnostic skill, a sensitivity for nonverbal communications, as well as the appropriate timing for interventions, a capacity for taking risks, and a desire to experiment with different tactics, strategies, and styles than she may have used in the past. Her plan will demand a high level of persistence and patience from her. She will need to be sufficiently committed to the intervention plan that she will practice it, in various permutations, over the long haul. Only after the plan has been given enough time, enough testing, enough fine tuning that any fair observer would say that she had given it a reasonable chance for success, could she abandon the plan.

CONCLUSION: LIMITATIONS OF THE POLITICAL PERSPECTIVE

Thus far we have examined Evelyn's dilemma solely from a political perspective. While we endorse the use of additional models for understanding organizational and managerial behavior (for example, the structural, human relations, cultural, and action frames of reference have a great deal to offer), the political perspective is important for its capacity to describe organizational life as many players themselves see it. We need to recognize and be able to cope with organizational politics not only because of its pervasiveness, some would say universality, in American work organizations, but also because politics represent the standard modus operandi. The exchange model of influence in particular suggests ways of manipulating others at work that are considered acceptable, appropriate, and normalizing. From a different vantage point, however, we find that the exchange model relies upon the segmented work roles and instrumental reasoning inherent in the bureaucratic tradition. In other words, in most work organizations we do not deal with the whole person; management is concerned only with how an individual performs a work role. Similarly, a worker like Tammy is regarded as a tool to be used in the quest for goal accomplishment.

As they are most frequently used, the strategies and approaches described in this chapter possess limitations in that they permit the user to cope more effectively with an existing environment, as opposed to changing the ways organizations accomplish work. The resulting repertoire of managerial skills is thus reformist in its assumptions. No amount of political expertise and talent will help change the "system" to reduce the negative consequences of politics. No matter how skilled and effective a woman can become in her managerial and supervisory performance, she will still encounter resistance to her efforts to change the system. If she remains in the organization long enough, she will eventually encounter obstacles that cannot be addressed by using the vantage provided by the political perspective, such as the intimidating capacity of bureaucracies to fight to stay the same (Schon, 1971). The strategies presented thus far are insufficient by themselves to guide us in changing system values and culture, so the next chapter will focus upon the issue of empowerment. In chapter 6, we will look at Evelyn and Tammy's case from another perspective in an effort to reframe Evelyn's problems and generate a different set of recommendations. More broadly, we will explore how women can be empowered to negotiate bureaucratic systems and, in the process, transform our work organizations.

NOTE

1. In addition to bystanders (scoring low on most influence strategies) and tacticians (with average to high scores on three or four strategies), Kipnis and Schmidt (1982) describe two additional profiles for influencers. Captives have high scores on only one or two influence strategies but are low on the remainder. These individuals tend to be limited in their choice of strategy. Regardless of

what they want to accomplish, they invariably use the same few influence strategies. Shotguns have high scores on most influence strategies. Unlike captives, those fitting this profile use a wide range of strategies but are probably not as successful as they would like. They use too many different strategies without knowing what is best considering their native style as well as the demands of the situation.

REFERENCES

Belenky, M., B. Clinchy, N. Goldberger, and J. Tarule. 1986. *Women's Ways of Knowing: The Development of Self, Voice, and Mind.* New York: Basic Books.

Bolman, L., and T. Deal. 1984. *Modern Approaches to Understanding and Managing Organizations.* San Francisco: Jossey-Bass.

Carr-Ruffino, N. 1985. *The Promotable Woman: Becoming a Successful Manager.* Revised ed. Belmont, CA: Wadsworth.

Catalyst. 1986. *Female Management Style: Myth and Reality.* New York: Catalyst.

Chodorow, N. 1978. *The Reproduction of Mothering.* Berkeley: University of California Press.

Cohen, A., and D. Bradford. 1989. "Influence without Authority: The Use of Alliances, Reciprocity, and Exchange to Accomplish Work." *Organizational Dynamics*, Vol. 17, No. 3, Winter, 5–17.

Dahl, R. A. 1957. "The Concept of Power." *Behavioral Science*, Vol. 2, No. 3, July, 201–18.

Dubrin, A. J. 1978. *Human Relations: A Job-Oriented Approach.* Reston, VA: Prentice-Hall.

Fairholm, G. W. 1985. "Power Tactics on the Job." *Personnel*, Vol. 62, No. 5, May, 45–50.

French, J.R.P., and B. Raven. 1959. "The Bases of Social Power." In *Studies in Social Power*, ed. by D. Cartwright. Ann Arbor: Institute for Social Research, University of Michigan.

Gilligan, C. 1982. *In A Different Voice: Psychological Theory and Women's Development.* Cambridge, MA: Harvard University Press.

Hennig, M., and A. Jardim. 1977. *The Managerial Woman.* Garden City, NY: Doubleday, Anchor Books.

Hirschman, A. O. 1970. *Exit, Voice, and Loyalty: Responses to Decline in Firms, Organizations, and States.* Cambridge, MA: Harvard University Press.

Horner, M. 1968. "Sex Differences in Achievement, Motivation, and Performance in Competitive and Noncompetitive Situations." Ph.D. diss. University of Michigan, Ann Arbor.

Isenberg, D. 1984. "How Senior Managers Think." *Harvard Business Review*, Nov.-Dec.

Kanter, R. 1977. *Men and Women of the Corporation.* New York: Basic Books.

———. 1983. *The Change Masters.* New York: Simon and Schuster.

Kaplan, R. 1984. "Trade Routes: The Manager's Network of Relationships." *Organizational Dynamics*, Vol. 12, No. 4, Spring, 37–52.

Kipnis, D. and S. Schmidt. 1982. *Respondent's Guide to the Profiles of Organizational Influence Strategies.* San Diego: University Associates.

Kohlberg, L. 1973. "Continuities and Discontinuities in Childhood and Adult

Moral Development Revisited." In *Collected Papers on Moral Development and Moral Education*, L. Kohlberg, ed. Cambridge, MA: Moral Education Research Foundation, Harvard University.

McCall, M. 1979. "Power, Authority, and Influence." In *Organizational Behavior*, ed. by S. Kerr. Columbus, OH: Grid.

Martin, P., et al. 1983. "Advancement for Women in Hierarchical Organizations: A Multilevel Analysis of Problems and Prospects." *Journal of Applied Behavioral Science*, Vol. 19, No. 1, 19–33.

Mintzberg, H. 1983. *Power In and Around Organization*. Englewood Cliffs, NJ: Prentice-Hall.

Morrison, A., R. White, and E. Van Velsor. 1987. "The Narrow Band." *Issues and Observations*. Greensboro, NC: Center for Creative Leadership, Spring, 1–2.

Rizzo, A. M., and C. Mendez. 1988. "Making Things Happen in Organizations: Does Gender Make a Difference?" *Public Personnel Management*, Vol. 17, No. 1, Spring, 9–20.

———, and D. Brosnan. 1990. "Critical Theory and Communication Dysfunction: The Case of Sexually Ambiguous Behavior." *Administration and Society*, Vol. 21, No. 4, May.

Schon, D. 1971. *Beyond the Stable State*. New York: W. W. Norton.

Vilkinas, T. 1988. "Do Women Use Different Influences?" *Women in Management Review*, Vol. 3, No. 3, 155–160.

Chapter 6 _____

Using Action Training to Empower Women Managers: Lessons from an Experimental Workshop*

Chapter 6 asks how human resource development (HRD) can foster change in organizations. How do we work with employees with varying levels of experience and states of readiness to persuade them to want to change? The authors explore how trainers can encourage employees to assume responsibility for issues and problems at work and begin to "own" their organizations, in the hopes that in the process, both the individual and the system will be transformed.

The Evelyn and Tammy case introduced in the last chapter is revisited here from several additional perspectives: action theory, critical theory, and dialectical analysis. An experimental workshop wherein the authors tried to translate these concepts into practice is described here in detail.

TRAINING AS LEARNING

Although training and education are frequently used to address the problems of women, most training conducted in the workplace emphasizes teaching employees the requisite policies and procedures, tasks and technical expertise on an as-needed basis. Workers' deficiencies or flaws are remediated when those responsible, usually supervisors or management, recognize that these deficits pose an obstacle to effective organizational performance. For the most part, technical training is based on instrumental learning assumptions. Instrumental learning is what commonly occurs when people learn how to do a job or task, usually one deemed by authorities as central to organizational functioning, in an im-

*An earlier version of this chapter was presented to the 1989 American Society for Public Administration Conference in Miami, Florida.

proved fashion. For example, when corporations become aware that illit-
eracy rates among employees are rising and that job performance suffers
as a result, literacy training may be proposed as the answer to the problem. However, this version of literacy training will encompass only those
aspects of reading and writing considered essential or instrumental to
on-the-job performance. After being given specific directives, trainers
typically proceed by defining and delimiting which aspects of the literacy
problem they should address; they then design a program and plan (perhaps in concert with trainees) a course of action for learning to read and
write, conduct the sessions, and evaluate the results. In this manner, instrumental learning implicitly endorses linear, analytic, step-like, scientific
models of managerial and employee development.

Although undoubtedly the most commonly found type of employee
and professional training, technical training or, as we shall see, even
skill training, possesses some distinct drawbacks. One is that technical
training in particular is founded upon a deficit model of education
wherein poor performance or lack of promotability is assumed to be the
direct result of a lack of specific and concrete information, skills, or
knowledge. If only women, or any other group, possessed these characteristics or skills, this reasoning goes, they would be able to climb the
organizational ladder as quickly and easily as men. Therefore, the logic
of the medical model maintains: prescribe the appropriate medication—
assertiveness training or confidence building, to name two common
examples—, take as directed, and the employer's responsibility in contributing to organizational learning is discharged.

More sophisticated training models are based upon the notion that
learning is more complex, continuous, dynamic, and multifaceted.
Learning in organizations occurs informally, incidentally, and in a non-
routine manner (Marsick, 1987). Many causes, direct and indirect, complex and simple, and varying in salience are most likely responsible for
flawed performance or promotability dilemmas. Unlike technical training or narrow skill training, where one or two compartmentalized issues
may be addressed, training models based on noninstrumental types of
learning can investigate more amorphous, nonlinear issues, such as
leadership, organization climate, type of work culture, and personal
interpretations of goals.

In contrast to instrumental learning, dialogic learning (Marsick, 1987)
is directed toward interpreting consensual norms that occur when employees learn about their work culture or when they interpret policies
and procedures. The emphasis on this kind of learning is an improved
understanding of one's situation; for example, being able to validate
perceptions about what is going on in organizational life with others.
Another kind of learning involves self-reflection directed at personal
change. Its purpose is critical reflection about one's identity in a partic-

ular environment and involves a "transformation in meaning perspectives, that is, integrated psychological structures with dimensions of thought, will, and feeling which represent the way a person looks at him or herself and relationships" (Marsick, p. 17). None of these types of learning—instrumental, dialogic, or self-reflective—can be easily separated and all overlap considerably; most training models currently in practice aspire only to instrumental goals. While dialogue and self-reflection can accompany learning the most simple task, technical training programs typically devalue or undermine the importance of these divergent types of learning.

This chapter considers how those in HRD professions might go about designing contexts that facilitate the growth and empowerment of women at work. Since most approaches to HRD assume an instrumental orientation, readers' attention will be directed to alternative approaches, particularly the self-reflective and, to a lesser extent, dialogic types of learning, which we feel promote a special quality of identification and involvement with a workplace. Rather than serve merely to enhance the existing mission of an organization, these perspectives contribute toward enhancing "the capacities of people in everyday situations to investigate, understand, and if they wish, to change those situations in an ongoing fashion with a minimum of external help" (Morgan and Ramirez, 1983, p. 9). Building on these perspectives, this account will address those strategies and approaches that empower people, thus enabling organizations "to learn from their own experience, and to modify their structure and design to reflect what they have learned" (p. 4). Finally, a workshop that we designed to empower women managers will be described and assessed.

ACTION THEORY: A FRAMEWORK FOR DEVELOPING MANAGERS

Organizational learning is concerned with the predominant modes in which organizations correct errors or learn from experience. As Argyris and Schon (1978) have observed, organizational learning begins with individuals; individuals are the agents of organizational action, so they are also the agents for organizational learning. To transform organizations, then, one must begin with their members. To begin to understand that change process, Argyris and Schon have refined the notion of theories of action: how people learn to become competent in taking action and learn from reflecting on their actions. When asked how they would behave under certain circumstances, most people would respond with a preferred, even ideal, set of behaviors. Some will relate what they think others want to hear or what they believe will make them appear competent or effective. This is known as espoused theory. The theory that actually governs actions is known as theory-in-use. One can construct theories-in-use from directly observable behavioral data, which in turn generate models of action theories for individuals.

For most individuals, theories-in-use, once discovered and owned, will be found to contradict their espoused theories in obvious ways. For example, when Evelyn reported to the class that none of her strategies worked to improve her secretary's performance and that she chose to avoid her, we probed her day-to-day dealings with Tammy. It was inaccurate to describe Evelyn as refusing to deal with Tammy. We found that Evelyn did respond to the secretary's behavior in indirect ways, through sarcasm, jibes, and gossip about her. Passive aggressive behavior, one component of her theory-in-use, may have served to ventilate her frustrations but also probably contributed to Tammy's impression that she controlled the situation, not only through her external political connections but as reenacted daily through her direct encounters with Evelyn.

At first, when examining this case study, most of the manager's classmates advised her to take control of the situation in as direct a manner as she could muster: "Be assertive! Take charge! Let her know that you're the boss." Or, later in the course: "At least air the conflict and [discuss the undiscussible] confront her with your feelings!"

As one might suppose, the manager had already experimented with various forms of assertive and authoritative behavior, all of which were met with resistance or, worse, no response. She had even gone to her own superior but her complaint was met with "That's the way it is. Learn to work with her or leave." The problem was too complex and deeply embedded in the web of everyday work patterns to be easily manageable.

Of more immediate interest, however, is that we in the class were focusing on a narrow range of issues closely resembling what Argyris and Schon call single-loop learning. This type of learning is invoked when, in order to accommodate pressures and influences from the internal and organizational environment, most people in organizations are encouraged, even trained, to detect errors that, if corrected, will enhance the organization's effectiveness. Continual efforts at doing things (that is, theory-in-use) usually will result in patterns of behavior that perpetuate the central features of that theory-in-use (Argyris and Schon, 1978, p. 18). However, single-loop learning considers only organizational strategies and assumptions that accommodate a constant framework of management philosophy, procedures, and techniques. We deal with, or "manage," only problems deemed solvable or "doable"; this concern with effectiveness impedes efforts to resolve problems of a more fundamental nature—those that allow for redefining organizational norms and restructuring strategies and assumptions associated with these norms. When the latter process, known as double-loop learning, can occur, not only are the norms that define effective performance open to question and redefinition, but the process through which people inquire into the nature of current norms and explore new ones modifies how they confront and resolve conflict over these fundamental issues. Outcomes of a double-loop learning process may include setting new priorities and different weightings of norms, as well as changes in the norms themselves, accompanied by changes in strategies and assumptions.

Viewed in this light, Evelyn's dilemma was not simply that she expected and depended upon effective performance from the secretary. She needed to be able to inquire jointly with her into their incompatible work behavior and, in so doing, foster a new understanding of their work requirements, the sources of errors, and consequences: "understandings which then [can] become embedded in the images and maps of organization" (Argyris and Schon, 1978, p. 24). Evelyn, indeed all learners, must be able to discover the sources of errors, and must be permitted to discover how error derives from strategies and assumptions in existing theories-in-use. Learners must be supported in inventing "new strategies, based on new assumptions, in order to correct error. They must be permitted to develop those strategies and once invoked, evaluate and generalize the results of that new action" (Argyris and Schon, 1978, p. 19). Much of what we feel is needed to resolve her dilemma fits into what is called a Model O-II behavioral world. The reader can compare Model O-II action strategies, listed in boldface, which can enable individuals to focus on questions of increased long-term effectiveness, with Model O-I, the norm in most organizations (adapted from Argyris et al., 1985, p. 99):

1. **Design situations or environments where participants can be origins and can experience high personal causation.** This contrasts with Model I strategies that advise: design, manage, and control the environment;

2. **Tasks are controlled jointly.** Model I thinking is: own and control the work, guard the right to define problems, and rule on the appropriate execution of tasks.

3. **Protection of self is a joint enterprise and oriented toward growth.** Examples include speaking in easily observable terms, seeking to discover one's own inconsistencies and incongruities. Model I thinking is: unilaterally protect yourself. Act and speak on the basis of self-interest as opposed to directly observable behavior; be blind to impact on others and engage in defensive actions.

4. Bilateral protection of others, as opposed to Model I thinking in which one unilaterally protects others from being hurt. Paternalistic behavior includes withholding information, creating rules to censor information and behavior, and holding private meetings.

We have described an interesting and texturally rich dilemma: the secretary has perhaps violated the official code—the espoused theory, if you will—that we expect high performance from our employees; she did not violate the Model O-I theory-in-use that severs the connection between performance evaluation and retention. If the secretary were to change to such an extent that she began meeting her work obligations, we would have a single-loop solution to what can also be interpreted as a double-loop problem. Yet, ultimately without substantial change using either frame of reference, it is primarily Evelyn, not Tammy, who is censured for ineffective performance. She is criticized by co-workers for not exercising sufficient unilateral control (that is, she is not effective by Model O-I behavioral standards). She is counseled by classmates to protect herself and wait for the secretary to "hang herself." She regards herself and is viewed sympathetically by classmates as a victim of the system and believes that a Model O-II espoused theory would not be respected at work even if she could behave accordingly.

Evelyn does not think it possible that she could be an "agent" capable of feeling empowered to cope with managerial problems. Paradoxically, both she and even the secretary feel like victims of the other's intentions. Both would probably question whether they could become empowered to take responsibility and control over their lives. As things stand, it is safe to say that both undoubtedly lack feelings of control and the critical awareness of how they can better share their immediate work environments to move away from the destructive, nonproductive work climate that inhibits their learning and changing.

Since most work organizations are best described by Model O-I theories-in-use, it is widely argued that Evelyn is not likely to learn a Model O-II posture at work. Most likely, if she learns these concepts as empowering strategies at all, she will have encountered them in the classroom.

KEYS TO ACTION LEARNING

Action learning can be described from many starting points. This treatment will begin with one goal of action theory: the empowerment of the individual. One way of describing the empowered individual is that he or she possesses feelings of control, heightened by ownership of an issue or problem and the perception of efficacy or the ability to have impact. The empowered can critically analyze the social and political environment in an effort to acquire a deeper, more subtle, and thorough understanding of the nature of power relationships.

In order to analyze in this manner, however, something more is required: the ability to reflect on oneself and one's experience, or to "see one's self in relationship to one's object of attention, be it a material object, another person, a concept, an ideological constraint on thought or action, or an unconscious constraint on thought or action." This self-reflection provides us with a vantage point from which we can evaluate "the truth and desirability of our relationship to things in our environment" (White, 1982, p. 98). The purpose of empowerment acquired through self-reflection is that "human beings—as individuals, groups, or classes—can engage in action consistent with their interests" (Morgan, 1983, p. 4). Empowerment is therefore a formulation combining feelings of power, control, and efficacy with the special kind of emancipation gained through self-reflection and critical insight into power relationships.

Which contributes to empowerment? Judging from the outcomes of our teaching and training, certain skills, knowledge, and abilities[1], most directly derived from fundamental action theory concepts, appear to be linked with feelings and perceptions of empowerment.

- Learning from experience or, more precisely, from reflections on experience. Through reflection, one can come to terms with the powerful forces toward reification that exist in the social world as well as within us (Harmon and Mayer, 1986, p. 325). This quality of understanding is empowering. Empowerment is not measured merely by success but by failure as well; through reflection on successes and failures, one can acquire deeper understanding of the true nature of one's circumstances (Couto, 1989, p. 245) and ultimately release oneself from an unconscious dependence on reified power structures.

- taking risks in meaningful activities where prospects for both learning and failure are higher than usual.

- participation in choice-making, which presents the genuine opportunity for making impact upon one's environment, thereby enhancing one's prospects for efficacy.

- owning a problem or "mess" that lacks closure and "neatness," and taking responsibility for its articulation, legitimation, follow-up, or solution.

- reframing or experimenting with different frames of reference, which includes using different methods of gathering information to supplement, refine, or alter a world view in ways that transcend official rhetoric. As many (Mitroff, 1983; Schon, 1983; Bolman and Deal, 1984) have noted, the way one frames basic problems is critical in determining the way they will be solved. We refer to this in short as reframing and suggest that for many seeking empowerment, experimenting with different perspectives continues in a given situation until a frame is found which, in terms of that situation, is more adequate or sufficient in its explanatory power, logical cohesiveness, and comprehensiveness.

- discovering where ideology (information and views that perpetuate the interests of the powerful) ends and understanding begins concerning apparent contradictions in organizational life, such as domination that is taken for granted by workers.

- analyzing a work or political situation on both the surface (that is, the taken-for-granted, everyday world of organizations) and deep structural dimensions (including the material conditions of production and the unexamined beliefs and values upon which the surface structure rests) and being able to appreciate his/her part in sustaining both worlds.

Here, we borrow heavily from dialectical analysis, which views all change as the product of tension between opposites or contradictions. Voiced in the context of our training workshop, the contradictions to be examined involve not the polar opposites of female and male or the dualism between instrumental and expressive dimensions, but those between organizational structure and roles, between official policies on equality, justice, and fairness and actual practices of inequality, injustice, and unfairness. Such contradictions raise the question of confrontation between opposing or incompatible ways of arranging social life.

A good contemporary example would be discovering a "mommy track" in an organization, by which working mothers (and in lesser numbers, family-oriented men) opt out of the "fast track" up the career ladder in order to devote greater time and energy to raising their children. Identifying such a practice points up contradictions regarding fair treatment of the sexes at work (Schwartz, 1989). Unfolding these contradictions also means discovering the combinations of social forces that allow for transforming organizational life. The question is, can we change how we conceptualize the possibilities (scenarios of the future) by recognizing, in the spirit of mutual causality, our interdependence with others? Should differences in the treatment of "mommy track" women and "career primary" women be tolerated and supported, not only for the benefit of family-identified women but in the interests of our society's children as well?

In a very real sense, dialectical analysis describes how the management of organizations always involves the management of contradiction. Evelyn's situation is an all-too-common, perhaps even typical dilemma, more so certainly than she realizes. During a period of crisis, when competing values and logics have the opportunity to emerge clearly, we can cast our choices for the kind of contradiction that will shape social reality (Morgan, 1986). Evelyn could focus on the contradiction between the official chain of command and legitimate authority versus the consistent undermining of her authority; she could consider her situation from the vantage point of the public-private distinction, which attempts to separate the secretary's personal life and, by extension, her political connections, from her formal work assignment and how she carries out her duties and responsibilities. Another contradiction is expressed in the presumably causal link between performance and retention: why, if Tammy is performing below standard, is she retained?

An action theorist might reframe the dilemma and pose different questions: Why are Evelyn and Tammy operating under assumptions (Model O-I governing variables) that are so clearly counterproductive to both parties' long-term effectiveness? Evelyn cannot get her unit's work accomplished and feels subverted; Tammy must survive in an openly hostile work climate. Each of these contradictions, while phrased at an organizational level of analysis (official versus operative, public versus private, performance versus retention), relies on the surface and deep structure distinction. As mentioned, both surface and deep structures interact with and reinforce each other, which admittedly confounds our efforts to capture the precise nature of the dilemma. More central to our purposes, however, Evelyn and Tammy must account for buying into and sustaining both worlds as well. Indeed, of the contradictions mentioned, it is the tension between the actors' espoused theories and theories-in-use that, according to action theory assumptions, should attract the most attention for it is the contradiction most within their control and most within their ability to change directly. For the usual complex reasons, however, in reality, it has received the least attention. The situation has shown little improvement, and Evelyn is currently on the search for a new employer. Her expressed hope is that she can find a position where she "can have some real influence for a change."

Most trainers and HRD personnel will find Evelyn's scenario commonplace. In teaching and training managers, we encounter more examples like these than we care to count. The challenge here is what we can do to set forces in motion through which the empowerment skills and abilities described, as well as knowledge directed toward realizing the potential of the individual, can be cultivated, integrated, and practiced.

It should be clear from the foregoing that empowerment, in its goal of emancipation, differs qualitatively from standard management development goals of enhanced competencies or advanced skills. The empowered manager must be open to learning new ways of looking at problems in his field of professional practice. To accomplish this, he must invoke qualitative or naturalistic concepts of: hypothesizing about the work world, testing the validity of what he sees, experimenting with different interpretations as well as trying out new behaviors, and reflecting upon the results. This quality of theorizing does not come about easily, however. Those dedicated to conducting this form of inquiry find that reflection-in-action begins with tacit knowledge and intuitive understanding and then tries to delve both deeper beneath the surface as well as farther beyond accepted horizons. Our special challenge in training involves how to create an action learning environment with appropriate enabling mechanisms that will promote the acquisition of action theory concepts and foster the empowerment of managers.

PREMISES FOR A TRAINING DESIGN

Elsewhere (Argyris and Schon, 1974, p. 28), it has been said that an interventionist is a person struggling to make a particular vision or model of human nature come true. In our case, we found an opportunity to experiment with a training workshop as a mode for testing our ideas concerning action learning and empowerment. In the spring of 1988, we published an article exploring how male and female managers compared concerning their choice of organizational influence strategies (Rizzo and Mendez, 1988). The head of HRD for a large metropolitan public utility called after reading the article and asked us to train about 160 managers and professionals—all women—in strategies for influencing their organizations. As long-time trainers, we were well acquainted with the all-too-common version of training that offer "pop" management techniques of the day—"the solution to your most fundamental management problems"—and that inevitably produce little genuine or enduring behavioral change. When we presented her with our conditions for agreement, we were reassured that they wanted management *development*: long-term cultivation and enhancement of the managers' human relations skills that emphasized core behavioral change. Our interest in challenging the way people think and behave would be appropriate and accepted (at least by the HRD manager), even if it required working through individuals' areas of greatest resistance to change.

While still a little leery about our prospects, we were challenged and provoked by some questions: Could we make inroads into altering the ways these women conceptualized or "framed" their organizations and simultaneously enhance their feelings of efficacy? Would we find participants who were receptive to our notions of taking responsibility and empowerment? Would we find committed participants or just another audience of managers wishing to be entertained? And what about an all-female series of workshops? Would our research findings that only minor or subtle differences distinguished female from male managers be welcomed here, or would these particular individuals prefer being treated as a special class, with training needs that we had not anticipated?

We began designing the workshop series with the premise that some problems in women's work experience were due to individual failings and were therefore of the kind that lent themselves easily to remediation. Most management workshops that focus on competence and skill acquisition fit this category. We refer to such workshops as skill training, a type of training similar in orientation to technical training in that it too frequently results only in instrumental learning. One such example involves the acquisition of "political" skills and knowledge. In our workshops, this translated as: being able to identify the common games that superiors, co-workers, and subordinates play, as well as the behavioral skills and strategies for coping. Another example is human relations skills and knowledge needed for dealing with "difficult people"; still another problem area targets the awareness of different influence strategies and developing the ability to know when it is appropriate to use which strategy.

While these topics form the bulk of most workshops about women, they are also relatively easy problems to resolve. Once acquired, these necessary skills do not guarantee professional and managerial success. More importantly, we maintain that they are insufficient by themselves to contribute significantly to the desired goal of empowerment. As Denhardt has observed, "The central question is no longer how the individual may contribute to the efficient operation of the system, but how the individual may transcend that system" (1981, p. 131).

Managerial skills and competencies, however necessary they are to work world survival, do not explain women's lack of advancement in organizations, the professions, and society. Even with mass remediation of skill deficiencies, women could become qualified, or more qualified, and still experience underutilization or discrimination in greater numbers in the future. Blum and Smith (1988) call this the individual personality, or failings, model. They argue that it fails in large part to account for the overwhelming, almost universal pervasiveness of mobility problems experienced by women (Hennig and Jardim, 1977; Horner, 1972). As suggested by emerging models that employ the analytic tools of dialectical reasoning and critical discourse to the exploration of women's special dilemmas, interests, and identification of societal and organizational contradictions (Glennon, 1983; Ferguson, 1984; Rizzo and Brosnan, 1990), we must make efforts to probe the common situation of women in order to acquire a deeper, fuller understanding of these issues. Ferguson addresses this need:

Real social change comes about when people think and live differently. Feminist discourse and feminist practice offer the linguistic and structural space in which it is possible to think, live, work, and love differently, in opposition to the discursive and institutional practices of bureaucratic capitalism. (1984, p. 212)

We have referred to the type of training that devotes attention to critical thinking and self-reflection as action training. In the case of these particular workshops, we had to come to grips with our own assumptions about human nature and the way we have chosen to handle the issue of gender differences. We summarize our position through these propositions:

Proposition 1:

Physiological, social, and psychological differences between men and women lie beneath the surface of all social behavior at work, yet when these differences appear, they are more likely to be manifested in subtle and indirect ways and vary from individual to individual. We leave the question of the overall saliency of these differences open to speculation.

Proposition 2:

In terms of what we want trainees to gain from these workshops, they will experience greater opportunity for empowerment if they can reflect upon: their own behavior, how they are seen by others, and how they might not only influence others' behavior but also realistically contribute to changing their work world in seemingly small, reflexive, long-term ways.

Proposition 3:

As a result of the first two propositions, we want them to become empowered as change agents. We wanted them, in Morgan and Ramirez's words, to "become critically conscious of their values, assumptions, actions, interdependencies, rights and prerogatives so that they can act in a substantially rational way as active partners in producing their reality" (1983, p. 9) To serve that end, we are interested in their developing analytic and conceptual tools; that is, to be able to use our "keys," which will facilitate their empowerment. We want them to use the gender overlay and appreciate how it operates in organizations as a starting point to explore other contradictions in organizational life.

Differences between men and women, including the special situation of women working in a "man's world," are therefore just one way among many—taken-for-granted domination is another—to segment organizational life. These contradictions offer a "lens" through which we can begin to capture critical insight into power relationships. We expected the workshop participants to "try on" or test these lenses and frames of reference in the hope that they might discover more adequate explanations of what they encounter or find confusing about organizational life. We felt we could offer the participants these conceptual and analytic tools, experiential exercises to provide context, and the modeling of Model O-II reasoning. We would rely on both skill and action training techniques to guide our choice of learning activities. We hoped that these methods, approaches, and techniques could provide them with more than the usual repertoire of success-driven behavioral skills and limited strategies. These remedies might help them survive organizational politics but would not enable them to become empowered, stand on their own, think independently, and resist organizational pressures to conform to Model O-I values (define goals, win-lose strategies, minimize negative feelings, be rational). Nevertheless, in designing the many training programs we have delivered as a team, we have adopted a rather cautious point of view toward the question of any training program's effectiveness. We have gradually come to agree with the Socratic maxim: the most important things cannot be taught but must be discovered for oneself in one's own way and, we add, in one's own time (Argyris et al., 1985, p. 92). From this perspective, much depended upon the commitment, sincerity, readiness, and risk-taking capabilities of the trainees. Were they ready for new ways of viewing their organizations?

THE WORKSHOP: DEVELOPING ORGANIZATIONAL STRATEGIES: A TWO-DAY WORKSHOP FOR WOMEN PROFESSIONALS

Day 1: Making Sense of Work Organizations

When we began planning this series, we provided a needs assessment survey to the HRD staff for distribution to prospective trainees. Its purpose was to obtain a reading of who the participants might be, how they described their interests and problems, and especially how they saw their organization. We then designed the activities with these responses in mind. When we began our workshop, we asked participants to describe their ideal work organization. This activity involved participants in groups articulating espoused theories ("e.t."), at least in a general sense, from which to measure one's personal espoused theories and theories-in-use ("t.i.u.") at a later time. As one would expect, participants generated descriptions that they readily acknowledged sharply deviated from practice. We devised this exercise for the additional purpose of setting an agenda: we wanted to find out whether they would or could incorporate these ideals into their individual list of goals to achieve. In Table 6.1: "Day 1: Making Sense of Work Organizations," we list the keys to empowerment that we hoped would enhance their abilities to analyze a work situation on both the surface and deep structural dimensions.

After this introduction, we polled each class to find out who they were, asked why they had come, and tried to determine from this exchange how committed and open they were to new ideas and what we had to offer. We quickly discovered that very few of our participants

Table 6.1
Day 1: Making Sense of Work Organizations

Learning Activity	What We Hoped to Accomplish	Keys to Empowerment	Types of Training
I. activity: "Describe an ideal work organization..."	I. espoused theory/ideals; can these be incorporated into goals?	I. analyzing a work situation	action
II. 1. diagnosis: "Ways of learning about organizations"	II. 1. reframe views of organizations	II. 1. analyzing a work situation as deep or surface structure	action
2. group discussion of instrument: How did they respond (show of hands)	2. get a reading of participants' views	2. discovering where ideology ends; reframing	action
III. activity: How to tell a business-man from a business-woman	III. is biology relevant? gender differences at work: are they real, pervasive, influential, important?	III. discovering where ideology ends and under-standing begins	skill
IV. how organizations really operate; the role of politics	IV. espoused theory and theory-in-use: demystifying "the system"	IV. analyzing a work situation as deep or surface structure	skill and action
V. 1. goal-setting: work on one goal	V. 1. apply skills and knowledge throughout workshop to improve chances of reaching goal	V. 1. owning a problem; participating in choice making	action
2. analysis and critique	2. get group to help refine goal and give feedback	2. reframing	action
3. the assertive script	3. write behavioral objectives: what requires action to achieve goal	3. owning a problem	skill and/or action

had received or responded to the pre-workshop needs assessment; indeed, we had planned the series around the expectations of employees who never did attend. Paradoxically, the politics and controversy surrounding HRD's offering a training series solely for women influenced who was permitted to attend a workshop on understanding organizational politics.

Undaunted, we proceeded to section II with distribution of the diagnostic instrument, designed for the workshops, called "Ways of Learning About Organizations." As described earlier, the foundation for this instrument is Belenky's book concerning women's patterns or stages of self-awareness and apprehending the world around them (Belenky et. al., 1986). These levels range from silence through received knowledge (listening to others for counsel and knowledge), subjective knowledge (including intuition), procedural knowledge (separate and connected knowing), to constructed knowledge (in which previous levels are integrated and consolidated). One of us designed a simple instrument that asked participants to "choose the perspective which most accurately describes how you try to understand your work organization." If the individual selected paragraph C, as did seven of the trainees,[2] she felt that this view closely matched her own (Refer to chapter 7 for complete survey.):

Most of the time in my work organization, I feel like I never understand what is really going on. I mean, I know what work I am supposed to do and everything but I don't understand why things happen the way they do and I can't tell you what will happen next or why. Other people know these things but I don't.

Some (fifty-three) chose paragraph F, which read:

Many times if I'm to get at what's really going on, I need to make up my own version of events. It might be from a combination of what I see, what I feel, what a few people tell me or checking out my impressions with someone. Sometimes it means asking the right questions until I understand the situation and the personalities. Then I know how to make the connections that will tie things together.

The accompanying answer key scored answers using a developmental approach that explained, "as we grow in experience we usually progress through various stages of understanding. Each stage is progressively more capable of explaining events than the last. Look at the paragraph you selected on Part I and find its corresponding explanation on the answer key." The individual would find a brief description of her view accompanied by some suggestions about adding to or changing that view for purposes of improving the adequacy and comprehensiveness of her understanding. Paragraph B corresponded to the silence orientation. The description on the answer key read:

An employee with this perspective feels unable to understand what is going on to her satisfaction and may appear quite passive about her role in the organization. One who is silent feels she has little or no influence or control over understanding external events.

Compare that orientation with constructed knowing, where all previous stages are incorporated in a manner unique to the individual's mental constructs:

The employee with this perspective feels that she needs to reconstruct events or problems to determine what is going on. She may use a variety of methods: experience, intuition, social networks, knowledge of political games, and/or data gathering to uncover patterns in events. Quite often, she will ask questions which others consider unorthodox or radical, that question "the way things are done around here." She feels a need to clarify the organization's complexities and her place in it and, as a result of some success in doing so, feels empowered to act."

After completing the answer key, participants discussed how they responded, why they did so, and how they interpreted their results. Discussion ranged from whether the results met their expectations to what prevented their scoring at a "higher" orientation. The latter is especially revealing since, early in each of the workshops, we observed a quite common tendency in participants to displace, deflect, or disown responsibility for their inadequacies or problems. This lack of ownership extended to how they thought about organizational life.

In one respect, the HRD manager's plan to sponsor all-women workshops, however well-intended, afforded the women the comforting rationalization that all their problems in climbing the career ladder were due exclusively to being female. As one participant put it, "It's a male-dominated department and I have no access to those in the know because I'm the only woman." This diagnostic instrument was admittedly unscientific; we had not had the opportunity to validate it thoroughly or check for reliability before the workshop series. Consequently, we concluded that due to its transparency, an inordinately large number of participants responded to the instrument according to how they "should" respond and that, as one example, paragraph six was the "best" choice. They preferred to think of themselves as constructivists, whether or not this was confirmed through observation or practice. Others may have responded honestly but found easy excuses for what they interpreted as inferior orientations, such as silence or received knowledge.

Not having anticipated this, we had prepared the next section (III) to deal with gender differences. We had originally developed this portion of the workshop with the idea of placing gender differences in proper perspective. Gender is, after all, only one way—albeit an important and frequently neglected way—to segment organizational reality. There are other typifications that serve to produce discrimination; by these means, the haves impose their picture of the world on the have-nots. We discovered, however, that a sizable group of participants in each of the workshops felt comfortable discussing women's status and problems as special and unique. This view was consistent with the widespread tendency on their part ot disown responsibility for their problems. In each workshop, many began to argue for why employees, particularly women, could not do anything about their situations and the way in which "they" (they being men, management generally, or simply those with power) viewed the participants as what needed changing. Fortunately, the section that followed (IV) dealt with demystifying who "they" were and was directed at compelling participants to account for the part they played in perpetuating what they labelled "the system" by focusing on examples of power scenarios from their own experience. They were to assess how organizations really operate, in contrast to official versions of how they are supposed to function. We also wanted them to understand that politics is universal in organizations, normal, and can be analyzed and dealt with effectively depending upon the frame of reference one chooses to adopt.

In section V, we asked them to choose one goal they wanted to pursue and describe it in some detail, using behavioral guidelines that we designed. After writing their goals privately, they met in groups to provide feedback concerning the definition of the problem. Was it clear? Specific? Was the stated problem the real source of difficulty? Discussion was targeted toward refining the goal. Enabling individuals to see their problems from others' perspectives drew heavily on the notion of framing and reframing problems. Sometimes, participants were more willing to hear what they could do about the problem from a co-worker who had witnessed the incident or was familiar with the people or work situation than they were from perceived "experts" like the trainers. The point, of course, was to develop their own expertise and encourage them to look at old problems in new ways. Crucial to this component of the workshop was the premise that they look at themselves as responsible, take-charge people capable of making an impact.

Empowerment is a term that trainers might use to describe what we think or hope results from this kind of education; to the participants, we were, in their words, "energizing" or motivating them. In each activity in Section V, we challenged them to own a problem, to make it theirs, to identify elements that were within their control to influence, and to change how they regarded the event or the people as well as how they behaved given those conditions. In some cases, our expectations were met and occasionally exceeded. Particularly for those open to new views, who believed that they could act and were willing to take the risk, the first day may have produced genuine, long-lasting learning of the double-loop variety.

Day 2: Using Political Strategies to Get What You Want

The second day's training was generally received with greater enthusiasm than the first. Perhaps world-view talk (section II) earlier in the workshop was regarded as too abstract and/or threatening. Written evaluations suggest that the reframing section, including "Ways of Learning About Organizations," was perceived by some as too theoretical to prove interesting or useful. Whatever the reasons, we began with a relatively "safe" concept—each individual's profile of organizational influence strategies (see Table 6.2, section I).

Table 6.2
Day 2: Using Political Strategies to Get What You Want

Learning Activity	What We Hoped to Accomplish:	Keys to Empowerment	Types of Training
I. 1. POIS: 6 strategies people use to influence	I. 1. identification of individual profiles	I. 1. reflection-in-action; participation in choice-making	skill
2. skills to cultivate: what additional strategies do you want to learn/use?	2. expansion of influencing repertoires	2. continued as above	skill
3. group mirroring: get feedback from coworkers/group members	3. double-loop learning	3. reframing	skill
II. 1. case study: "Murdock the Maneuverer"	II. 1. discuss espoused theory in "Murdock"	II. 1. analyzing a work situation;	skill
2. use Diagnostic Style Survey from Hersey and Blanchard	2. examine factors in analysis: empathy, predictive power, your predominant style, comfort level using different styles, timing, leverage, limitations of intuition	2. analyzing a work situation;	skill & action
3. handout: Isenberg's "How Senior Managers Think"	3. describe examples of level 5 constructivists	3. conceptualizing organizations	action
III. 1. handout: "Recognizing Common Types of Difficult People"	III. 1. demonstrate Model O-I thinking	III. 1. reinforcing the making of choices	skill
2. strategies for coping	2. shift to Model O-II	2. continued as above	skill & action
3. scenario discussion: involving the lazy worker	3. can they integrate what they've learned to focus on Model O-II action strategies and double-loop learning?	3. reflection-in-action	action
IV. quiz: Are you an ethical employee?	IV. place politics in context; justify use of level 5 and Model O-II governing variables	IV. reframing	action
V. wrap-up: What will you do differently?	V. reinforcement and positive group support	V. owning a problem; taking risks	action

The diagnostic instrument used here, the Personal Organizational Influence Survey (POIS) (Kipnis and Schmidt, 1982), looks at seven strategies—reason, friendliness, bargaining, assertiveness, coalitions, appeal to higher authority, and, employed only with subordinates, sanctions—that can be used to influence co-workers, subordinates, and managers (superiors). POIS has respondents rate themselves on their first attempt to influence co-workers, subordinates, or managers and, if that attempt does not succeed, choose which strategies to try the second time. While our research on a broader population of women and men suggests that most managers attempt to include a variety of tactics and strategies in their influencing repertoire, women differed from men only in relying on assertiveness less frequently (Rizzo and Mendez, 1988). In all four workshops, the women exhibited patterns diverging from our findings: some scoring low in all strategies, especially those scoring as silent on the "Ways of Learning About Organizations" survey. A sizable group scored the same on the second attempts to influence as the first and thus in practice may fail to influence by not varying their strategies. Perhaps members of the latter group were not aware of other strategies, did not know how to employ them, or could not analyze what the situation required. Groups of five to six then processed the POIS scores and discussed whether each individual might need to learn additional strategies to deal with the specific problem identified in section V of the previous day.

A group-mirroring exercise followed, which was aimed at augmenting the participants' understanding of their predominant influence strategies. We asked co-workers to provide feedback, recording their comments using felt-tip pens and poster-sized sheets taped around the classroom, identifying which of six strategies they thought a participant did rely on at work. (Since sanctions are used only with subordinates, we eliminated them with these participants.) Pointing out specific examples of her behavior in a particular circumstance was most helpful for participants to own these concepts. Still, while a substantial number now knew what they should be doing, such as analyzing the situation or varying their strategies, they could not mobilize their resources and apply these skills when needed. They did not know how to act. The groups moved to deal with these issues in section II.

First, a case study called "Murdock the Maneuverer" (Christie, 1978) was distributed to review how they analyzed an upwardly mobile manager who uses political tactics (informal contacts, circumvention of the personnel recruitment and selection system, covert cultivation of prospective bosses) to get ahead. They discussed the difference between the case's organizational espoused theory, such as using official channels, apprising your superior of your plans, etc., and Murdock's theory-in-use, although both clearly exhibited Model O-I values and behavior in different guises and with varying degrees of emphasis. Interestingly, the overwhelming majority endorsed Murdock's choice of tactics, even though he circumvented his superior, alienated co-workers, and could be interpreted as using an outside bid for his services to force a job offer within his company (referred to as "highway robbery"). A few commented on Murdock's ethical standards and observed that he could have accomplished the same objectives by being "up front" and open with all parties who would be affected if he pursued a promotion. Murdock was also described as assuming from the outset that he was the only one concerned about his job satisfaction; he assumed that his only recourse was to protect himself unilaterally concerning his career prospects. For some trainees, Model O-II thinking seemed to be sinking in.

Rounding out the modeling of "analyzing a work situation" was Hersey and Blanchard's Leadership Effectiveness Adaptability Description (LEAD)-Self Survey. Trainees scored management situations according to which of four styles or alternative actions they would use to deal with that set of conditions. They completed the survey first as individuals; then we reviewed each situation with a class as a whole. For example,

Your subordinates are no longer responding to your friendly conversation and obvious concern for their welfare. Their performance is declining rapidly. *What do you do?*

a. Emphasize the use of uniform procedures and the necessity for task accomplishment

b. Make yourself available for discussion, but don't push your involvement

c. Talk with subordinates and then set goals

d. Intentionally do not intervene (Hersey and Blanchard, 1982, p. 99)

The LEAD was selected not only for its ability to measure self-perception in terms of leadership style, style range, and style adaptability, but also because it stresses a variety of elements that must enter into how one can most competently diagnose a situation. In this respect, the LEAD's value lies in the variables and priorities that the reader uses to judge which style is most appropriate. What was important to us was how individuals reasoned through each situation. For that purpose, we added several factors in our whole group review of each case that we asked the participants to consider: how well you predict outcomes generally, predominant leadership style, comfort level with different styles or style adaptability, timing of the behavioral strategy, leverage you may have at your disposal, benefits and limitations of intuition, how to validate your reading of the situation, empathy for others in the situation, etc. Our intention was to use the entire group to reason through each dilemma to demonstrate to them the comparison between what we hoped would be constructivist reasoning and the reasoning they used when they had completed the instrument as individuals. In this manner, we tried to model constructivist thinking. To reinforce the notion that effective managers rely on a variety of methods to reason through a dilemma, we also recommend that they read "How Senior Managers Think" (Isenberg, 1984).

In section III, we targeted specific problem situations to test how the participants would apply the tools and techniques we had presented. The handout, "Recognizing Common Types of Difficult People," was an adaptation of common types of people who pose problems at work, among them, Sherman tanks, exploders, super-agreeables, complainers, and clams (Bramson, 1981). Many of these problems can be dealt with, or as Bramson says "coped with," using Model O-I governing variables and action strategies. He recommends such strategies as control turf, minimize expressing negative feelings, and unilaterally define goals and protect yourself. However, such strategies inhibit double-loop organizational learning in the long run. In some cases, difficult people can be coped with only by using Model O-I strategies, such as appropriate passive behavior in the face of physical threat. Nevertheless, these cases are admittedly few. We asked groups and later the whole class to analyze what to do in a hypothetical scenario involving the lazy worker and hoped that they could shift to Model O-II thinking.

Participants' performance during this exercise was primarily characterized by wanting the trainers to provide the answers. What did we think was right to do? It appears all too frequently that trainers' expertise is suddenly respected and called upon precisely when the trainers hope most that the transfer of their knowledge and its accompanying authority will be complete. In contrast, section III's quiz on ethics produced a different result: most participants seemed comfortable with their choices of action in hypothetical ethical dilemmas. Perhaps this is due to the extreme distancing of ethical considerations from most employees' everyday work lives. If this is true, it is a sad commentary on most work cultures: unlike supervisory competencies, ethics is not deemed an essential commodity in managers' promotability or effectiveness. Consequently, our trainees, not aware of either congruence or incongruence between personal and organizational ethics but cognizant that ethical considerations generally are devalued, were not anxious about the correctness of their responses in the same way as when considering the adequacy of possible approaches to coping with difficult people.

Finally, the workshop concluded with reviewing the goals formulated on the first day. What, if anything, would the participants do differently as a result of what they now knew?

SPECIAL CONDITIONS FOR EFFECTIVE ACTION TRAINING

Some Commonalities with Organization Development

We maintain that both critique and innovation are possible. With action training, we felt we could combine the value of critique with the problem-solving potential of training that focuses on double-loop learning. It is arguable, however, whether the training workshop as typically construed provides a suitable framework for promoting this kind of learning.

There are several reasons to evaluate the workshop format. As was true in the case reported here, most management training is approved by HRD or personnel officers who are required to legitimate the need for a training program or even justify their unit's existence using the accepted standard reasoning that such training will further the success of both the individual and the organization, most importantly the latter. Action models, however they are conceived and executed, ranging from Argyris and Schon's to neo-Marxian applications, are tied together in part by the shared assumption that the transformation and empowerment of the individual is the key to long-term effectiveness. This argument suggests that although the pay-off for organizations may be far in the distant future, empowerment will be well worth it in terms of overall effectiveness of the organizations' members. Action models treat short-term effectiveness, framed in terms of utilitarian value to the organization, and managerial success-driven strategies as generally inconsequential or at best, of secondary importance. Contracting for workshops such as the series discussed in this chapter frequently raises such a divergence in expectations between trainers and contractors.

With the benefit of hindsight, we can see that our psychological contract with the HRD manager omitted what later became important influencing factors on the program's outcomes. First, our discussions with the HRD manager, which seemed precise and candid at the time, failed to bring out some important political considerations, such as her interest in legitimizing her programs. In an effort to justify workshops solely for women, she felt compelled to coerce recruits to attend the women's programs. The number of attendees became critical. To complicate matters, the professional women who had originally completed the pretraining needs assessment, dropped out as a group out of concern that they would be rejected by their male colleagues who comprised the overwhelming majority in that unit and were not permitted to attend the training. As a result, once the workshops were in progress, we found that we had few volunteers attending and even fewer middle- and upper-level professionals than expected. A distinct majority had been required to attend. One woman was called to attend while at home in the middle of an official maternity leave. Once the workshop was completed, she resumed her maternity leave. Axiomatic in management training is that trainees not be pressured to attend for fear of losing their jobs, or their maternity leave, but that they are permitted to attend out of genuine interest in learning. Only with free choice surrounding training possibilities are you likely to recruit participants open to the level and quality of experimentation our design offered.

These findings lead us to an essential condition for action training: participation should be voluntary, or if not voluntary, all members should participate in training as in a full-scale organization development effort. They should want to work together, come prepared to pursue common goals, be willing to work through resistance to change (be willing to "unfreeze"), and be interested in exploring how they, not those outside the workshop, can improve their respective situations. As support that these are realistic expectations for training, Pierce's Management Workshop (1987) teaching empowerment strategies, self-discovery, and holistic perspectives at work, provides evidence that such workshops are doable.[3]

A related condition: participants need to understand and buy into the behavioral norms and goals of action learning (ownership, taking responsibility, giving and receiving of feedback, collaborative or joint inquiry, working through resistance to change, to name a few) as part of the psychological contract between trainers and trainees. We speculate that much of the willingness to buy into these norms and goals may be predicated upon the participants' degree of readiness for a radically different and, to some, threatening learning experience.

Revealing in this regard was the number of participants who spoke with us after and in between sessions and offered spontaneous evaluations, expressing appreciation and even enthusiasm for what they were learning. We recognized that many of these individuals had previously scored high on the "Understanding Your Organization" instrument and observed that those open to action learning at the outset appeared to have gained the most satisfaction from the training. We recognize that self-confidence, initiative, autonomy, and interest in self-discovery may play an influential role in maximizing action learning.

According to Ravid (1987), a key factor in readiness for self-directed learning and, by extension, action learning, is the openness of the organizational climate as perceived by employees, to the innovations, ideas, and approaches acquired through training. If employees perceive that new ideas can be experimented with in a receptive, responsive organization, their initiative and incentive for learning may improve. External sources notwithstanding, readiness for action learning also involves internal, psychological sources of resistance to self-discovery and change, issues that we can only mention briefly here. Those considering the appropriateness of action training for a given organization should survey the extent of members' readiness for action learning in the event that interventions that address resistance to change are needed.

Another grievous omission in our informal contract with the HRD manager was the lack of clarity concerning content. The manager was less enthusiastic about our interest in changing the way women viewed organizations and in developing new, more effective theories-in-use than she was about delivering what she called "substantial training." Most of the other workshops in the series for women turned out to range from dressing for success to oral communications and presentation skills. While the need for such programs was debated by the three of us, the manager's agenda was to treat our workshops as the "intellectual" component; other classes would provide entertainment value, thereby attracting the necessary numbers and justifying the need for the series. We, however, were not interested in intellectualizing; we were there to promote and facilitate empowerment strategies and to teach reframing, reflection-in-action, and related skills and strategies. As in organization development programs, action models are based on value assumptions, which must not only be transmitted wholesale and practiced as a package, they must also be endorsed, supported and, one would hope, aspired to by top management as well. Lack of explicit agreement concerning these outcomes served as a signal that any long-term commitment by the organization to fostering change in participants' practices was highly improbable. A related condition for effective action training therefore concerns the essential requirement of obtaining top management support for the goals of action learning.

Another problem raised by the delivery of this kind of program using a workshop model concerns the time dimension. If organization development training that culminates in long-term behavioral change requires certain necessary conditions and assumptions, these qualifications also apply to action training. Under preferred conditions, organization development requires top management support, a long-range focus, an emphasis upon targeting problem-solving and renewal (that is, learning) processes using applied behavioral science theory and technology (French and Bell, 1984, p. 17). Meetings, workshops, and consultation sessions offered over a long period of time provide opportunities where people can learn new views, skills, and strategies. In the interim, participants can experiment with new views, conceptual and analytical skills, and behavioral strategies, reflect on the outcomes of these efforts, and return to the program group to report on their findings, seek advice, and receive reinforcement and support. Another condition then would be: an effective program cannot be presented on a one-time or intensive basis but must be offered over periods as long as six months to a year for maximum benefit.

THE CRUX OF THE DILEMMA: ORGANIZATIONAL PRAXIS

Time to revisit organization members also means that the facilitators have time to reflect and learn, to clarify misconceptions, and to explore their own espoused theories and theories-in-use. As usual, we learned more from our mistakes presenting this program than from our successes. The transparency of the understanding organizations instrument raised some fundamental problems addressed in the praxis elements of action theory, such as the cleavage between thought and action. We learned a great deal from the varied inconsistencies revealed in the participants' reasoning and through discrepancies between their thought or intentions and actions. For example, if so many participants thought like sixes, why did they not behave like sixes? We questioned earlier whether most of these respondents are true constructivists (sixes); transparency problems would seem to be the culprit here. Testing this instrument with two graduate public administration classes before the workshops might or might not support the transparency hypothesis; it is true that in graduate classes where students held little stake in the survey's outcome, we received far fewer constructivist responses.

A related question is why some who scored six on this instrument did not score as tacticians on the POIS? When we asked for a show of hands from trainees concerning scores on the POIS, the results revealed very few tacticians, actors capable of strategizing effectively and using a variety of influence styles to meet problems at work. This finding deviated from their responses on the "Understanding Your Organization" instrument. Whether or not the sixes were genuine, we postulate that most people who are capable of thinking like constructivists fail to behave as empowered people. This raises some of the fundamental problems addressed in action theory. One problem for such people may lie in knowing how to assess what they actually do; another is that they know what to do but need help and the self confidence to do it.

Another dimension to this problem was suggested by a few individuals checking two responses on their survey: some said they were sixes within their work unit, but fours or ones outside it; another thought she was a six with her own subordinates, a five, or "politician" as she described it, when acting externally. Comments such as these, written in the margins of surveys, provoke thought. For those individuals for whom acting according to stage six is possible, even comfortable in some situations, the dilemma is how to transfer what they can do effectively there to those anxiety-provoking adversarial relationships and crisis situations. For these individuals, we hope that placing their actions within a Model O-II context and discussing conflicts between their espoused theory (comment in the survey: "my real nature is best represented as a '6' ") and theory-in-use ("I'd like to be empowered in every situation but events and people beyond my control prevent this") may have encouraged risk-taking behavior. Since many of the problems with reification stem from this subject-object split, we hoped that encouraging participants to strategize how to overcome resistance to change from within the self, as well as from others, would propel innovation in the appropriate direction.

As was mentioned earlier, having all employees undergo such training helps provide a shared experience and form bonds among those attempting to change their context, which in turn proves essential in sustaining behavioral changes as well as reinforcing the use of new skills and strategies. Encountering and overcoming such multi-layered sources of resistance to change is a common charge for organization development and action trainers. We witness an ongoing struggle against reification, as we rediscover with every program and course.

The cleavages between thought and action as well as subject and object are focal points in organizational praxis. Heydebrand's work (1983, p. 307) specifying different types of innovations into organizational life is instructive in this regard. He describes imposed or adopted innovations as a result of the interaction between organization and environment. These behavioral innovations, although they may contribute to structural change, are merely adaptations to a changing environment. When intervening in organizational action, defined as the more subjective, goal-directed activity oriented toward problem-solving and the transformation of the environment, innovative forms of conscious strategies change the conditions of action. It is only at the level of organizational praxis, however, that innovations are targeted not only at the transformation of the work environment but at self-transformation as well. Heydebrand states that organization as praxis:

refers not only to the technical transformation of the environment and to the solution of practical problems, but also to the conscious self-transformation of collective actors. This requires a high level of understanding and insight into the motivational and causal links among actors, social structures, and history. Thus, organizing activity, cooperation, undistorted communication and domination-free interaction are central to the concept of organizational praxis. (1983, p. 306)

The power of the action model can be summarized through this concept. As Heydebrand continues:

the idea of organization as praxis involves not only organizational self-transformation, but also the previous moments of understanding, explanation, and critique. Praxis-oriented analysis merely makes available the articulation of alternative strategies for the resolution of complex and contradictory situations. But each of the strategies represents a practical program that is only part of the resolution. *Since the collective actors and their analysts are to various degrees involved in concrete situations, they must achieve a very high level of self-understanding and self-criticism in order to be able to participate creatively in their own self-transformation and self-organization, instead of merely reacting to crises or engaging in particularistic strategies.* (1983, p. 319; emphasis added)

High levels of self-understanding and self-criticism thus provide the catalytic force for the reflection-in-action process. Recalling Evelyn's dilemma with Tammy, the intransigent secretary, exposure to action learning ideally would promote sufficient self-understanding and constructive self-criticism that Evelyn could choose creative ways of exploring the layers of meaning embedded in her complex work environment. Relatedly, she would want to test her understanding of her environment, enjoy the self-confidence to experiment with personal theories of action, and possess enough forbearance and persistence to endure in the face of adversity. We would hope to convince her that ultimately, "change unfolds through circular patterns of interaction" and that she serves as its author (Morgan, 1986, p. 247). For Evelyn and the thousands of practitioners like her, such programs may help in some small way.

EPILOGUE: A FINAL NOTE ON THE CASE OF EVELYN AND THE SECRETARY

Evelyn's progress in influencing her secretary was relatively uneven during the course. When we would periodically check on students' experimentation with different strategies or tactics in dealing with their case dilemmas, she would report on trials with innovative techniques. Once, for example, simple assertiveness in communicating her feelings appeared to have penetrated the secretary's barriers. In her view, however, what really succeeded in increasing the secretary's respect for her as a supervisor and a person was a fortuitous event. A fellow student in the course was the mayor's assistant and was well acquainted with the secretary's source of power, a political appointee who worked in his office. After hearing Evelyn's story, he took it upon himself to offer a few well-chosen comments during the natural course of office conversation. The substance of the conversation found its way back to the secretary, and her demeanor and attitude suddenly improved—a Model O-I solution to what was generally interpreted in the class to be a Model O-II problem. Most recently, Evelyn reports that her secretary is still not performing at her potential but now assumes the mask of the professional employee and is at least pleasant to work with. Unlike most of her fellow students, Evelyn is, for the time being, willing to settle for a Model O-I behavioral world. She remains discontented nevertheless; she is currently pursuing a cautious job search to "test the waters" regarding her marketability. Now, we think, she is aware of the possibilities.

APPENDIX I

Supplemental Methods: Maps of Action, Reframing the Evelyn Case Study

Since the original design of the workshop was delivered, opportunities to experiment with and fine-tune some of the activities have uncovered

what promises to be an effective learning tool for trainees like ours who
resist change. This tool, called maps of action, is described and illustrated
here in an effort to provide readers with another strategy for apprehending action theory concepts.

Maps of action form a framework for envisioning familiar managerial
dilemmas (Argyris, 1985, pp. 79–80) in a new way. As a learning tool,
they enable the researcher, or in our case trainees, to enlist Evelyn in
frame-breaking. This device may be most useful when an individual like
Evelyn persists in interpeting her motives as a rationalized response to
victimization by another. If she resists other students' or trainees' efforts
to track interactions initiated by Evelyn toward Tammy (in the form of
feedback loops) as well as how Tammy's behavior is interpreted, coded,
and acted upon by Evelyn, the method of charting or scripting Model
O-I dynamics on paper appears to help. Evelyn can see how her reactions
feedback to reinforce previous assumptions and escalate dysfunctional
behavior.

In the mapping process we construct scripts that attempt to make
sense of factors such as behavior or attitudes that contribute pressures
and constraints to an individual's problem situation. Argyris describes
the mapping process in specific, concrete, and clear terms, and it is the
explicit nature of the mapping process that may mark its superiority as
a learning technique for managers over other, more general and less
focused methods used in the workshop series described earlier in this
chapter, such as the assertive script. We will rely on Argyris' example
in charting a Model O-I map for Evelyn.

For Evelyn's case, fellow trainees would undertake the task of using
analytical and critical skills to reflect upon her problem. To serve this
end, they would therefore need to be trained in special human resource
skills of giving and receiving feedback, active listening techniques, and
simple components of measurable behavioral objectives in order to help
critique and analyze the problem in a reflexive manner. Partly as a result
of this analysis, Evelyn would be able to clarify not only her own way
of framing and defining the problem but her approach to dealing with
Tammy. Eventually, she may be able to create an action map which
more closely resembles Model O-II thinking and behavior.

Trainees might begin by listing contributing factors or the pressures
and forces that shape the problem situation summarized in column 1 of
Figure 6.1. Next, they could identify the structural solutions Evelyn
might use to deal with them. Judging from reactions to similar exercises
such as the reflective case study, these might include "divide tasks,"
"supervise closely," and "define your authority/your expectations and
ensuing punishments." It would then be up to Evelyn's skills in double-
loop learning to critique any or all Model O-I solutions posed by others
in terms of her long-term effectiveness. Some solutions might be to avoid

Figure 6.1
Model O-I Reaction Map for Evelyn

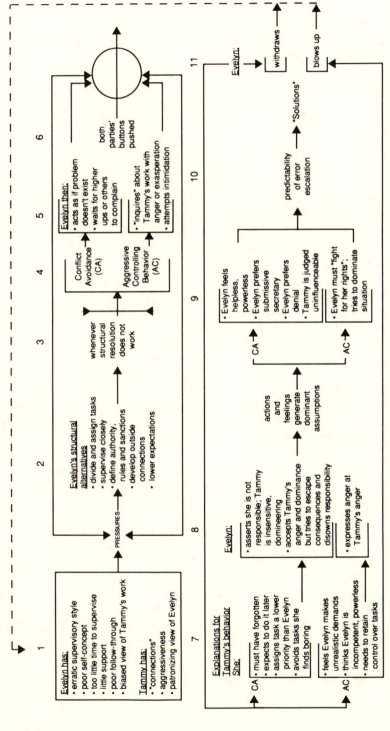

Source: Adapted from Argyris, 1985, pp. 79–80.

conflict and outlast Tammy; others would probably include direct confrontation and indirect tactics such as engaging in behind-the-scenes maneuvering. These are summarized in column 4. In column 5, Evelyn's most typical reactions are recorded (to the best of Evelyn's recollection; these are only as good as her objectivity and accuracy in describing the observable behavior of the secretary). The typical reactions of the secretary and Evelyn are then played out in column 5; again, students need to serve as objectivity monitors. In other words, if Evelyn tries to control Tammy (in column 4), she might try to intimidate her or, more likely, engage in passive-aggressive, complaining behavior (column 5).

When Evelyn confronts Tammy directly and assertively, Tammy's responses have varied from ignoring Evelyn to escalating the conflict through counterattack. All of these reactions, according to Argyris, feed back to reinforce previous assumptions. The feedback processes in Model O-I thinking are not error-correcting but error-enhancing. One way to cope with these difficulties is to explain them in terms of the other's dysfunctional behavior (column 7). This explanation might take the form that Tammy may have several motives for her behavior. Evelyn feels victimized and controlled by Tammy; there is nothing that she can do about her situation (column 8). Alternatively, Evelyn's efforts to engage the secretary meet with short-term change although Tammy's long-term behavior remains unpredictable, so confrontative tactics are concluded to be generally unreliable (column 9). These conditions lead Evelyn to conclude that Tammy is difficult to influence and change, that escalating error and a sense of helplessness are a way of life (column 10). The outcome for Evelyn is to endure Tammy's blowups and recalcitrance, if she can avoid blow-ups herself, to withdraw and insulate herself further (column 11).

Argyris recommends a program of change which, among other things, fosters the testing of, inquiry into, and constructive confrontation of the actor's (both Tammy's and Evelyn's) actions (Argyris, Putnam, and Smith, 1985, p. 102).

PROGRAM OF CHANGE

1. I know how I believe that you (or I) should behave given the difficulties identified, and I will communicate* that to you.

2. I will act in ways to encourage you to inquire* into and to confront* my position.

3. I will expect* that you will inquire into and confront my position whenever you believe it is necessary and I will tell* you my position if you ask.

4. I will check* periodically to see whether you are inquiring and confronting. I will hold you responsible for continual designed congruence between your actions and your thoughts.

5. If I infer incongruence between thoughts and actions, I will test* it with you openly.

6. a. If I learn* that the incongruence is unintentional, then I will act to help you by going back to number 1.

   b. If I learn* that the incongruence is intentional and you are knowingly hiding this fact, then I will feel that I cannot trust you and will go back to number 1.

(Starred words should be executed in a Model O-II manner.)

With some fairly concrete behavioral recommendations such as these, which serve to anchor a manager's new theory of action, each student can begin developing a personal theory of action based on Model O-II thinking that is capable of producing genuine behavioral change.

NOTES

1. Couto has commented that without the understanding that empowerment is first and foremost a radical political concept there is a:

danger of reducing empowerment to an individual phenomenon and training "helping professionals" to empower others. This . . . undermines the group and community element of empowerment. It also risks making empowerment a professional competence and creating an expertise about a process that (by definition) involves demystification of expertise and less deference to experts (1989, pp. 246)

This chapter tries to bridge the distance between empowerment as a radicalizing agent and empowerment as a professional skill; we do not hold that they are mutually contradictory.

2. The complete breakdown of participants classified into each orientation stage was as follows: 1, silence: 7 percent; 2, received knowledge: 3 percent; 3, subjective knowledge: 3 percent; 4, procedural knowing/connected: 18 percent; 5, procedural knowing/separate: 15 percent; 6, constructed knowing: 53 percent. The cumulative total adds to 99 percent due to rounding errorrs. The total population of respondents from the four workshops was 151.

3. Gloria Pierce's Management Workshop (1987) emphasizes some of the same issues as the series described in this chapter: self-discovery, empowerment, and holistic approaches toward work. Unlike our workshops, however, the Management Workshop is attended by employees at all levels in the same corporation and is five-and-a-half days in length.

REFERENCES

Argyris, C. 1985. "Making Knowledge More Relevant to Practice: Maps for Action." In *Doing Research That Is Useful for Theory and Practice*, ed. by E. Lawler III, Allan M. Mohrman, Gerald E. Ledford, Jr., Thomas G. Cummings and Associates. San Francisco: Jossey-Bass.

———— and D. Schon. 1974. *Theory in Practice: Increasing Professional Effectiveness.* San Francisco: Jossey-Bass.

—— and D. Schon. 1978. *Organizational Learning: Theory of Action Perspective.* Reading, MA: Addison Wesley.

——, R. Putnam, and D. M. Smith. 1985. *Action Science.* San Francisco: Jossey-Bass.

Belenky, M., B. Clinchy, N. Goldberger, and J. Tarule. 1986. *Women's Ways of Knowing: The Development of Self, Voice, and Mind.* New York: Basic Books.

Blum, L., and V. Smith. 1988. "Women's Mobility in the Corporation: A Critique of the Politics of Optimism." *Signs,* Vol. 13, No. 3, 528–545.

Bolman, L., and T. Deal. 1984. *Modern Approaches to Understanding and Managing Organizations.* San Francisco: Jossey-Bass.

Bramson, R. 1981. *Coping With Difficult People.* Garden City, NY: Doubleday, Anchor Books.

Christie, J. 1978 "Murdock the Maneuverer." In A. Dubrin. *Human Relations.*

Couto, R. 1989. "Catastrophe and Community Empowerment: The Group Formulations of Aberfan's Survivors." *Journal of Community Psychology,* Vol. 17, July. 236–248.

Denhardt, R. 1981. "The Administrative Journal: Theory and Method." In *Innovations in Teaching Public Affairs and Administration,* ed. by R. Heimovics and A.-M. Rizzo. Kansas City, MO: University of Missouri.

Dubrin, Andrew, 1978. *Human Relations: A Job Oriented Approach.* Reston, VA: Prentice-Hall.

Ferguson, K. 1984. *The Feminist Case Against Bureaucracy.* Philadelphia: Temple University Press.

French, W., and C. Bell. 1984. *Organization Development: Behavioral Science Intervention for Organization Improvement.* Englewood Cliffs, NJ: Prentice-Hall.

Glennon, L. 1983. "Synthesism: A Case of Feminist Methodology." In G. Morgan, ed. *Beyond Method.*

Harmon, M., and R. Mayer. 1986. Organization Theory for Public Administration. Boston: Little, Brown and Company.

Hennig, M., and A. Jardim. 1977. *The Managerial Woman.* Garden City, NY: Doubleday, Anchor Books.

Hersey, P., and K. Blanchard. 1982. *Management of Organization Behavior: Utilizing Human Resources.* 4th ed. Englewood Cliffs, NJ: Prentice-Hall.

Heydebrand, W. 1983. "Organization and Praxis." In *Beyond Method: Strategies for Social Research,* ed. by G. Morgan. Beverly Hills: Sage, 306–20.

Horner, M. 1972. "Toward an Understanding of Achievement-Related Conflicts in Women." *Journal of Social Issues,* Vol. 28, No. 2, 157–175.

Isenberg, D. 1984. "How Senior Managers Think." *Harvard Business Review* Vol. 62, No. 6, Nov./Dec., 80–90.

Kipnis, D., and S. Schmidt. 1982. *Profiles of Organizational Influence Strategies.* San Diego: University Associates.

Marsick, V., ed. 1987. *Learning in the Workplace.* New York: Croom Helm.

Miles, R., and W. Randolph. 1985. *The Organization Game: A Simulation. Administrator's Guide.* 2nd ed. Santa Monica: Goodyear.

Mitroff, I. 1983. *Stakeholders of the Organizational Mind: Toward a New View of Organizational Policy Making.* San Francisco: Jossey-Bass.

—— and R. Kilmann. 1975. "Stories Managers Tell: A New Tool for Organizational Problem Solving." *Management Review*, Vol. 64, No. 7, July, 18–28.

Morgan, G. 1986. *Images of Organization*. Beverly Hills: Sage.

———, Ed. 1983. *Beyond Method: Strategies for Social Research*. Beverly Hills: Sage.

——— and R. Ramirez. 1983. "Action Learning: A Holographic Metaphor for Guiding Social Change." *Human Relations*, Vol. 37, No. 1, 1–27.

Pierce, G. 1987. "Management Workshop Toward A New Paradigm." In V. Marsick. *Learning in the Workplace*.

Ravid G. 1987. "Self-Directed Learning in Industry." V. Marsick. *Learning in the Workplace*.

Rizzo A.-M., and C. Mendez. 1989. "Uses of Training for Empowerment: Reflections on Possibilities for Action Training and Observations on Workshops for Women." Paper presented to the American Society for Public Administration Conference, Miami, Florida (available from author).

———, and C. Mendez. 1988. "Making Things Happen in Organizations: Does Gender Make a Difference." *Public Personnel Management*, Vol. 17, No. 1, Spring.

———, and D. Brosnan. 1990. "Critical Theory and Communication Dysfunction: The Case of the Sexually Ambiguous Behavior." *Administration and Society*, Forthcoming.

Schon, D. 1983. *The Reflective Practitioner: How Professionals Think in Action*. New York: Basic Books.

Schwartz, F. 1989. "Management Women and the New Facts of Life." *Harvard Business Review*, Vol. 67, No. 1, January/February, 65–76.

White, J. 1982. "Public Policy Analysis: Reason, Method, and Praxis." DPA Dissertation, George Washington University. Available from George Washington University.

PART IV _____

Ideas and Approaches for Personal and Organizational Change

This final section combines some tested and well-known techniques and strategies with the more experimental techniques of action training to promote the participation and empowerment of employees in the workplace. Beginning with the outline of the two-day workshop on empowering women managers in the last chapter, chapter 7 lays out the techniques themselves, accompanied by instructions and recommendations concerning their use. Chapter 8 reviews non-training techniques useable by two sets of prospective facilitators: direct supervisors, as well as other interested parties without authority over the employees. The techniques covered in this final chapter are typically one-on-one, informal strategies but are nonetheless considered powerful catalysts to initiate personal and, perhaps in the long run, system-wide change. Chapter 8 closes with some thoughts about what workplace revitalization in microcosm implies for democratic cultures.

Chapter 7 _____

Tools, Strategies, and Approaches for Trainers and HRD Professionals

Effective workshops depend partly on whether the methods and techniques are suitable for meeting participants' needs. We provide some of the tools, methods, and approaches used in our workshops in this chapter for the reader's consideration and use. Some concepts used in our workshops, such as job politics or situational leadership, may not be new but will perhaps be employed in a different way. A few are borrowed wholesale from their sources, which we share with the reader. Other materials we developed especially for action training and may be regarded as experimental. Finally, we offer some suggestions concerning the presentation and use of the materials discussed in this chapter.

TRAINING FOR EMPOWERMENT

This chapter presents a variety of instructional methods and techniques that can be used in training workshops and classrooms. The tools described here accompany the workshop design for developing organizational strategies outlined in chapter 6 and are designed to accomplish that program's goals and purposes. They range from descriptive vignettes, case studies accompanied by questions for reflection and discussion, and survey instruments with scoring and interpretation, to lecture notes and handouts, as well as suggestions for presentations. We describe in detail only the original tools we have developed or those adapted from other materials. We know that they have been tested and fine-tuned in our training programs; therefore, we can recommend with some assurance how they might be executed and with what likely or possible results. Additional resources are suggested as directions for locating alternative tools to the ones described here.

These tools can be used in either piecemeal fashion or as a complete training package. *Our purpose in providing these tools is to encourage experimentation with action training.* We believe that those who employ these techniques within an action framework may discover the value of changing individuals' postures toward organizations and the virtues of treating empowerment as a major goal, if not the primary purpose, behind HRD training. For this reason, the ways in which these old and new training methods should be applied ought to promote emancipation through self-reflection and critical insight into: 1) power relationships generally and 2) how we contribute to perpetuating our environment so that the current state of affairs appears unalterable rather than subject to change and improvement. To recap from the earlier section on empowerment, our goals in training are to encourage participants to:

• learn from experience,
• take risks or consider doing so at work,
• encourage making choices where one may not only have impact but also in turn contribute toward one's prospects for efficacy,
• own problems, reframe problems, and experiment with using new or different perspectives,
• discover what the organizational ideology is and be able to explore and regard its inherent contradictions as possibilities for change, and
• be able to analyze a work or political situation in both the deep and surface structural dimensions.

We begin with a personal goals survey for workshop participants. The Roman numerals preceding the capitalized headings correspond with major headings on Tables 6.1 and 6.2, outlining our instructional plan of action for Days 1 and 2 respectively of the workshop series.

MAKING SENSE OF WORK ORGANIZATIONS

SUGGESTED SCHEDULE FOR DAY ONE

I. Introduction: Surveying Participants' Goals and Interests
   9:00–10:00
   1. Pairs introduce each other—name, title, unit, why they are here; groups form at this time
   2. Participants describe the ideal organization
   3. Participants describe personal goals and interests in the workshop
   4. Instructional objectives for the workshop; refer to outline

II. Diagnosis: Ways of Learning About Organizations

10:00–11:00

1. Complete survey: "How You Understand Your Organization"
2. Introduce Belenky et. al. research
3. Provide answer key and scoring
4. Groups: case study analysis and discussion
5. Applications, limitations of each stage: discussion

III. Views of Work World and Careers: How to Tell a Businessman from a Businesswoman

11:00–12:00

1. Questionnaire on perceived stereotypes
2. Differences and similarities in behavior and attitudes
3. Gestures of power and privilege
4. Special problems: working with male bosses; male co-workers; male subordinates

IV.   A. Defining Political Dilemmas and Problems

1:00–2:00

1. Definitions
2. Perform in pairs/dyads
3. Discuss a political game or condition you would like to see changed

IV.   B. Demystifying Organizational Politics: How Organizations Really Operate

2:00–3:00

1. Factors contributing to politics
2. Handout: "Games Employees Play"
3. Handout: "Political Strategies"
4. Groups: Describe some appropriate political tactics: give a hypothetical or real example. How would they use it?

V.   Personal Goal-Setting for Organizational Problem-Solving

3:00–4:00

1. Groups: Redefine problems into political goals
2. Participants complete The Strategy Script Worksheet
3. Groups offer feedback about participants' Worksheets

VI. Homework assignment

1. POIS
2. Read "Murdock the Maneuverer"

I. SURVEYING TRAINEES' INTERESTS AND GOALS

Describing an ideal organization requires both introspection and reflection on the part of those employed by the organization. Employees need the chance to look at their current situation and see both the positive and negative aspects of the organization in which they work. Through this process, we anticipate that at least initially the organization will be seen as the problem in which the employees are victims of forces that they cannot control. In other words, we will witness the process of reification. To overcome feelings of powerlessness and victimization, the workshop should begin by charging participants to compare the desired organization or ideal to the organization in which they work. Once this ideal is expressed in concrete terms, individuals begin to develop a sense of ownership in the process and see possibilities for personal involvement. Through this process, participants also begin to formulate goals that describe how the organization would have to change to improve. The trainer should serve as a sounding board or collator of these ideas and impressions to help design the framework for individual change later in the workshop.

This simple exercise was intended to provide the opportunity for interacting with co-workers in an environment where their opinions or beliefs could not negatively affect their jobs or positions. In the beginning of the workshop, trainers can divide the whole group into small groups of four or five participants and ask them to list at least three specific characteristics that they agree are essential to an ideal organization. In completing this task, participants begin to test their personal ideals and to refine their perceptions of what is fundamental for an organization to enable members to be effective performers.

The workshop then reassembles, and each group reports to the workshop as a whole about the three essential ingredients of an ideal organization. In many cases, a few of the requirements will probably be repeated from one group to the next; in others, the requirements may be specific to a department or unit. Nevertheless, the result should be a clear understanding of the ideal. With this shared foundation, trainers can begin to develop individual initiative so that participants can begin to move their organization closer to the ideal.

With the ice broken, participants can also discuss with their group members why they chose to attend this workshop and the goals they want to pursue, then present those comments to the workshop as a whole. From this information, trainers can begin to adapt and fine-tune techniques and strategies to the needs and requirements of the particular workshop members.

II. ACTIVITIES FOR WAYS OF LEARNING ABOUT ORGANIZATIONS

Survey on Ways of Learning About Organizations

GENERAL INSTRUCTIONS: Review the following list of six quotations. Then read the following case studies and answer the questions. You will be asked to choose the quotation that you feel best describes your overall efforts to make sense of that dilemma and choose how or whether to act. Please be sure to read all six choices and select the one you really feel most often, not what you think is the "best" answer of those listed. Be prepared to explain and defend your choice.

A. "If someone in a position of authority tells me why things happen in this organization, I can usually depend on this information and know that this is the way things really are."

B. "When I try to understand what's really going on, I never take anything anyone says for granted. I just tend to look at it all as a sort of game. The more you can understand what the game is or how it operates and figure out the rules, the better off you are."

C. "Most of the time in my work organization, I feel like I never understand what is really going on, I mean, I know what work I am supposed to do and everything but I don't understand why things happen the way they do and I can't tell you what will happen next or why. Other people know these things but I don't."

D. "If I'm trying to come to grips with what's going on and I talk to someone who has another way of explaining it, I'll usually try to look at events from that person's point of view, see how she could say that, why they think they're right, why it makes sense. Sometimes if I talk to people I trust, I can grasp the logic behind what caused what to happen. But almost everyone has something to lend to explaining complicated events. It's important to see a whole lot of different points of view on things."

E. "I can usually rely on my intuition for guiding me to the truth in events. I don't need to check it out with anyone, I just feel it, I know it in my heart, or the idea rings true in some way. It's like I have a little voice inside that tells me what's really happening around me and why. And I can trust this little voice."

F. "Many times if I'm to get at what's really going on, I need to make up my own version of events. It might be from a combination of what I see, what I feel, what a few people tell me or checking out my impressions with someone. Sometimes it means asking the right questions until I understand the situation and the personalities. Then I know how to make the connections that will tie things together."

CASES

Information—Asset or Liability

You have been an employee of this organization for fifteen years. During this period you have been promoted from an entry-level position to an upper-middle management post. Your responsibilities have increased dramatically, as have your contacts with individuals at all levels of the organization. Most of these relationships are very positive and reflect your acquired knowledge, ability to do what you promise, and knowing how to keep quiet when appropriate.

The vice-president to whom you have reported for the past five years has retired, and the organization has promoted an individual from a branch office to take his place. The new vice-president has had little personal contact with the home office and has a limited working knowledge of its general office procedures. His previous responsibilities had been very narrow in focus with emphasis being placed on only one part of the organization's operation.

Your track record in assisting fellow employees and subordinates has helped in developing strong feelings of trust and personal respect. At times of crisis or unusual circumstances, you were consulted about personal or confidential issues and were given information to be used at your discretion. In the past, you were able to pass this information on to the vice-president, knowing that neither you nor the individual providing the information would be identified as the source and that the information would not appear in a different context.

The current vice-president has consistently asked you about information that is coming to you through the grapevine, office gossip, etc. You have given him some of this information, but have not been as open as in the past. You have begun to hear feedback that the information given to him has been used in a questionable manner. You cannot tell whether things are slow in the office or if people are not talking to you as much as before.

Address the following questions privately before discussing them with members of your case study group.

1. How do you determine to whom you should give information? Is whatever you learn the property of the organization or is personal discretion the determinant of your distribution?

2. How do you gain distance from the situation without alienating either your supervisor or your co-workers?

3. Your expertise and position reflect in part your participation in a communications network that has not only provided you with access to those in positions of power but information; the network no longer functions as it did, so where do you go from here?

4. Turn to the Survey on Ways of Learning About Organizations and, considering how you decided to deal with this case, choose the most appropriate quotation.

Be prepared to discuss your responses and supporting arguments for your viewpoints with members of your case study group.

Alleged Harassment and the New Supervisor

You are a recently appointed supervisor of a copy department in an up-and-coming advertising agency. You supervise over twenty professionals of diverse backgrounds who, due to the complex nature of the work, must collaborate as members of a team. Your predecessor left his position suddenly because, according to most accounts, he could not handle the interpersonal conflicts in the department. This is the first time the supervisor of this unit has been a woman.

This morning Sara Johnston, one of your subordinates, informs you that another subordinate, June Ramirez, has been the victim of unwanted sexual advances. The man responsible is an associate vice-president named Harry Wolfe, to whom you have been introduced briefly. You ask Sara why Jane has not come forward with a complaint. Sara replies that she thinks Jane is uncertain about what to do. Harry is, after all, an associate vice-president with stature and a good reputation with the company. After asking questions, you find that Jane has never complained to Sara; Sara has observed Harry's behavior and thinks it is sufficiently serious that she has taken it upon herself to report these events. Sara thinks Harry's behavior qualifies as sexual harassment. You, on the other hand, feel pretty knowledgeable about sexual harassment yourself. You know a supervisor's responsibilities to prevent your work unit from becoming a "hostile environment" where workers cannot perform their jobs due to harassment and intimidation. Nevertheless, you are unclear as to whether Harry's behavior qualifies as sexual harassment.

There are other factors that influence your thinking. You are new to the agency, you are the first woman in this position, and you have heard other women in the agency referred to as "wild-eyed radical feminists." You ruminate about whose reputation warrants protection: Harry's? Jane's? The Agency's? How do you decide what to do?

Address these questions privately before discussing them with members of your case study group.

1. Do you wait for events to unfold? After all, the third-party charges might be fiction or may disappear. Or do you choose to act in some way?

2. If you decide to act, what would you do first? What factors would figure prominently in your choosing one strategy?

3. Turn to the Survey on Ways of Learning About Organizations and, considering how you decided to deal with this case, choose the most appropriate quotation.

Be prepared to discuss your responses and supporting arguments for your viewpoints with members of your case study group.

Circles of Power: In or Out?

You are a staff assistant in a highly political public agency. You work for a politically shrewd department manager who prides himself on having the best information before anyone else. A neighbor of yours happens to be a rather highly placed member of the staff of a legislative oversight committee, and he is quick to provide you with information of your own. Last night he told you that he had just heard that your program's sole source of funding was slashed to 40 percent of this past fiscal year's allocation. He firmly believed that this was reliable information, and his intention was to forewarn you that bad times might be ahead. As one of the most recently hired staff, you are concerned about the old maxim "last hired, first fired" applying in your case. You also, however, do not want to be seen as a rumormonger or as an insecure, defensive employee. And, finally, you are loath to let on that you knew this before the boss.

Address these questions privately before discussing them with members of your case study group.

1. Given the circumstances, would you seek additional information to find out what is happening to your program and your job?
2. If your answer to the above question was yes, how would you go about finding out? If your answer to 1 was no, skip this question and proceed to the next.
3. Knowing what you now know, what, if anything, would you do with this information?
4. Turn to the Survey on Ways of Learning About Organizations and, considering how you decided to deal with this case, choose the most appropriate quotation.

Be prepared to discuss your responses and supporting arguments for your viewpoints with members of your case study group.

Move It or Lose It

The head of the engineering department has resigned under pressure. Jules Livingston, a senior engineer with the department, has been appointed interim director, pending the outcome of a national search. Upper management felt that Jules was the ideal choice because of his technological experience and his ability to manipulate data and complete assignments. Jules thought that the job would be challenging and the kind of position that he would like on a permanent basis. Also he felt he could handle the responsibilities because he had always been successful in setting and reaching his goals. One drawback, however, was that Jules in all his years as an engineer had never supervised professional employees.

Of all the responsibilities facing the interim director, Jules felt that the plan to review the current staffing of the department and the development of a proposal to maximize the productivity of the unit were the most important. The department had performed at a more or less mediocre level and was seen by the organization as more of a liability than an asset.

Since Jules wanted to be named permanent director, he realized that he had to do a first-rate job. For that level of quality, he would need some help in this project. He had often depended on Tony Greene for assistance in identifying problems and assessing personnel decisions, and he felt that Tony could be helpful in the restructuring process. Tony was also interested in being considered for the permanent directorship, so he agreed to participate in the project. He felt that this would be an opportunity to showcase his skills and demonstrate his administrative abilities. He felt that this kind of visibility was just what he needed.

Jules decided to follow a plan of attack that was geared to meet the rational criteria ingrained in most engineers. A great deal of emphasis was placed on designing organizational charts, program goals and objectives, and evaluative instruments. He felt that Tony's work was in most cases too superficial and based on commonsense knowledge, and Jules decided either to ignore it or move it to the appendix. Tony was concerned because he felt that by ignoring some of the issues that he had raised Jules was demonstrating how he would behave as a permanent leader.

This feeling of concern was one that was felt by the other engineers in the department. Jules no longer had time to eat lunch with his colleagues and was far too busy to share a beer after work. People no longer seemed to matter to Jules; concerns of a personal nature were sacrificed in favor of producing a quality report and presentation. Jules had concluded that this was a fair trade-off: he saw this as exchanging short-term neglect of his subordinates' priorities for the long-term goals of greater efficiency and enhanced prestige for the department. Tony, on the other hand, spent a great deal of time talking to the other engineers, trying to get a feel for what they felt was important, but also selling his point of view.

The presentation of the proposal to the department was the first step in implementing the plan. Jules' presentation was a visual masterpiece. His professional style of presentation, his visual aides, and his polished manuscript demonstrated his redoubtable skills and the amount of time and effort spent in preparation. During the presentation, the administrative formula for assigning personnel was referred to but not completely described. Some of the engineers were concerned with the limited information provided concerning the nature of the formula and its use and began to ask very pointed questions. Jules felt out of his depth and referred the question to Tony. For whatever reasons, Tony was not inclined to rescue Jules from questions that he had warned him about.

At first, Jules was at a total loss for words, but then he became furious. On realizing that he had lost control of the situation, he began to shout. This outburst stunned the group, an embarrassed silence followed, and the meeting disbanded spontaneously, as if by prearranged agreement.

Agreement was reached that day, not as to the direction or structure of the department or the program, but concerning the immediate need for a new director.

Address the following questions privately before discussing them in the case study group.

1. Individuals employed on interim appointments can have an impact on an organization, albeit in different ways than a permanent appointment. Understanding the nature of Jules' appointment and knowing that he was interested in being the permanent director, where do you feel that he should have focused his energies?

2. In designing any major effort that will affect all members of the department, where would you go for information and how would you validate it?

3. What are the implications for Jules of taking on the bulk of the responsibility himself and delegating the remainder to Tony?

4. You could argue that Jules' case was lost not because he did not do his homework but because he ignored the political environment in which he was operating. What would you have done differently?

5. Emotional outbursts can be deadly, but to defend against them, what should Jules have done?

6. Turn to the Survey on Ways of Learning About Organizations and, considering how you decided to deal with this case, choose the most appropriate quotation.

Be prepared to discuss your responses and supporting arguments for your viewpoints with members of your case study group.

Answer Key to Survey on Ways of Learning About Organizations

This questionnaire asks you to choose the perspective that most accurately describes how you try to understand particular events and problems in your workplace. This answer key is designed to interpret your choices in a developmental context. That is, as we grow in experience, we usually progress through various stages of understanding. Each stage is progressively more capable of explaining events than the last. While there are no "right" or "wrong" answers as such, those who use certain postures tend to enjoy certain advantages. Look at the quotation you selected for each case, then find its corresponding explanation.

If you chose C, your predominant orientation would be:

1. SILENCE.   An employee with this perspective feels unable to understand what is going on to her satisfaction and may appear quite passive about her role in the organization. One who is silent feels that she has little or no influence or control over understanding external events.

If you chose A, your predominant orientation would be:

2. RECEIVED KNOWLEDGE.   An employee holding this perspective relies heavily upon experts and/or persons in authority as her primary source of knowledge.

If you chose E, your predominant orientation would be:

3. SUBJECTIVE KNOWLEDGE.   This employee relies on intuition and instinct to the exclusion of other methods such as gathering facts. She usually feels that "intuition doesn't lie" and is more dependable as a way to acquire understanding that what social networks or so-called experts may reveal.

If you chose B, your predominant orientation would be:

4. PROCEDURAL KNOWING/SEPARATE.   An employee with this perspective feels that organizations operate as systems or games, and that one must know the rules or procedures to acquire a complete picture of events. Once she acquires a sense of the rules and clarifies the way the system works, she may feel more capable and play a greater role in organization activities but will do so in keeping with "the rules of the game." Unlike the connected employee (level 5), this individual chooses to remain separate from events. "You must play the game whatever it is, but the gameplayer is not really you." Separate thinkers explain their behavior in terms of their changing role in games.

If you chose D, your predominant orientation would be:

5. PROCEDURAL KNOWING/CONNECTED.   This employee respects social relationships (friends, mentors, social networks) as an integral part of understanding what is going on in an organization. Relationships provide different vantage points on the same event, all of which may contribute part of the explanation as to why things are the way they are. She may experience a need to "connect" with others to verify her impressions or articulate her views.

If you chose F, your predominant orientation would be:

6. CONSTRUCTED KNOWING.   The employee with this perspective feels that she needs to reconstruct events or problems to determine what is going on. She may use a variety of methods: experience, intuition, social networks, knowledge of political games, and/or data gathering to uncover patterns of events. Quite often, she will ask questions that others consider unorthodox or radical, that question "the way things are done around here." She feels a need to clarify the organization's complexities and her place in it and, as a result of some success in doing so, feels empowered to act.

Interpreting Your Results

Given any case, you could have selected silence, received knowledge, subjective knowledge, procedural knowing/separate, procedural knowing/connected, or constructed knowing as a response. Let's say for "Alleged Harassment and the New Supervisor" you chose quotation e. You can then interpret your approach in dealing with that case or that class of events as relying heavily on subjective knowledge.

Now determine whether there is a pattern among your choices. Do you select the same quotation for each case or different ones? If you choose subjective knowledge for all or most of your cases, your ability to act effectively may suffer for not using a variety of ways to make sense of these dilemmas. This is sometimes referred to as adaptability. Note especially if you have chosen levels 1, 2, or 3 in at least three of the cases. If you chose silence, received or subjective knowledge more or less consistently, this pattern suggests that your general orientation does not promote understanding and could be enriched. If you selected mostly quotations at levels 4, 5, or 6, (for example, three out of four cases produced this level of response), your capacity to understand organizational dilemmas is more comprehensive and can produce relatively more adaptable and effective action strategies.

As mentioned, many individuals will find that they choose different responses or levels, depending upon the particulars of the situation. Using Kipnis and Schmidt's terms, they can be called tacticians. Others will choose one type of response (silence, received, or subjective knowledge, procedural knowing/separate and connected) consistently, regardless of the situation. We can describe these individuals as captives. They try to understand what is going on by using the same approach, no matter what is presented by the situation. A few, however, will consistently choose level 6 for all or most cases but, due to the special nature of constructed knowing, these individuals are not prisoners of this orientation in the same way as levels 1 through 5. A special feature of the constructive approach is that it both subsumes and builds upon all other, lower levels. At the same time, the constructive perspective transcends levels 1 through 5, resulting in a description of reality that is personally grounded and original.

Individuals who choose level 6 for all cases have been able to adopt a proactive stance and consequently have moved beyond the silence phase. They can consider the advice of experts (received knowledge) and frame that advice within certain self-imposed parameters. While they have cultivated nonrational skills, such as intuitive techniques (subjective knowledge), they are able to confirm their instincts either by consulting experts or using higher order approaches. Consistent constructivists are able to appreciate political games and understand their workings, even if they do not play them well, and can also use networks to see problems from others' viewpoints and to validate their own impressions. Those who select three or four different orientations for the cases (for example, levels 1, 3, 4, and 6) are relatively limited by others' standards and expectations about how they should think and behave. In a sense, their ability to understand events and define problems may be only as good as their sources, the soundness of their intuition, or their gamemanship. Ultimately, they must rely on methods of confirmation that are external to themselves and beyond their control. Consistent constructivists, on the other hand, have developed personally grounded systems of apprehending the world and consequently enjoy a kind of independence and security that others lack. Unlike our speculations about Evelyn in the last chapter, these individuals not only know what to do when faced with a dilemma, they can put it into action. The greater the likelihood that you choose constructivist responses, the more we feel you can rely on your own capacities for making sense of organizational dilemmas.

Recommendations for Practice

As mentioned, this is not a valid or scientific measure of how you try to understand your organization. This survey only suggests or indicates how you conceptualize problems and how you see how you fit into your organization. Nevertheless, for those who feel that this may accurately describe your perspective, you should be aware that certain strategies can promote progression through these stages. You might try the following:

- Participate in new or different tasks or projects that allow you to "stretch" yourself, not only in understanding how the organization functions but also your own capabilities.
- Experiment with new methods of gathering information or try methods you rarely use. For example, if you think you are a "silent" employee or one who relies almost exclusively on intuition (subjective knowledge) to judge your environment, try seeing events in terms of political games. Ask questions of trusted co-workers regarding how they would explain a particular event or circumstance, and try seeing it from their points of view. "Try opposing viewpoints on for size."
- You may need to take some risks in "owning" problems and following them through to some resolution.

For example, a computer engineer widely regarded as a leader for his innovations revealed his "personal best" leadership performance. It began when he realized that major manufacturing defects were not being corrected anywhere in the company, and complaints were flowing into the engineering division in such great number that engineers were unable to work on design problems. He decided to channel all complaints to himself, even though he was not a supervisor or manager. He said, "I had no standing (authority) to do this, but once I did, we not only freed up people to focus on solving the engineering part of the problem, we also established how serious the problem was and began to enlist the involvement of the production people." Through much-needed cooperation and communication between engineering, production, and related units, he not only obtained valuable information concerning the problem; he was able to acquire a deeper understanding of the nature of the design flaws. As you might guess, his volunteering for this assignment eventually won him a promotion (reported in Kouzes and Posner, 1987.)

To supplement this section, trainers may want to use exercises from Morgan's *Creative Organization Theory* (1989). Morgan calls these exercises mindstretchers, because they may assist participants in broadening their interpretations as well as stretching their views of organizational "reality." Specifically, refer to chapters eleven through thirteen: Developing Multiple Interpretations; Understanding Different Viewpoints; and Escaping from Dominant Ideas.

A common approach to involving trainees and students in a subject is to analyze cases of real or hypothetical events similar to what they typically encounter or may face at work. Cases have the advantage of simulating real life and therefore directly engage participants' interest in the subject in a nonthreatening way. Four case studies are provided here, each of which presents different topics and problems. Each is written to elicit different points of view and to emphasize different slices of organizational life, thus enabling participants to employ alternative or new frames. One case deals with sharing grapevine information with a possibly untrustworthy superior, another with third-party allegations of sexual harassment, a third with political information that would be considered sensitive and valued by a well-connected supervisor, and the last with the exploitation of a necessary employee. Some cases place the participant in the case; others ask her to observe as a third party. Some roles are as the supervisor or manager, while others are staff.

While there is no recommended, right or wrong answer to any of the case questions, each set of questions should be addressed individually and privately first, to gauge individuals' thoughts accurately without the influence of peer group pressure. Then we recommend that small groups of no fewer than four and no more than seven members discuss the questions freely and openly. The purpose of group discussion is to generate insight into the meaning of the case and its many possible interpretations, and afterwards to broaden the array of strategies and solutions that could be used in each case. Groups should be informed as to the purpose of these discussions so that they do not attempt to force agreement from members. If case groups are used, individuals can then share their responses and justifications and witness how other members choose to place their priorities, weigh evidence, and derive solutions or draw strategies from selected information. In this manner, the case group brings out how different individuals take the same information, process it differently, and model ways of framing the case that challenge some of the other interpretations. If the trainers or instructors can raise questions and issues focusing on reframing and raising the level of discussion to a macro-perspective, this enables participants to reframe how they had viewed the event or problem in the case privately. Just as importantly, participants have the opportunity to discover if case groups display connected behavior. Members should rely on "real talk" to stimulate ideas and provoke insight; this was contained in the Survey on Ways of Learning About Organizations.

III. HOW TO TELL A BUSINESSMAN FROM A BUSINESSWOMAN

We enter the workplace with an assortment of personal baggage: previous experiences, unconscious biases, preconceived ideas, and, in many cases, untested assumptions. Often, we are not aware that this baggage exists or the ways in which it can shape our actions or behavior. In the following exercise, participants identify stereotypes that are often mistaken for accurate descriptions of women's and men's behavior.

QUESTIONNAIRE ON PERCEIVED STEREOTYPES

Each of the following statements can or may suggest behavior that is typically used to describe men or women in our culture. Fill in the blank with the appropriate letter: M for male or F for female.

1. _____ managers aren't afraid to say what they think; they understand the system and really know what is happening.

2. _____ managers are pushy; you'd better give them what they want or else they'll get emotional.

3. _____ managers exert authority diligently, and are concerned about meeting the needs of the organization.

4. _____ managers rarely lose their tempers, but when they do, it usually is for a good reason.

5. _____ managers have used methods other than productivity in achieving their current positions.

6. _____ managers have had to overcome their natural nurturing instincts and, partially to compensate, are usually tough as nails and unwilling to give an inch.

7. _____ managers are human; they know how to balance concern for productivity with sensitivity.

8. _____ managers have the courage of their convictions; they are willing to take a stand on the tough decisions and support the implementation of those decisions.

After completing the questionnaire, the group should review the preceding stereotypes and determine if all the participants were able to identify the listed behavior by gender. Even if one does not agree with the description, the behavior usually can be attributed to either males or females. Open discussion as to the nature and purpose of these generalizations allows participants to question not only the values behind these statements but offers an opportunity to determine to what degree stereotypes are used for identifying acceptable behavior. Expected or acceptable behavior should not carry with it gender implications. Discussion of this simple exercise should teach an important lesson. If different norms apply to women, these norms limit the range of behavioral options open to women that are available for men. Or, as Cook and Mendleson advise:

1. Do not generalize about people! Finding one "bad apple" (one ineffective man or woman manager) does not mean the rest are spoiled. Generalizations toward groups of people always have exceptions.

2. Throw out stereotypes! Stereotypes build inaccurate expectations from fellow workers and could eventually lead to a self-fulfilling prophecy within the organization. The statement, "Women have to work ten times harder than men," could be because they have to jump the "stereotype hurdles." Women in management have proven that they can manage in spite of the stereotypes and should be able to manage better without the stereotypes. (1984, p. 27)

IV. A. DEFINING POLITICAL DILEMMAS AND PROBLEMS

Political dilemmas and problems faced in individual organizations will vary not only from organization to organization but from within internal units or departments. Individuals within organizations will differ on what they perceive to be a political problem. Consequently, it is up to the trainer to provide a general review of the areas that could be defined as problematic and allow individuals working in pairs to identify one or two specific examples to be addressed. Refer to chapter two for definitions and examples.

By working in pairs or dyads, the group will have the opportunity to identify specific political games or conditions that are found in the unit in which they work. One can anticipate a greater amount of intimacy that encourages freedom of expression and interaction and serves as the initial testing ground for investigating personal perspectives or concerns. This arrangement will encourage feedback that either reinforces the individual's perspective or refocuses the situation or the political dimensions of the games being played. In assessing the use of political games by members of the organization, the dyad as part of its discussions should choose a specific game that would benefit from change. This discussion should include an examination of the game, why it exists, possible ways to modify the way the game is played, the support needed to implement these changes, and ultimately the feasibility and probability of achieving change.

IV. B. DEMYSTIFYING ORGANIZATIONAL POLITICS: HOW ORGANIZATIONS REALLY OPERATE

As presented in chapter 6, this topic was covered by a brief lecture about strategies and tactics used to deal with organizational politics. Borrowing from Dubrin's book, *Human Relations: A Job-Oriented Approach* (1978) as well as other resources, we made transparencies of the following techniques to guide the lecture and discussion. These labels can also be used to develop handouts.

POLITICAL TECHNIQUES TO AVOID AND ANTICIPATE

BLACKMAIL

CHARACTER ASSASSINATION

REMOVE THE OPPOSITION

DIVIDE AND CONQUER

THE SET-UP

RECEIVE UNDUE CREDIT

STRATEGIES TO LEARN AND USE

HELP BOSS SUCCEED

DISPLAY LOYALTY

VOLUNTEER

PRAISE

HUMOR

BECOME INDISPENSABLE

V. PERSONAL GOAL-SETTING FOR ORGANIZATIONAL PROBLEM-SOLVING

Instructions to the workshop participants: Think about some problems at your work that you would like to change. In considering alternatives make sure that you do not rule out important problems because you feel that you lack control over their resolution. Many problems can be dealt with by adopting a change approach with a variety of tactics and strategies over a long enough period of time to have an impact on others, but it is YOU who must initiate the change and YOU who must give your new approach a chance.

Once you have narrowed your list of problems, select one and write it down on your Strategy Script Worksheet. Working with an overhead projector, the trainer can outline instructions to facilitate the exercise.

THE STRATEGY SCRIPT WORKSHEET

A. DESCRIBE what you would like to happen; for example, to change a person's behavior or a situation. Describe your preferences specifically and objectively.

B. EXPRESS how you feel about what will happen if you do not reach your goals. Focus on how badly you want this to happen and develop some commitment toward reaching your goal.

C. SPECIFY how you can arrive at your goal. Break it down into time sequences and stages. Evaluate the possible impact of influencing factors (such as: your superior; co-workers; subordinates; demands and/or goals of the organization; outside stakeholders; job demands, power of setting a precedent; personal and professional ethics).

D. CHOOSE what you will do in the long run; in the short term; when the timing is right. Try to anticipate different scenarios in which you may encounter variations of this problem. Anticipate positive and negative consequences as a result of your strategies. Be careful to be adaptable.

E. REWARD yourself for the little steps you accomplish. Take stock periodically and come to terms with what you have yet to accomplish. Evaluate what worked and what did not. Store this information for future use. You may need to set new, more specific goals before you can say you have dealt with this problem effectively.

FINALLY, keep this worksheet and add new ideas, skills, tactics, and strategies throughout tomorrow's workshop. You should keep experimenting and trying to look at this problem in new ways (Kelley, 1979).

Now each of you should discuss your choices with your discussion group. Discussion group members are to ask constructive questions of the problem identifier to help her refine the precise nature of the problem:

- Is the problem as stated within the individual's control to change?
- Is it a serious problem or trivial in importance?
- Is the written problem the true source of difficulty or is that unstated or implied?
- Is the written statement clearly written and comprehensive? Is it specific?

VI. HOMEWORK ASSIGNMENTS

At the conclusion of this workshop, two assignments are announced. First, participants must complete the POIS surveys distributed at this time. Trainers can choose from three forms: Influencing Your Manager, Influencing Your Co-Worker, and Influencing Your Subordinate. To save time as well as focus the next session's discussion, we recommend that participants complete only two scales. Usually the Manager and Subordinate scales cover a sufficiently broad range of influence situations to be considered a representative sample of the participants' behavior.

The second task is to distribute the case study "Murdock the Maneuverer" and direct participants to read it before the next session. Tell them that when they return, they should come prepared to discuss their answers to the questions that follow the case.

USING POLITICAL STRATEGIES TO GET WHAT YOU WANT

SUGGESTED SCHEDULE FOR DAY TWO

I. POIS

9:00–10:00. Presentation

2. Participants read illustrative stories

3. Case groups may discuss stories or role play the stories using the suggested technique and alternatives

4. Process: Compare self-concept, POIS, and Survey on Ways of Learning About Organizations. Are they complementary or dissonant?

II. Factors in Diagnosing Dilemmas/Problems in Job Politics

10:00–11:00

1. "Assessing Your Diagnostic Skills"

2. LEAD—using the situational approach

3. Factors to consider in analysis

4. Case study and discussion: "Murdock the Maneuverer"

III.   A. Coping with Difficult People

11:00–12:00

1. Handout: "Recognizing Common Types of Difficult People"; discuss

2. Strategies for coping

3. General recommendations

III.   B. The Strategy Script Worksheet Revisited

1:00–2:00

1. Group discussion: Use LEAD, POIS, diagnostic factors, difficult people, political strategies, and Belenky to define and analyze problems

2. Group members provide feedback to participants concerning soundness of planning strategies

IV. (ETHICS) When Playing the Political Game Should Stop and Personal Ethics Begin

2:00–3:00

1. Cases on ethical dilemmas

2. The power of support groups: When a pat on the back is a must

V. Wrap-Up: What Changes Will You Make Back On the Job?

3:00–4:00

1. Groups announce strategies for problem-solving

2. Get feedback from workshop members

3. Workshop evaluation

I. THE PROFILES OF ORGANIZATIONAL INFLUENCE STRATEGIES (POIS)

An important part of broadening and deepening the employee's repertoire of influencing and leadership skills is the POIS. Instrumentation, scoring, and interpretation are available from University Associates, Inc.

A brief lecture can be delivered concerning Kipnis and Schmidt's seven organizational influence strategies. Again, consult University Associates for the original materials, including a respondent's guide and trainer's manual. These materials will be essential in developing your lecture. In summary, the influence strategies are as follows (Kipnis and Schmidt, 1982).

SEVEN ORGANIZATIONAL INFLUENCE STRATEGIES

REASON:
- Relying on data and information to support one's request; planning, preparation, and expertise are required
- Base of power—influencer's knowledge and ability to communicate information

FRIENDLINESS:
- Causing person to think well of influencer, acting friendly
- Sensing mood of target before making request
- Based on influencer's personality, interpersonal skills, and sensitivity to moods and attitudes of others

BARGAINING:
- Influencing through negotiation and exchange of benefits or favors
- Tactics used based on social norms of obligation and reciprocity
- Past favors or future concessions influence trades (own time, effort, skill, or organizational resources that the influencer controls)

ASSERTIVENESS:
- Influencing by forceful manner, making demands, and setting deadlines
- Expression of strong emotions (temper)
- Based on legitimate authority

COALITION:
- Mobilizing other people in organization to assist in influencing target
- Power in numbers—unified support increases success
- Strategy based on alliance with co-workers
- Complex strategy requires skill and effort

APPEAL TO HIGHER AUTHORITY:
- Relying on chain of command, appeal to people higher up in organization who have power over target person
- Indirect means of influence, informal request, or source of information to higher management regarding issue

SANCTION:
- Using rewards or punishments to attain desirable goal
- Depends on influencer's access to rewards or punishment and ability to deliver them

An overhead transparency can be used and/or a handout can be distributed at the time of the lecture. Since Kipnis and Schmidt's instrumentation explains the seven strategies in some detail, the handout may be helpful only for easy reference. The overhead, however, is useful to focus attention on the strategies as you describe them. We recommend making overheads with this information.

STRATEGY	BEHAVIOR
REASON	Relies on data, discussion, and logic
FRIENDLINESS	Demonstrates interest, good will, and esteem to create a favorable impression
BARGAINING	Relies on negotiation and the exchange of benefits or favors

ASSERTIVENESS	Relies on direct and forceful communication
COALITION	Mobilizes other people in the organization to support requests
HIGHER AUTHORITY	Invokes the influence of higher levels in the organization to back up requests
SANCTIONS	Uses rewards and punishments derived from organizational position

Cases to Illustrate Use of Each Strategy

Reason

The telephone equipment being used by your department borders on the archaic. This is the only unit in the organization that has resisted changing to a comprehensive system. Your department head has put such pressure on the organization to keep this system in place that no one wants to hear the complaints. Some of the staff have speculated that she does not want to commit such a huge sum of money since the department would then need to stretch its budget to the limit for the next two years. What she may not realize is that a new system would be the kind of investment that in the long run could pay off handsomely. For now, however, the department faces a situation where the addition of three new fax lines will severely strain telephone access. As it is, the support staff can barely handle calls, and the capacity to increase the number of stations is inadequate.

Previous discussions with the manager have not helped alleviate the problem. In the past, you had complained about the unfairness of the situation and the need for change to maintain sanity. Rather than try this emotional tug on the heartstrings again, you have decided to plan a strategy that maximizes your chances of getting a new system. Your first priority is to compile any available data on the limits of the current system, the availability of other systems, and the projected costs of remaining on the current system. Once this information is in place, you plan to review possible options and determine which would be the most cost-efficient in providing immediate service for the department. Market studies done by the planning department will also be reviewed so that the needs associated with anticipated future growth can be met by the system.

Planning the presentation requires a great deal of effort. You know that it has to be concise and to the point. You schedule the presentation at a time when the manager has the least amount of distraction and will be willing and able to devote attention to the subject.

Last and possibly most important, you present the facts in a professional manner and are able to anticipate and respond to questions.

Friendliness

Office paperwork can often be tedious, especially when there is more work to do than time available. Spending a few extra minutes with some of the support staff is particularly helpful when you need to get something accomplished quickly. This is useful when dealing with the third floor. The manager of that department is overburdened and under such stress that few people remain for any length of time; consequently the turnover rate is higher there than in any other unit. There are a few employees who have weathered the storms and still manage to get their jobs done. However, one can only notice that work does get prioritized.

Your first contacts with people in that office were brisk and to the point. Needless to say, you found yourself waiting for responses to questions that should have been readily forthcoming. After limited success, you began to change tactics. What used to be conversations focused on 100 percent business developed into discussions that included a few personal comments and then the request for needed information or support. You now find yourself being included in some of the inside jokes and are no longer perceived as an outsider pressuring your colleagues for quick responses. Friendships have developed from this association, and periodically you stop by the third floor to see how everyone is doing and to get to meet the new people on the floor. Now when you call for assistance, it is available, and, perhaps the most amazing part, you usually get it immediately.

Bargaining

Three years ago, I was promoted from staff assistant to assistant director for public relations. Moving up the ranks in any hierarchy provides an individual with more than an increase in salary or an office with a view. It more often than not gives you access to perquisites that can be used to trade with co-workers. When one has little to trade, one must often be content with what has been assigned. My job can be done at any time during the day, so should I want to come in at 10:00 and leave at 7:00, I can adjust my hours accordingly. However, I am willing to give up that flexibility and be available for more conventional hours when I can exchange my knowledge, talents, and skills for support from co-workers or subordinates who are not assigned to help me.

Attending a meeting for a co-worker at 7:30 is not my idea of a great way of starting the morning, but I will stand in for someone whose outside responsibilities makes arriving at work early impossible. This provides me with the opportunity to ask a favor in return. I tend to choose this option especially when I want to obligate someone with valuable resources to exchange. In support positions, people will frequently trade time for answering telephones, xeroxing, or running messages. However, as one gains broader and higher level responsibilities, what is traded—for example, substitute representation at an inter-departmental meeting—can have an impact beyond the bargaining partners' shared domain. That is, the outcome of the trade can affect others' performance and the organization's effectiveness generally. I find that what is traded has ranged from office equipment to collaboration on high-level projects; the choice of "currency" to trade partly depends on what resources you have at your disposal as well as what is valued by the party you want to obligate. This strategy will work only if everyone involved follows the social norms of obligation. It is important that the parties involved in these exchanges believe that payback is fair and correct.

Assertiveness

Stella hated to be perceived as being pushy or obnoxious, so she kept quiet. She would smile and hope the problem would disappear, but one thing became clear: it was not going away, it was getting worse. Everyone in the office would dump work on her and, since she was so unwilling to object, they often did not realize how overextended she had become.

She was passing a construction site on the way back from lunch when a particle of dirt got under her contact lens. As she was hurrying back to the office to clean her lens, she was waylaid by Stan, the department's budget director. Stan told her that he was desperate and needed her help immediately. She tried to protest, but he literally dragged her down the hall. The emergency consumed most of her afternoon. By the time she had a minute for herself, it was time to go home.

The next morning Stella could hardly see out of her injured eye and could not put in her lens. But at work no one noticed that she was wearing glasses rather than her contacts, and she did not think to tell anyone about her problem. Before she had a chance to catch her breath, she was asked to pitch in and help out. Her eye began to throb, and she realized that she would have to go to see her ophthalmologist. By sheer chance, she was able to get an appointment during her lunch hour. On the way out the door, she ran into Stan who began to rant and rave about a new emergency. All she managed to get out was "Not now" before the elevator closed in his face.

The doctor examined her eye and told her that she would not be able to wear her contact lens for at least a week. But before she left, he made Stella promise him one thing—that she stop and think about what she was allowing others to do to her. Rather than take a bus, she hailed a cab to go back to the office, but at the last minute changed her mind and gave the driver her home address.

After a long painful weekend, Stella realized that she had been passive for so long that to gain any respect she would have to change her behavior radically and at once. As she was walking down the hall to her office, Susie, the receptionist, asked whether she could catch the phones for a second. Stella smiled at her and said, "Yes, my eye is much better, thank you," and continued down the hall. Susie looked rather perplexed because she had not realized that Stella had a problem with her eye.

On reaching her office, she was met at the door by her secretary who began to tell her what had happened after she had left on Friday. Stella calmly told her to hold her calls and to give her half an hour to go through her mail before she came in for her assignments. Her secretary shook her head and went back to her desk.

Stella sat down at her desk, turned on her terminal and began to list the projects that she needed to complete and items to be anticipating. As she was working, Stan burst into the office, shouting "You have to help me." Stella turned to him and said, "I would appreciate it if you would knock on my door if it is closed," and turned back to her terminal. Stan was so shocked that he went outside and knocked on her door. On reentering the room, Stella told Stan that she would be glad to help him, but that he should begin sketching out the problem and she would help him fit in some of the pieces later.

Stella realized that being assertive was not as hard as she had thought it would be. Her biggest problem was not others, but herself.

Coalition

The company had undergone financial restructuring in the last quarter because of a change in the national economy. Money that had previously been available to fund travel to the national sales show had dried up. Only two people from this office would be able to attend this year's meeting, one being the sales manager who was making a speech at the opening meeting. It was not clear who the second participant would be or what the criteria would be to choose to determine him or her.

Sean had been with the company for three years, but his lackluster career had only recently begun to blossom. Last month he actually led the office in sales. Rumor had it that some of those sales had been gained at the expense of Frank, who had been hospitalized because of a blood disorder. No one could ever accuse Sean of not knowing what he wanted. Apparently, what he wanted most was to be chosen to represent the company at the meeting.

The sales manager listened to Sean's case and felt that he would be an ideal representative for the company. He would send Sean, because he certainly was enthusiastic. Two or three of the other sales representatives got wind of Sean's prospective trip and became very concerned. They realized that the manager did not want to get too involved in making the decision and would rather let things evolve; more importantly, once the sales manager made up his mind, it was almost impossible to change it. The sales reps got together and discussed their options. They decided that letting Sean attend the meeting without any kind of a fight would be irresponsible on their part. Through informal conversations with the other sales reps, they realized that they had reached consensus and were willing to present their case at the weekly wrap-up meeting. Delores led the group in expressing their concern about the process being used to choose the participant. Not only did they express their feelings, but they outlined a process that would be fair and reward the most productive member of the sales force. The manager was taken aback by the unanimity of their action, so taken aback that he said that he would reconsider sending Sean.

Appeal to Higher Authority

Joe was a great golfer and the perfect kind of partner: consistent, accurate, always shot under par, and never got angry. This ability had come to the attention of R. J. Smith, vice-president of marketing, who felt that the country club was the best place to sell their product. Joe became R. J.'s partner and spent Wednesday afternoons and Saturdays on the course, weather permitting. They had been golfing buddies for the past two years, and Joe began to confide in R. J. Most of their conversations centered on ways that Joe could improve his status within the company.

Joe had never taken advantage of his preferred status within the organization, because he prided himself on being able to take care of himself. Over the past few months, he had noticed that the revenue from their unit had been declining. He could not understand why this was happening, because from his vantage point, it looked as though the company was actually doing better than in the past. But numbers never lie, and those numbers were down. On returning to the office one evening, he noticed that one of his file drawers had been left open and one of the folders had been inserted backwards. He noticed that the folder held the account of an individual who worked directly with Joe's supervisor and that it had been placed in the wrong office. He sensed that something was wrong, something more serious than a misfiled folder. His curiosity made him open the file and look inside. The contents of the folder were on first appearance pretty clean. But as he flipped through the pages, he saw small check marks in the margins. On close inspection, he realized that these marks were next to entries that made little sense in terms of the type of account and notations. After careful review, he realized that this file represented only a small portion of the accounts in question.

Joe now understood that he had not stumbled into anything by chance, but that someone had realized what was happening and felt that Joe could do something about it. Joe now faced a major dilemma—should he confront his supervisor and face possible firing, or should he go to talk to R. J. and get his advice. After weighing his options, he realized that he had little choice but to talk to his golfing buddy without disclosing the name of his supervisor.

Sanctions

The supervisor had a limited amount of money to distribute for raises. He could divide the dollars equally among all the employees and give everyone a token reward for their unequal efforts. Or he could finally do what he had been trying to for years—reward the two hardest-working people in the unit with substantial increases.

The time had come not only to reward exemplary efforts, but also to send out a strong warning that just getting by was not good enough.

II. FACTORS IN DIAGNOSING DILEMMAS/PROBLEMS IN ORGANIZATIONAL POLITICS

We define job politics as efforts by one or more individuals to influence or control another's behavior on the job through subtle or overt, formal or informal means with the perpetrator's conscious or unconscious awareness of intent. The target of job politics does not need to be aware of or accept the behavior directed at him or her for this behavior to qualify as job politics. To analyze various dimensions of job politics, "Murdock the Maneuverer" (Christie, 1978) is read before this session.

Discussion about Murdock is usually lively and provokes many insights into the wide range of political tactics acceptable in most work settings, as well as into Murdock's debatable ethics. Our purpose in examining Murdock's case is to model the analysis of a lifelike work dilemma and practice framing the problem. In addition, we ask participants to consider Murdock's espoused theory and theory-in-use: might even he detect the inconsistency in how he behaves in contrast to how he would like to think he behaves? If everyone used Murdock's tactics, would Murdock feel victimized or vindicated?

Next, we administer the Diagnostic Style Survey (Hersey and Blanchard, 1982) for the reasons cited in chapter 6. We follow this with a discussion of Isenberg's "How Senior Managers Think" to reinforce the concept of extra-rational approaches to capture the nature of organizational problems and nonrational methods for problem-solving.

III. COPING WITH DIFFICULT PEOPLE

Moving on, a lecture on "Recognizing Common Types of Difficult People" is presented, accompanied by a handout. These materials on difficult people are attributed to Bramson's work on the subject (1981). Because Bramson is so comprehensive in his identification of problem types, as well as his coping strategies, we recommend that you read his *Coping with Difficult People.*

SEVEN TYPES OF DIFFICULT PEOPLE

HOSTILE AGGRESSIVES: THE SHERMAN TANK
- Sherman Tanks come out charging
- They are abusive, abrupt, intimidating, and overwhelming
- They attack you in an accusing manner
- Tanks have strong needs to prove to themselves and others that their opinions are always right

COPING WITH SHERMAN TANKS
- To cope with Sherman Tanks, you must stand up to them without fighting
- Give them a little time to run down
- Do not worry about being polite; get in any way you can
- Get their attention (call by name, sit, or stand)
- If possible, get them to sit down
- Maintain eye contact
- State your own opinions and perceptions forcefully
- Do not argue with what the Tank says or try to cut the Tank down
- Be ready to be friendly

COMPLAINERS
- Complainers point out real problems but in a manner that elicits placating or defensive responses from others
- They believe that they are powerless to help themselves
- They have a strong sense of how others ought to behave and feel anger when they do not conform
- In blaming others, complainers can continue to feel personally "perfect" while disowning responsibility for the problem

COPING WITH COMPLAINERS
- Listen attentively to complaints, even if you feel impatient
- Acknowledge statements by paraphrasing and checking out your perception of how they feel
- Do not agree with or apologize for their allegations even if you think they are true
- Avoid the accusation-defense-reaccusation pattern
- State and acknowledge facts without comment
- Move toward problem-solving by asking specific, informational questions
- If you supervise:

- assign limited fact-finding tasks or
- ask for complaints in writing
- If all else fails, ask, "How do you want this discussion to end?"

SILENT AND UNRESPONSIVE: THE CLAM

- Clams will not or cannot talk when you need their input
- Their silence is difficult to understand
- They are often silent and visibly nonresponsive

COPING WITH CLAMS

- Get the Clam to open up
- Ask open-ended questions
- Wait calmly for a response; do not fill in the silence
- Plan enough time to wait with composure
- Get agreement on or state clearly how much time is set for the interchange
- If you get no response, comment on it. End your comment with an open-ended question
- If you still get no response, wait, then comment on what is happening, and wait again
- Try to keep control by dealing matter-of-factly with "Can I go now?" and "I don't know" responses
- When the Clam opens up, be attentive and hold your comments and praise
- Keep to the original topic
- If the Clam stays closed, avoid a polite ending. Terminate the meeting and set up another appointment. State in detail what you will do since a discussion has not occurred

SUPER-AGREEABLES

- Super-Agreeables have strong needs to be liked and accepted
- Because it is useful for gaining acceptance, they make others feel liked and approved of
- They are difficult only when their friendship needs conflict with negative aspects of reality
- Rather than risk rejection, they will commit themselves to actions on which they cannot or will not follow through

COPING WITH SUPER-AGREEABLES

- You must work hard to surface the underlying facts and issues that prevent Super-Agreeables from taking action
- Let them know you value them by:
- telling them directly
- asking or remarking about nonwork topics (but only if you are sincere)
- Ask them about those things that might interfere with your good relationship

- Ask them to talk about any aspect of your product, service, or self (only if appropriate) that is not as good as the best
- Be ready to compromise and negotiate if open conflict surfaces
- Listen to humorous remarks for hidden messages

NEGATIVISTS
- Negativists are people who have a deep-seated conviction that any task not in their own hands will fail
- Their negativism is prompted by another's attempts to solve a problem or improve a procedure

COPING WITH NEGATIVISTS
- Be alert to being dragged down into despair
- Make optimistic but realistic statements about past successes
- Do not try to argue them out of their pessimism
- Do not offer alternatives until the problem has been thoroughly discussed
- Raise the negatives in an alternative yourself
- Be ready to take action and announce your plans to do so
- Do not ask them to act before they feel ready

KNOW-IT-ALL EXPERTS: THE BULLDOZER
- Bulldozers believe that knowledge provides stability in an unpredictable world
- Because they believe that most of the power to affect their lives resides in them, they see the ideas of others as irrelevant
- Often the "expert" quality that was equated with strength by their parents has become associated with both superiority and certainty of knowledge

COPING WITH BULLDOZERS
- Do your homework, carefully reviewing and checking facts
- Listen carefully and provide feedback main on points of his/her proposals
- Avoid dogmatic statements
- To disagree, be tentative, yet do not equivocate; use questions to raise problems
- Listen for Bulldozer tendencies in yourself
- Convey appreciation for the Bulldozer's knowledge
- Use delays to gain time for each party to review the other's proposals
- Know that as a last resort, you can choose to subordinate yourself to build an improved relationship for the future

INDECISIVES: THE STALLER
- The Staller is super-helpful but indecisive
- Stallers postpone decisions that might distress someone. This "works," because in time, most decisions, if unmade, quickly become irrelevant
- Stallers hint and beat around the bush to avoid both being honest and hurting anyone

COPING WITH STALLERS
- Encourage Stallers to surface conflicts or reservations
- Listen for hesitations, indirectness, and omissions
- When the Staller's reservations are about you:
- acknowledge any past problem
- state relevant data nondefensively
- propose a plan
- ask for help
- If you are not part of the problem, help the Staller examine facts and put them in priority order
- Give support after the decision is made
- If possible, keep action steps in your hands
- Watch for signs of anger or withdrawal. If you see them, try to remove him/her from the decision situation

Usually, presentation of this information and discussion adequately covers this material. Nevertheless, instructors may choose to encourage discussion about a hypothetical problem. For example, the participants can brainstorm possible techniques or ways to be used by a supervisor for making a lazy worker more productive.

IV. THE STRATEGY SCRIPT WORKSHEET REVISITED

The groups refine the information recorded in their Strategy Script Worksheets during the previous workshop (Day 1, section V, entitled Personal Goal-Setting for Organizational Problem-Solving). Since that time, they have been presented with the LEAD as a guide to identifying important diagnostic factors, the seven organizational influence strategies, and special techniques for coping with difficult people. To the original information, they can now add relevant skills, information, strategies, and approaches that can help them to own the problem as well as develop the confidence, and wherewithal to take responsibility for dealing with it. Often, people are more willing to take risks once they see that something can be done and that they themselves can do what is needed.

Another way of crystallizing what participants can accomplish is to ask them to complete a questionnaire entitled "Analysis for Action," which helps them to create action alternatives to improve organizational and personal effectiveness. This questionnaire (Morgan, 1989) taps the participants' reading of their current roles in terms of their visibility, autonomy, relevance, and relationships and emphasizes what needs to be changed for their future effectiveness. Generally, this section of the workshop focuses on making choices about strategies and plans and on refining and integrating an informed plan of attack, so that participants can not only have an impact but at the same time enhance their efficacy.

V. ETHICS AND JOB POLITICS: REINFORCING THE GROUNDED EMPLOYEE

Of growing concern are the implications associated with the number and range of ethical choices facing employees in both the private and public sector. The ability to make ethically responsible decisions and to incorporate ethics into daily decision-making requires balancing the goals of the organization and determining what is best for the general public. Consensus of opinion though a goal, can serve only as a guide; there is no clear prescription to assist in ethical decision-making. However, a general guideline would serve as a framework or baseline that would demonstrate that a consensus has been achieved, that these standards are known to the community as a whole, and that individuals are reinforced for upholding values that are held in common.

Individuals will face the dilemma of choosing not between good and evil,but between two acceptable variables. Each of the acceptable variables carries with it implications for the individual and the organization. The matter of choice would be much easier if our culture had a clearly defined set of values and standards that were agreed upon by all members. But, lacking that standard, one must be able to deal with difficult dilemmas on a case-by-case, situational basis or by a trial-and-error approach.

Case studies are excellent focal points in group discussions and put the ethical question in the context of decisions that everyone faces in one way or the other. The Harvard Business Case Studies publish some examples of ethical dilemmas in the private sector, while the National Institute of Justice publishes materials intended for the public sector.

VI. WRAP-UP

At the workshop's conclusion, participants and/or spokespersons will need to report their strategies to the workshop as a whole once more, this time taking into consideration the ethical factors involved. This is a logical sequence of events last completed during this workshop under section IV. The purpose in repeating this activity is to reinforce the intent to make changes back on the job in front of the entire workshop group. Finally, a written evaluation of the workshop should be distributed to assess whether the workshop met its stated objectives.

APPENDIX 1

Some additional resources that may fit your needs follow: Robert Denhardt's *Administrative Journal* is effective for prompting reflection on the part of practitioners. Some guidelines can be found in R. Heimovics and A.-M Rizzo, *Innovations in Teaching Public Affairs and Administration* (1981). Norma Carr-Ruffino's *The Promotable Woman* (1985) provides many creative and innovative exercises, most of which can be used in group settings and workshops as well as privately, as originally intended. University Associates publishes valuable training materials, some of which may interest the HRD specialist interested in action training. Their address is: 8517 Production Avenue, San Diego, California, 92121. In other workshops, we have used their Women as Managers Scale.

REFERENCES

Bramson, R. 1981. *Coping with Difficult People*. Garden City, NY: Doubleday, Anchor Books.

Carr-Ruffino, N. 1985. *The Promotable Woman*. Belmont, CA: Wadsworth.

Christie, J. 1978. "Murdock the Maneuverer." In A. Dubrin. *Human Relations*.

Cook, S., and J. Mendleson. 1984. "The Power Wielders: Men and/or Women Managers?" *Industrial Management*. Vol. 26, No. 2, March/April, 22–27.

Dubrin, A. 1978. *Human Relations: A Job-Oriented Approach*. Reston, VA: Prentice-Hall.

Heimovics, R., and A.-M. Rizzo. 1981. *Innovations in Teaching Public Affairs and Administration*. Kansas City, MO: University of Missouri.

Hersey, P., and K. Blanchard. 1982. *Management of Organizational Behavior: Utilizing Human Resources*. Englewood Cliffs, NJ: Prentice-Hall.

Kelley, C. 1979. *Assertion Training: A Facilitator's Guide*. La Jolla: University Associates.

Kipnis, D. and S. Schmidt. 1982. *Respondent's Guide to Kipnis-Schmidt Profiles of Organizational Influence Strategies*. San Diego: University Associates.

Kouzes, J., and B. Posner. 1987. *The Leadership Challenge: How to Get Extraordinary Things Done in Organizations*. San Francisco: Jossey-Bass.

Morgan, G. 1989. *Creative Organization Theory: A Resourcebook*. Newbury Park: Sage.

Chapter 8

One-on-One Strategies: Even Small Successes Contribute to Change

Earlier chapters covered what HRD managers or executives/managers could do individually and collectively to involve people and, in the long run, improve organizational functioning. In this final chapter, we focus on what supervisors, managers, and peers can do to promote personal change in others. When employers choose to respond to personal problems such as substance abuse, they typically offer formal counseling and employee assistance programs as the solution. More often, however, employee problems and the larger issue of employee dedication and involvement are left to a supervisor's or manager's discretion and initiative. The authors propose that much can be accomplished even by co-workers and nonsupervisory personnel through one-on-one, informal strategies if they focus on the long term. The kinds of activities described range from programs targeting self-esteem, to modeling and coaching, to encouraging mentoring and networking.

With diversified workforce predicted in the next few decades, scenes like this one are likely to become more common.

When Ana McCormick recruits new employees for *Aetna Life & Casualty* these days, she does a lot more than collect applications. In the past few months, she found counseling for a new employee who came from a battered women's shelter. She helped arrange state subsidies for child care for another. For a third, she scrambled around to supply "a neat skirt and blouse" to wear to work and to make sure that transportation was available. "I had to dig into my own pocketbook for bus fare," she says. (Bennett, 1989)

Recruitment of employees raises one set of such problems; retention brings another. To keep competent, experienced workers, who frequently represent substantial investments by employers, personnel officers, HRD specialists, supervisors, and managers are forced to shift gears to devote attention to employee problems. These new priorities apply not only to the culturally diverse workforce, but to employee needs generally. The American workplace may have needed these employee-centered priorities for years, but the growing scarcity of competent, trained workers highlights this concern for the 1990s and beyond.

Inasmuch as employee involvement or organizational integration efforts target work relationships, change agents should ask: How do people evaluate how they work together, and what is the outcome of integration efforts? Like many other organizational development techniques, involvement efforts usually begin by surveying the attitudes, opinions, and behavior of employees concerning their perceived place in the organization. As recommended in the chapter on organizational integration, many change agents recognize that they must first assess where their employees stand. Frequently, however, even before these mirroring techniques are presented to members of work units, most experienced HRD manager/trainers will find their senses tuned to searching for potential obstacles, the people who resist or fight change. Too often, they do not have to look far.

One concern of the literature of organizational development and change is the pervasiveness of such obstacles, especially in the form of specific problems and "difficult" types of people. In a few organizations, counseling or employee assistance programs represent the institution's formal responses to such problems. Even in these institutions, an employee problem must recur on a large scale for it to warrant executive attention. However, when the problem is addressed at that level with the dedication of significant resources, it makes supervisors', managers', and HRD officers' jobs that much easier. For example, AT&T's program for substance abusers means that most supervisors can refer affected employees to that program and depend on those professionals to take the lead in intervention. As beneficial as these programs are, they are unfortunately the exception rather than the rule. Most organizations are not large enough or sufficiently profitable to justify formal programs. Others fail to recognize the widespread nature of the problem or possess a less than progressive attitude about assuming responsibility for employee problems. In many work settings then, supervisors and managers may find that they have only themselves to rely on concerning how to deal with employee problems or difficult individuals. Since formal programs may not be feasible, we need to explore informal strategies that can be invoked to accomplish the same, or similar, goals.

This chapter is addressed to the initiator or, as referred to earlier, change agents. A first line supervisor, a manager, an HRD officer, or even a dedicated co-worker can qualify. What can one do to help an employee with difficulties or one who is performing admirably but needs assistance and support in reaching career goals? In part I of this chapter, we focus on a range of strategies for the individual holding supervisory authority over another individual who either has a problem or requires support. Here we discuss informal, one-on-one strategies for the employee who suffers from a problem or set of problems. Part II concerns informal strategies that can be invoked by a manager or peer in a non-supervisory capacity, that is, one without authority over the individual in question. An HRD officer or a co-worker may choose to offer assistance or support; perhaps no one else is willing to take the initiative. While some of the strategies in part II can be successfully employed for difficult subordinates, we try to distinguish between specific approaches available to managers and supervisors in direct command of difficult individuals and those broader strategies available to HRD officers, managers, and peers who choose to assist anyone needing support.

PART I: AUTHORITY AND PERSONAL CHANGE: TOOLS AND STRATEGIES

Let us say that you are a supervisor with direct command over the usual assortment of subordinates with a range of talents, expertise, and experience, and the usual variety of personalities from a diversity of cultural backgrounds. This section is addressed to your interests.

What Makes Good Supervisors?

We begin by stating that what we judge to be good supervision may differ from the interpretation of others in your organization. Competent supervision means that you are able to get work done through people and that if "people problems" intervene, you deal with them so that ultimately your workers can get the job done. Even if this behavior is interpreted as "soft-headed" thinking, or "humanistic" from the most cynical perspective, you know that your approach gradually contributes to an effective team. If a subordinate suffers from a problem or need that you think warrants attention, you at some point decide to assume responsibility for problem-solving and take the initiative. Without formal employee assistance programs outside your unit, you have only your own resources to draw upon and are aware that you must first survey the territory to know the nature and extent of the problem facing you. It could be substance abuse or a range of personal matters that influences the employee's performance on the job. We also commonly find work-related disorders such as the negative thinker or the "steamroller" who continually poses obstacles in forging cooperative work relationships (Bramson, 1981). Whatever the nature of the problem, the person with the problem can be described by a range of attitudes that you will have to deal with. These attitude sets are described by the following list. Your troubled employee:

• is mentally healthy or she is not;

• is aware or not at all conscious that a problem exists;

• knows the impact that her behavior or attitudes have on others at work or she does not;

• relatedly, cares about solving the problem or she does not;

• is sincerely concerned about the welfare of the organization and her future in it or she is not;

• disagrees with decisions or actions for reasons of principle or disagrees with the intent to destroy prospects for cooperation and consensus.

All of these descriptions should influence your diagnosis of the problem. The mentally healthy individual who is aware of the problem and its influence on others, who is committed to solving the problem and is dedicated to pursuing what is in the general welfare, and finally, who objects to actions on the basis of principle will merit different approaches, perhaps more in the form of support and guidance, than one with the opposite qualities.

Turning our attention to difficult people (such as Sherman tanks, exploders, snipers, or bulldozers) or troublemakers, these individuals typically fall on the right-hand side of our attitude sets. They may be mentally unhealthy, be unaware of their problem or its influence on others, not care about solving the problem, be unconcerned about others' well-being, and continually engage in destructive and unhealthy behavior: "lying, cheating, stealing, harassing, intimidating, and purposely hurting other people" (Kilmann, 1984, p. 165). Troublemakers are not likely to resign; they instead require some intervention before their behavior gets out of control or before the damage they cause becomes irreversible. The main goal is to get such an individual to care about how she is seen and how her behavior affects others so that she *wants* to change.

Counseling: Toward an Employee-Centered Dialogue

Counseling is frequently recommended as a means of problem-solving as well as a way of contributing to the self-confidence of the client. While coaching is typically used to identify errors and correct deficiencies in performance, counseling emphasizes issues of a more global nature with emphasis upon seeing them from the worker's point of view. To demonstrate its benefits, one study (Hill, 1984) reports that counseling either formally or informally results in employees who feel more satisfied on the job, believe supervisors perform adequately, and approve of their superiors' approach to motivation. Counseling not only aids in improving employee identification with the organization, but focuses dialogue on the usually seldom-discussed issues of employee needs, problems, and interests. It also can act as a safety valve for whatever frustrations evolve from work relationships.

Kilmann (1984) recommends a four-step counseling process for troublemakers: listing the troublemakers, conducting a first feedback session, conducting follow-up sessions, and concluding the sessions. Drury (1984) recommends using a special format for problem-solving. Summarized in chapter 7, in the Strategy Script Worksheet, Describe, Express, Specify, Choose and Reward helps to disclose how the problem identifier feels and what should be the objective of the consultation. While these approaches are included here to suggest the kind of assistance available, the reader should be assured that there is a substantial body of literature available for reference.

Rewards Revisited

In addition to supervisory counseling, those with authority can (according to path-goal theory) manipulate rewards to make "satisfaction of workers' needs dependent on effective performance" (Carr-Ruffino, 1982). By additionally providing a supportive work environment through coaching, guidance, and support, employees are aided in reaching mutually agreed-upon goals. The key is to use rewards appropriately, consistently, with proper timing, for desired behaviors. The worker must appreciate that the reward will be worth the effort, as well as the risk of failure.

Giving Feedback

Feedback is another tool that, although it can be used by others in nonsupervisory capacities, is central to a manager's repertoire of skills. Van Houten's (1980) rules of feedback summarize what to do:

Rule 1. Select an appropriate, measurable index of performance.

Rule 2. Provide immediate feedback as soon after the event as possible.

Rule 3. Provide feedback frequently.

Rule 4. Make feedback positive by delivering praise when appropriate.

Rule 5. Tie feedback to individual performance, rather than to an absolute standard. An employee should be allowed to compete with herself.

Rule 6. Provide group feedback.

Rule 7. When feasible, use public posting (charts) to display progress.

Rule 8. Graph your results.

Rule 9. Encourage comments relating to individual and group performance.

Rule 10. Provide additional rewards when warranted.

Rule 11. Select brief work intervals.

While feedback by itself has merit, it can be a very powerful tool for changing employee behavior when tied to the assignment of rewards and a plan for goal accomplishment. However, using these strategies—counseling, feedback, rewards, problem-solving—in a haphazard manner or through trial and error will not help you cope with a troublemaker or difficult person. The key is to use these approaches consistently and over a long period of time. Continual practice of these techniques will be required to enhance prospects for success. Even then, there is no guarantee that an appropriate technique exists that can solve all problems. Sometimes, the most realistic strategy is to try to cope with a serious problem.

PART II: PEER INTERVENTION: TOOLS AND STRATEGIES

For this set of approaches, we will assume you are an HRD officer or a manager who is in a position to hear about and witness firsthand many of the problems that employees experience. In training workshops, you observe employees acknowledging problems or describing difficult people and political games, which, while widespread in workplaces across the country, appear overwhelming and intimidating to the victim. You know that these problems seem entrenched in the company and will not be simple matters to resolve. Not only are the problems complex but the usual kinds of strategies available to commanding superiors are not available to you. You lack legitimate authority and day-to-day exposure to these employees. Since these workers are not accountable to you, you lack the carrots to motivate and reward their progress toward problem-solving. Consequently, your standing and influence with the employee rely solely on your dedication, caring, and human relations skills in helping him or her deal with that problem.

The kinds of tools available to a manager in this situation range from coaching and modeling to listening skills. We begin with what we feel is the core of the personal change cycle: building self-esteem.

Self-Esteem: The Key to Change

In arguing for the central importance of self-esteem in developing employee competence, Hill (1984, p. 8) cites the following evidence:

- Hackman's research demonstrating that personnel fail to take advantage of enriched jobs if they do not possess adequate levels of self-esteem;
- Lawrence's work concluding that a high correlation exists between job satisfaction and an employee's self-esteem;
- Strauss's conclusion that the key to the success of organizational development techniques lies in their capacity to contribute to self-esteem;
- McClelland's research observing that if management demands high performance, employees with high aspirations will find ways to reach those goals.
- Dalton's conclusion that personal and organizational change is based on an increase in self-esteem. Without an enhanced self-concept, workers tend to resist change and innovation.
- Finally, Korman's theory of motivation, which revolves around self-concept:
  1. people try to behave in ways consistent with their self-image,
  2. employees who consider themselves failures do not try, perform below standard, reinforcing their low self-concept; and
  3. improvement of employee performance largely rests on enhancement of their self-images.

While Hill envisions self-esteem as the first rung of the developmental ladder, others choose to place it higher in the causal chain. Knowledge acquired through experience and the testing of competencies can be described as a catalyst, initiating a cycle of empowerment. According to Josefowitz (1980), upon realizing that what we know is true and useful, we begin to augment our self-confidence. This results in attitude change: we begin to believe that positive outcomes are possible. In a kind of self-fulfilling prophecy, positive thinking in turn leads to greater risk-taking, creativity, initiative, and problem-solving. With the confidence to experiment comes the accomplishment of goals and finally empowerment. From Josefowitz's perspective, self-confidence forms the keystone of the cycle. The ways of knowing discussed in chapters 4 and 6 and the risk-taking mentioned in chapter 6 revolve around this essential quality of positive self-concept. Whether one believes that self-esteem appears early or late in the developmental cycle, it is difficult to deny its significance in providing motives for change and experimentation. Especially for women, historically identified as low in self-esteem (as discussed in chapter 1), the need for developing self-confidence becomes critical.

From a variety of studies, we can suggest several ways an individual can improve self-esteem: acting self-confident until self-confidence be-comes an integral part of the personality; improving one's stock of abil-ities; visualizing positive outcomes (mental rehearsal); learning new, constructive responses to cues that previously led to self-destructive behavior; rewarding oneself for new learning, new behavior, and improved accomplishment; and setting attainable goals for self-improvement.

What else can an interested party do to help? In addition to coaching, counseling, and regular feedback, Pierce and Dechant (1989) mention job enrichment and executive support groups, as well as creative spec-ulation of new scenarios of how troubled people want to act through techniques of fantasy, drawing, photography, theater, wilderness ex-periences, or music. Pierce and Dechant's primary objective is to improve critical thinking, making implicit beliefs and assumptions explicit so that employees are not destined to repeat dysfunctional patterns of behavior. While we agree in the author's objectives, in a lesser priority they rec-ommend the use of criteria analysis to require employees to identify how they know when they have performed well. Since most individuals can remember situations in which they have done well, they can use these events as steppingstones or as a foundation for reinventing their self-concept.

Listening and Attending: The Importance of "Being There"

Listening and attending skills complement efforts to enhance self-esteem, for many people are unwilling to accept another's mirroring of a new, positive self-concept unless they trust the change agent's inten-tions. Attending can be described as giving oneself entirely to "being with" the other, both physically and psychologically (Egan, 1975). In Egan's developmental model of helping and interpersonal relating, at-tending is used to set the stage for stage I. Here, the helper responds to another with respect and empathy in order to establish rapport and an effective working relationship. The client's goal is to explore expe-riences, behavior, and feelings and to reflect on the ways in which she lives ineffectively. During stage II, the helper builds on the data gen-erated by the client's self-exploration so that the client can find themes, eventually arriving at a larger picture of her behavior and inner re-sources. In stage III, the helper encourages the client to work out specific action programs and enables the client to act on new understandings of her capabilities. If the helper and the employee are committed to this interpersonal relating process, it is more likely that the helper will reflect, or mirror, a changed self-image to the client and that the latter will trust that the new image is true.

Envisioning Alternative Behaviors: Modeling

Modeling is another technique whereby learning occurs not through experience but through the employee's observation or imagination of another's (for example, the helper's) experience. In the most common form of modeling (Sims and Manz, 1982, p. 58), "the employee learns a novel behavior through imitating and substantially reproducing the behavior shown by a model." In another type, the employee learns about desirable or undesirable behavior through witnessing another's performance of that same behavior and observing its consequences. In still another type, a model might facilitate the acquisition of new behavior by encouraging practice through, for example, role play and rehearsal. Several guidelines are useful in establishing effective modeling. First, for a model to influence an individual, it must first capture the attention of the observer. Second, it must be presented simply, gradually, and repeatedly to ensure retention. Third, mental imagery should be cited and invoked during the rehearsal of a new behavior so that the modeled behavior can be established and later invoked by cues. Later, it can be more easily reproduced and transferred to a variety of settings.

Because supervisors are most closely associated with subordinates, they are natural candidates for modeling, although anyone perceived as successful and competent can be chosen by an employee as a role model. Sims and Manz (p. 61) find that "the behavior of successful executives is more likely to command attention, and therefore serve as a model. This conclusion points out the special responsibility that managers have in organizational life to make their own behavior exemplary of what they expect from subordinates."

Coaching for Peers

A related technique, coaching, is also designed to improve performance through observation and feedback. Unlike other techniques, coaching can be used by peers to help each other improve (Yakowicz, 1987). Joyce and Showers (1982) describe its several functions: companionship to reduce isolation and provide support; feedback on application of new practices or techniques; and assistance in deciding the appropriate timing for new practices and how to adapt and fine-tune a new practice for specific situations. Finally, coaching helps with stress reduction in introducing new ideas to prospective practitioners in a relatively nonthreatening "safe haven." It should be evident that coaching can be employed by superiors and immediate supervisors as well to correct special problems and introduce new practices. However, if peers assume the responsibility for coaching, this frequently provides a nonthreatening atmosphere especially conducive to learning. With the right measure of support and facilitative skill, collegial coaching can be effective in work units, especially those already open and receptive to quality circles and brainstorming sessions targeting performance problems.

Mentoring and Networking: Guidance from the Web

Mentoring or sponsoring represents another set of involvement strategies and addresses the problems of isolation and exclusion through an important mechanism: social networks at work. From most perspectives, social isolation at work is not constructive for anyone, even if self-imposed. For many normally cohesive groups or professions, the addition of "marginal" people or outsiders to social circles is met with greater resistance than might be found in less cohesive groups. In police work, for example, the exclusion of women has been documented as overt and organized, especially when the occupation is cohesive (Martin, 1980; Epstein, 1988). Using such evidence, some will argue that women may need mentors more than men because of discrimination. Kanter (1977), for example, argues that sponsors, which were important to men's career success (at Indsco), were critical for women." Sponsors might be supervisors, outside professionals, or organizational sponsors; whoever they might be, they help protegees broaden their experience and, through the demonstration of their talents, add to their visibility in their organization and/or profession. Unfortunately, some sponsors have difficulty in relating to potential protegees precisely because they are women. Partly as a consequence, Kanter (1983) remarks that multiple sponsors, each of whom may provide support and guidance only one time or assist in one or a few tasks, may be more realistic. So how can we promote mentoring? Considering that the best examples of mentored successes occur spontaneously, driven by the individuals' compatibility and rapport, and on a mutual, voluntary basis, should management attempt to arrange mentoring or merely encourage senior employees to "adopt" protegees and promote mentoring frequently and consistently? We recommend the latter alternative. Such matches cannot be arranged by management; the right people have to want to devote time and energy to mentoring and sponsoring people. Ideally, mentors need to:

- have a genuine interest in and empathy for others;
- hold the protegee's interests as a top priority;
- hold a high-level position that carries with it the right connections and knowledge of how informal systems work;
- have knowledge of people who could be helpful as well as the right information;

- be secure enough to withstand the protegee's succeeding beyond the mentor's dreams; and
- be able to find a personal pay-off for her efforts. (Spencer, 1989)

The right mentors alone cannot create supportive relationships. Aspiring protegees must play their part in the process by asking for assistance and support when needed. Again, Kanter's notion of multiple sponsors may be helpful when a protegee requires particular guidance on a specific concern. If the protegee does not know who can help, others may need to refer her to an appropriate resource person.

Management in turn can encourage these associations and reward them. Reward structures may provide one key to disseminating this particular innovation. If supervisors adopt incentives for senior, experienced employees to sponsor and mentor, then this may become widespread practice. Nonsupervisory personnel can make inroads by sponsoring protegees themselves and encouraging others to do so informally and incrementally. In some situations, it takes only a few minutes of time to offer advice and guidance to an individual in need. In work cultures where bonding is valued, even if limited, one-of-a-kind interventions can build to demonstrate sincere concern for individuals' well-being. If many adopt that attitude, mentoring and sponsoring may become part and parcel of how we attempt to involve workers.

Through mentoring, we see that maintaining the connections inherent in the web appears to be a universal key to success. Access to informal, "invisible" networks within an organization and across one's profession become almost indispensable for career advancement. Networking extends the goals and spirit of the mentor-protegee relationship to others in an organization or profession. Through informal, voluntary associations, a context is provided for peers to support and guide one another. Even the term networking suggests transition, a process of becoming. "The important part is not the network, the finished product, but the process of getting there—the communication that creates the linkages between people and clusters of people" (Naisbitt, 1982, p. 192). Networking is carried out through conferences, phone calls, the sharing of books, newsletters, articles, parties, workshops, grapevines, and mutual friends. Networks exist to promote self-help and self-reliance, "to exchange information, to change society, to improve productivity and work life, and to share resources" (p. 192). In transcending institutional boundaries and formal authority, networking offers ways for people to associate around their needs and interests in the search for creative solutions to problems.

For the fortunate women who have mentors, their guides are often men, since successful men outnumber women in most professions. In comparison, networking is typically women helping other women, both professionally and personally. Fear of exploitation, of victimization, or of being engulfed in the web are rarely issues for those using networks. Trust and caring form the basis of these relationships. Since this description highlights the voluntary nature of networks, people genuinely interested in networking frequently resist efforts to plan and organize them. Nevertheless, managers can refer individuals to networks and promote their use generally. By participating in informal systems, through their ties and accessibility to helpful people, managers serve as standard-bearers. By these acts, they signify that in this place, helping others is valued.

DEMOCRACY IN THE PLURALISTIC WORKPLACE: WORKPLACE REVITALIZATION FOR WHAT?

This book has attempted to clarify how people in organizations can involve employees and encourage their participation in activities and processes such as decision-making. Much attention has been paid to the special constraints of a pluralistic society in shaping the workplace. On the national scene, it is more difficult to imagine sweeping changes in a heterogeneous society such as the United States, as compared with Sweden or even the smaller scale of the United Kingdom. Nevertheless, economic and other arguments appear sufficiently compelling to cause employers to consider these organizational reforms. As mentioned, current workforce constraints shaping what a few employers now encounter have the potential of mushrooming into massive and widespread problems in recruitment and retention in the future. Due to increasing demand, workplace-based retraining and remedial education programs will expand, so that employers can continue to locate and hire essential workers. While developing good prospects for employment may not fully deal with or obviate the hardcore unemployed, steps discussed in this volume can help to reduce the growing masses of untrained and semi-skilled unemployed. According to many accounts, the level of employer involvement that will be required in the coming years should result in addressing a serious national problem in ways superior to present laissez-faire policies.

Workforce trends and conditions are quite appropriately forcing employers and human resource specialists to reexamine our stake in employees and reconsider our current approaches to human relations in the workplace. These issues also press us to examine our motives and purposes in making these recommendations to improve the quality of work life, driving us to a higher level of inquiry. Certainly, employers are motivated by their interest and need to augment productivity and are generally regarded as justified in doing so. Few genuinely concerned with a healthy national economy will quarrel with the centrality or salience of enhanced productivity. However, a few writers question the instrumental nature of the productivity argument (Denhardt, 1981). Following this reasoning, we can offer these recommendations not only because they benefit worker productivity or even because they promote employee job satisfaction, but because these reforms are capable of contributing to the processes that perpetuate and revivify a democratic society. Dahl reflects on this point.

> In an advanced democratic country the economic order would be understood as instrumental not merely to the production and distribution of goods and services but to a much larger range of values, including democratic values. The economic order would be seen as intended to serve not merely consumers but human beings in all the activities to which an economic order may contribute. (1989, pp. 324–325)

Relatedly, democratic values include not only the dignity of the individual, egalitarianism, and protection of minorities (and majorities) from arbitrary action but also enlightenment, empowerment, and emancipation. If workers do not possess rights at work, if organizational mechanisms of due process are not supported, if arbitrary and capricious acts constitute the norm, then the omission and failure to practice and uphold these values at work inevitably carries over to the realm of citizenship.

Recalling the action model in chapter 6, our efforts in presenting the techniques and approaches in this book have not been intended for the purpose of increasing the instrumental power of organizations but to educate and enlighten those who can, on the basis of their new understandings, act. Rather than continue in self-defeating ways that undermine both their own and others' dignity and efficacy, managers and workers try to ensure that employees can act and associate in fuller, more humane, and more satisfying ways. These actors can then change their collective arrangements through means that better realize their real interests and ideals (Fay, 1987).

With knowledge of their personal goals, employees can also discover how they mesh with the organization's sense of purpose and, if no overlap is found, understand what is capable of change. Demystification of gender differences, job politics, reification, and "the way things are"; reflecting about contradictions between espoused theory and theory-in-use; reframing; learning communicative competence as well as approaches discussed in this chapter can help to free individuals to understand how they can reconstruct the workplace. In considering these options, managers must regard themselves as educators and change agents in pursuit of realizing these democratic ideals in the workplace. If permitted by authorities and encouraged by superiors, use of these strategies may mean that eventually we develop employees who can responsibly reflect, deliberate, critique, and question the most fundamental assumptions about their own and others' behavior and actions at work. We in human resource development should become enablers in this process because it is the democratic and morally right action to take.

REFERENCES

Belenky, M., B. Clinchy, N. Goldberger, and J. Tarule. 1986. *Women's Ways of Knowing: The Development of Self, Voice, and Mind*. New York: Basic Books.

Bennett, A. 1989. "Aetna Schooling New Hires in Basic Workplace Skills." New York *Times*, November 10, B–1.

Bramson, R. 1981. *Coping With Difficult People*. Garden City, NY: Doubleday, Anchor Books.

Carr-Ruffino, N. 1982. *The Promotable Woman: Becoming a Successful Manager*. Belmont, CA: Wadsworth, 314.

Dahl, R. 1989. *Democracy and Its Critics*. New Haven: Yale University Press.

Denhardt, R. 1981. *In the Shadow of Organization*. Lawrence: University Press of Kansas.

Drury, S. 1984. *Assertive Supervision: Building Involved Teamwork*. Champaign, IL: Research Press.

Egan, G. 1975. *The Skilled Helper: A Model for Systematic Helping and Interpersonal Relating*. Belmont, CA: Wadsworth Publishing.

Epstein, C. 1988. *Deceptive Distinctions: Sex, Gender, and the Social Order*. New Haven: Yale University Press.

Fay, B. 1987. *Critical Social Science*. Ithaca: Cornell University Press.

Gilligan, C. 1982. *In a Different Voice: Psychological Theory and Women's Development*. Cambridge, MA: Harvard University Press.

Hill, N. 1984. *How to Increase Employee Competence*. New York: McGraw-Hill.

Josefowitz, N. 1980. *Paths to Power: A Woman's Guide From First Job to Top Executive*. Reading, MA: Addison-Wesley.

Joyce, B., and B. Showers. 1982. "The Coaching of Teaching." *Educational Leadership*, Vol. 40, October, pp. 4–10.

Kanter, R. 1977. *Men and Women of the Corporation*. New York: Basic Books.

———. 1983. "Women Managers Moving Up in a High Tech Society." In *The Woman in Management: Career and Family Issues*, ed. by J. Farley. Ithaca, New York: ILR Press.

Kilmann, R. 1984. *Beyond the Quick Fix: Managing Five Tracks to Organizational Success*. San Francisco: Jossey-Bass.

Marsick, V. 1987. *Learning in the Workplace*. New York: Croom Helm.

Martin, S. 1980. *Breaking and Entering: Policewoman Patrol*. Berkeley: University of California Press.

Naisbitt, J. 1982. *Megatrends: Ten New Directions Transforming Our Lives*. New York: Warner.

Pierce, G., and K. Dechant. 1989. "The Manager-Learner: Developing Critical Thinking in Managers." Paper presented to the Second Annual National

Conference for Management Development Professionals in Industry, Government, and Health Care. Boston.

Sims, H., and C. Manz. 1982. "Modeling Influences on Employee Behavior." *Personnel Journal*, Vol. 61, No. 1, January, 58–65.

Spencer, C. 1989. "Director's Column." *Women's Network*. American Society for Training and Development. Spring.

Van Houten, R. 1980. *How To Motivate Others Through Feedback*. Lawrence, KS: H & H.

Yakowicz, W. 1987. "Coaching: Collegial Learning in Schools." In V. Marsick, ed. *Learning in the Workplace*.

Author Index

Subject Index

About the Authors

ANN-MARIE RIZZO is Professor of Public Administration at Tennessee State University, Nashville. For the past fifteen years she has also trained practitioners in the public and private sectors and conducted workshops, with Carmen Mendez, for women managers and staff on ways of understanding organizations and job politics.

CARMEN MENDEZ is a Professor in the Department of Public Administration and the Director of Budget and Administration for the College of Education at Florida International University. She has been involved, with Ann-Marie Rizzo, in leading training workshops in both the public and private sectors, and served as Acting Director of the Institute of Government.